KT-198-616

30130504213293

The Faces of Germany

The Faces of Germany

by

MARGARET WIGHTMAN

HARRAP LONDON

First published in Great Britain 1971
by George G. Harrap & Co. Ltd
182-4 High Holborn, London W.C.1

Reprinted and updated 1978

ISBN 0 245 50399 4

Filmset by Photoprint Plates, Rayleigh, Essex
and printed by Redwood Burn Ltd, Trowbridge & Esher
Made in Great Britain

Preface

The greatest problem in writing about Germany lies in defining what Germany is and what is German. The answer to the question 'What is Germany?' has changed many times since Charlemagne first united a number of Teutonic tribes in the eighth century. Even in our own century no clear definition has emerged; the Germans have twice tried to extend their country and have twice seen their frontiers redrawn. The issue was further complicated by the failure to conclude a peace treaty after the Second World War, with the result that the theoretical extent of German territory and the actual area over which the Germans exercised sovereignty did not coincide. Indeed there are now *de facto* two Germanies. Again, there is no simple answer to the question 'What is German?', for the body of German-speaking people embraces the Swiss, the Austrians and some East European minorities.

In this book Germany is regarded for geographical, political and economic purposes as having the frontiers of 1945. The description of life in Germany is unfortunately restricted to West Germany.

M.W.

ACKNOWLEDGMENTS

The publishers wish to acknowledge the generosity of a number of organizations and firms who have provided photographs free of charge, in particular Lex Hornsby and Partners for the photographs of the German Democratic Republic; the Bundesbildstelle, Bonn and the Press Department of the Embassy of the German Federal Republic for the photographs on pages 27 (bottom), 34, 53, 54, 141 (top), 142, 143 (bottom), 144 (bottom), 148 (bottom), 149 (bottom), 181, 183 and 222; the Howaldtswerke-Deutsche Werft for the photograph on p. 13; Bayer AG Leverkusen for that on p. 16; Hoesch AG Dortmund for that on p. 29; J. A. Henckels Zwillingswerke AG Solingen, for that on p. 30; Schluchseewerk AG for that on p. 46; Fremdenverkehrsverband Ostbayern for that on p. 51; Volkswagenwerk AG for that on p. 70; Deutsche Messe- und AusstellungsAG for that on p. 74; and the Bildstelle (VWD) for those on pages 185 (top), 187, and 207. The remaining photographs were taken by R. P. L. Ledésert, R. Sawers and the author.

Thanks are also due to the following for permission to reproduce works of art: the Courtauld Institute Galleries for *Adam and Eve* by Cranach; the National Portrait Gallery for *Sir Thomas More* by Holbein; Rheinisches Bildarchiv, Cologne for *The Madonna in the Rose Arbour* by Lochner and *Trees in the Dusk* by Friedrich; the Staatliche Graphische Sammlung, Munich for *The Tiger* by Franz Marc; and Rembrandt Verlag, Berlin, for *Scholar reading* by Ernst Barlach.

Contents

Maps and Diagrams

I Geography

This chapter deals mainly with Germany within the present frontiers, for although the divisions brought about in 1945 were intended to be provisional, they have become fixed and are now generally accepted as permanent.

German soil is bounded by Lake Constance and the Alps in the south, the Rhine in the south-west, the Bayerischer Wald in the south-east, the coast in the north and the rivers Oder and Neisse in the north-east. The boundaries with Denmark, Holland, Belgium and Luxembourg are entirely arbitrary and in no way relate to natural frontiers. Germany is not then a complete geographical unit which can be dealt with as a separate phenomenon from the rest of Western Europe.

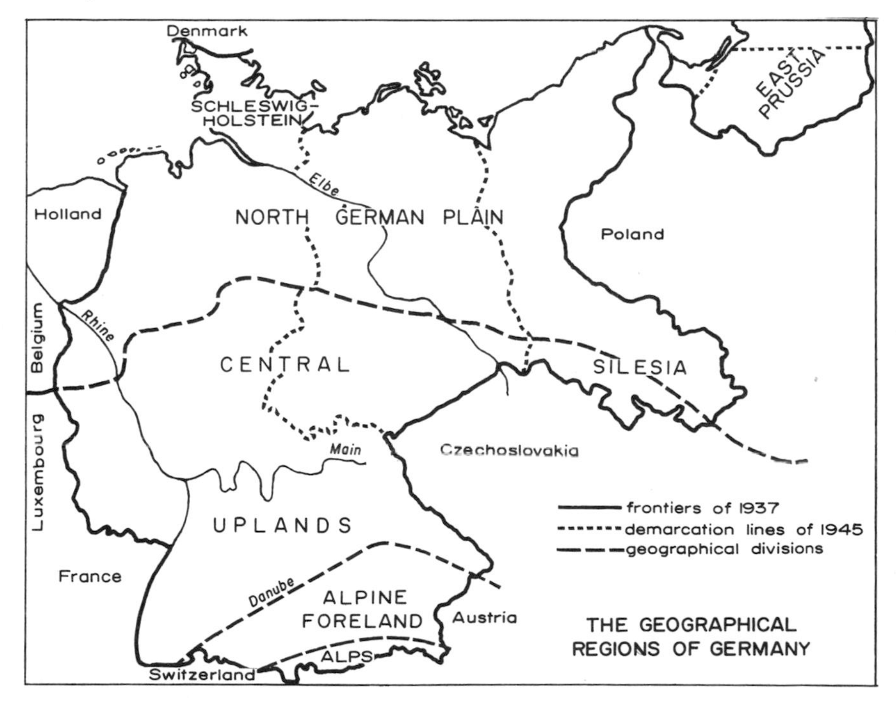

Fig 1

A glance at a relief map of Germany and the surrounding states reveals three distinct parallel bands running from east to west: in the north there is a wide lowland plain extending from the North Sea to the Ural Mountains; to the south of this plain is a band of uplands running from France across to Czechoslovakia. The third and most southerly band is formed by a chain of high mountains, the Alps, which extend from south-eastern France almost to Vienna. Only a small part of the Alps lies within Germany, although the Alpine foothills and foreland extend as far as the Danube.

The landscape in general was fixed by the Ice Age, when glaciers from the Alps and Scandinavia advanced four times. Each successive advance was less severe than the previous one, so that Germany was scarcely affected by the last phase of the Ice Age.

The Lowlands

The North German Plain west of the Elbe

Only occasionally does this plain rise above 150 metres; millions of years ago it lay beneath the sea and in places it is still below sea level. By the Ice Age the ground had risen above the surface of the water and became covered by the glaciers advancing southwards from Scandinavia. After the glaciers had receded, parts of the plain began to sink under the weight of water repeatedly driven inland by strong winds. The outermost ridge of dunes thus became separated from the mainland by a stretch of shallow water which at low tide reveals extensive mud flats *(Watten)*. The islands so formed *(Halligen)* were, however, inhabited, even though they were continuously being worn away by the waves; to raise their homes and stables above the level of flood tides the farmers built mounds 4–5 metres high. Farming on the islands consists principally of cattle- and sheep-rearing.

The larger sandy islands such as Borkum, Norderney and Sylt, also geographically part of the plain, are completely infertile and have achieved popularity as holiday resorts. Sylt has been connected to the mainland by the Hindenburg Dam, which serves the dual function of helping land reclamation and providing a rail link with the island.

Heligoland *(Helgoland)*, a red sandstone rock rising 58 metres out of the North Sea some 65 km north-west of

Cuxhaven, is the summit of a submerged mountain which escaped the effects of the Ice Age. Since 1890, when it was exchanged by England for Zanzibar, it has proved to be of considerable strategic importance, particularly to the German Navy. The harbour now provides a useful refuge for North Sea shipping, especially for the West German fishing fleet. Heligoland has also been developed as a holiday resort; it is popular with hay-fever victims and with day trippers attracted by the duty-free goods on sale in the shops. The island of Neuwerk at the mouth of the Elbe was acquired by Hamburg in 1969 for development as a deep water oil harbour. This scheme is necessary because the North Sea is too shallow for giant tankers near Germany's main ports.

The North Sea coast and the banks of the Elbe were once regularly flooded by high tides; occasional catastrophes drowned thousands of families and swept houses and livestock out to sea. From about A.D. 800 organized groups of farmers built dikes along the coast in an attempt to keep the sea out; a set of laws to enforce their upkeep is contained in the thirteenth century *Sachsenspiegel*. The last great inundation took place in 1570, when the entire North Sea coast of Holland, Germany and Denmark was submerged. Experience has since improved the design and construction of dikes, so that the land is safe so long as the dikes are kept in good repair; they are now maintained by the Federal Government. Much work was done on raising and strengthening the dikes after the near-disaster of 1962, when there was extensive flooding, especially

A farmhouse in the Elbe Marshland in spring

Fig 2

along the banks of the Elbe. Reclamation of the dangerous mud flats outside the dikes is also proceeding; mud is trapped by specially erected low fences made of interwoven twigs, which retain solid particles as the tide recedes. Later a protecting dike will be built and the land within the dike, known as a *Koog* or polder, will be left for a time under grass so that it loses its salt content. It will eventually become excellent agricultural land. The Elbe Marshland, or *Altes Land,* is especially famous for its fruit and vegetables, which find a ready market in nearby Hamburg.

Hamburg and Bremen, West Germany's two most important harbours, lie a considerable distance from the sea on the estuaries of the Elbe and Weser respectively. Both were members of the Hanseatic League and both are West Germany's only remaining free cities or city states. Hamburg's real prosperity began when the Hanseatic League declined, because it was favourably situated for transatlantic trade. It does, however, lack an industrial hinterland and relied before 1945 on communications with central Germany and Berlin. The division of Germany virtually halted barge traffic along the Elbe to Berlin, Saxony and Czechoslovakia, and Hamburg's communications system has had to be reorientated towards West Germany. It has nevertheless become the largest port in the Federal Republic with a freight turnover in 1973 of 49·3 million tonnes; it is an important industrial and trading centre and a cosmopolitan city with an excellent cultural reputation. The beautiful old city of Bremen never became as important as Hamburg and now the Weser is not deep enough to take the largest ships, which must dock in Bremerhaven, about 60 km. nearer the sea. Bremen now concentrates on containers and lightweight cargoes such as tobacco. Bremerhaven's importance grew considerably after the war, for besides being a passenger terminal for ocean-going liners and West Germany's largest fishing port, it became the American Forces' port of embarkation.

Other North Sea ports are Emden and Wilhelmshaven. The latter was developed originally as a naval base and is now a major oil harbour with a pipeline to the Ruhr. Emden is a

Hamburg : part of the Deutsche Werft shipyard. Shipbuilding is one of Hamburg's most important industries

fishing port and also handles bulk cargoes such as coal and ores for the Ruhr, to which it is linked by the Dortmund–Ems canal. The Volkswagen company has an extensive new factory in Emden, which makes cars for the American and Scandinavian markets.

Away from the coast the North German Plain is higher, very sandy and infertile, because early man stripped the area of its forest and thus ruined the soil. A feature of the *Geest*, as it is called, are the boulders (erratics), carried by the glaciers of the Ice Age from northern Scandinavia. They are seen to best effect in the megaliths marking Stone Age burial places *(Hünengräber)*. The *Geest* includes a large area south of Hamburg known as the Lüneburg Heath *(Lüneburger Heide)*, which was once an unbroken expanse of heather relieved only by occasional juniper and birch trees; it supported only a few herds of black-faced sheep and many hives of bees. As artificial fertilisers became available during the nineteenth century it became possible to grow certain crops such as rye and potatoes where once only heather flourished. When it was realized that the Heath was quickly disappearing, a considerable area was declared a National Park and preserved as an unspoiled recreational area from which the motor-car is excluded. Lüneburg itself, on the edge of the Heath, was once an important trading centre with a small harbour on the river Ilmenau. Salt mining, the very industry which brought prosperity in the Middle Ages, is now causing the decay of the beautiful town as the land is subsiding. The salt bubbles to

The Lüneburg Heath: heather and juniper trees

The Steinhuder Meer (known locally as 'Hanover's paddling pool' since it is only 10 feet deep)

the surface as brine; the saline springs of Lüneburg are also exploited for their healing qualities.

In parts the *Geest* is very wet; there are extensive marshes and peat-bogs. In some depressions there are shallow lakes, the largest of which is the Steinhuder Meer near Hanover *(Hannover)*. Once canals have been dug to drain the land, the vast expanses of marsh, moorland and peat-bog can be cultivated. One method is to remove the peat, then to fertilise the underlying soil; the peat is dried and used for fuel. Another method called deep ploughing brings up sand from beneath five feet of peat and produces a reasonably fertile growing-medium. The largest marsh in the whole of Germany, the Bourtanger Moor, lies south-east of Emden and extends into Holland. The Dutch drained and cultivated their part of the marsh over a century ago, but it is only since 1951 that Germany has begun to do likewise. Where once only heather and stunted birch trees grew, intensive cultivation is now possible and settlements are being built for farmers from all parts of Germany who wish to participate in this new venture. The farms are being built in a more practical version of the traditional local style and are being laid out to suit mixed farming.

Apart from the ports of Emden and Wilhelmshaven the only large town between the Weser and Ems is Oldenburg, a market for the poultry, cattle and eggs produced nearby. All other settlements are little more than villages. Near Aurich is a power station producing electricity for a large part of northern Germany by burning peat. The steam given off during the process is used to heat several hundred hothouses, which produce early fruit and vegetables.

Beneath much of North Germany there are important oil-fields, which have been exploited since about 1942, bringing better communications and employment to the area. The reserves have been estimated at up to 300 million tonnes. Between the rivers Weser and Ems natural gas has also been discovered. No major oil or gas strikes had been made by 1977 in West Germany's small share of the North Sea.

In the extreme west of Germany the North German Plain extends as far south as Cologne *(Köln)*. Here the Rhine leaves the hills and flows across a gigantic flood plain; the river banks have now been built up and its course straightened to reduce the danger of spring flooding. The 2,000-year-old city of Cologne is a thriving centre of industry, banking and trade and an important traffic junction. West of Cologne there are huge deposits of brown coal (lignite), which are now being increasingly exploited as a source of fuel and of raw materials for the chemical industry. To the north and west of Cologne lies an important textile-producing area; Mönchen-Gladbach specializes in cotton goods, Krefeld in silks and

Leverkusen: the Bayer chemical works on the Rhine just north of Cologne

Münster : the Prinzipalmarkt (reconstructed with great care after wartime damage)

Gemen : the moated castle, one of several fine examples in Westphalia

velvets and Aachen in woollen cloth. Düsseldorf, a short distance downstream from Cologne, is the headquarters of many large industrial enterprises and also has chemical and fashion industries; it is the capital of the *Land* or State of North-Rhine Westphalia *(Nordrhein-Westfalen)*, the most populous State in West Germany. Lower down the Rhine lie Xanten and Kleve, market centres for the dairy produce, vegetables and flowers of the plain.

East of the Rhine the uplands sweep round to enclose a wide 'bay', which takes its name from the largest town, Münster. The area is largely agricultural and supplies the industrial area of the Ruhr to the south (see pp. 28–31) with dairy produce, for which Münster is the main market; it is also a university town and now has some small industries.

Other large towns on the plain are Hanover and Brunswick *(Braunschweig)*, which grew up at points where medieval routes through the Central Uplands met the west–east route to Berlin. Hanover is the capital of the State of Lower Saxony *(Niedersachsen)*; it has long been an industrial and trade centre of importance and since 1945 it has become the scene of West Germany's industrial and trade fairs. It has well-known rubber and electrical industries. Around Brunswick a large industrial area has developed in the last fifty years, based on local raw materials, namely potash, low-grade iron ore and brown coal. Wolfsburg was chosen in 1938 as the site of the Volkswagen works, which were built alongside the Mittelland canal. Salzgitter houses an enormous foundry. Both towns have since 1945 absorbed large numbers of refugees from eastern Europe.

Schleswig-Holstein

Schleswig-Holstein, the most northerly State of the Federal Republic, has a long history of political instability; it occupies a strategic position at the base of the Jutland peninsula, guarding the shortest land (and since 1895 sea) route from

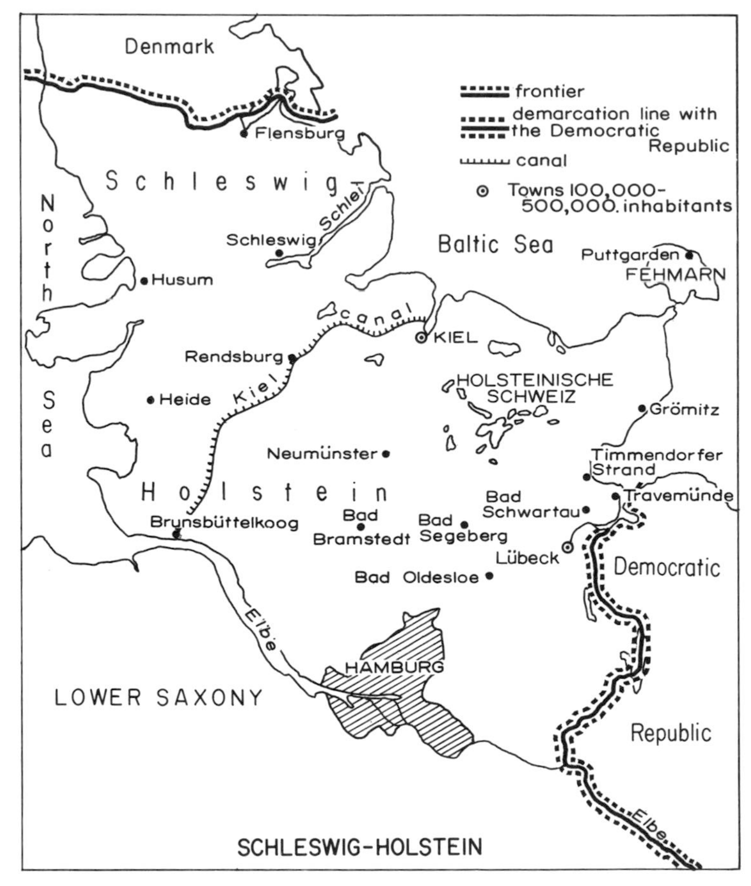

Fig 3

western Europe to Scandinavia. The present frontier just north of Flensburg dates only from the plebiscite of 1920 held in accordance with the terms of the Treaty of Versailles.

The west coast of Schleswig-Holstein is flat, bleak and wet. The chief sources of livelihood for the local people are dairy-farming, horse-breeding and fishing; towns such as Husum have grown out of fishing villages. The discovery and exploitation of oil have however brought additional employment to some areas; there is, for example, a large refinery in Heide. Many of the smaller towns and villages have flocks of nesting storks in late spring and summer which help to attract tourists, who provide an additional source of revenue.

Midway between the west and east coasts of Schleswig-Holstein the land is sandy and infertile *(Geest)*. There is some industrial development in Neumünster and Rendsburg and there are also important spas with saline springs, Bramstedt, Oldesloe, Schwartau and Segeberg. Bad Schwartau is also known for its jam. Immediately behind the east coast there is a group of low hills known as the *Holsteinische Schweiz* where pastureland alternates with woodlands and fields of grain. These hills are the moraines left by the last phase of the Ice Age.

The east coast is washed by the Baltic *(Ostsee)*, which is an enclosed and hence almost tideless sea. A milder climate and the peaceful nature of the sea produced ideal conditions for the development of seaside resorts such as Timmendorfer Strand and Grömitz, which extend in almost unbroken line from Travemünde to Flensburg. Flensburg's industrial development has been hindered by its proximity to the Danish frontier; it concentrates almost exclusively on shipbuilding.

Even though the Baltic, which contains hardly any salt, can freeze completely in a severe winter, the harbours of Kiel and Lübeck-Travemünde are of considerable importance. Kiel, the capital of Schleswig-Holstein, lies at the head of a deep inlet *(Förde)* that forms a natural harbour; it also provides an ideal setting for the 'Kieler Woche', one of Europe's leading sailing regattas. The Baltic coast has many of these inlets, formed during the Ice Age by rivers flowing beneath the ice; Schleswig at the head of the Schlei is 50 km. from the sea. Kiel is a base of the West German Navy and a centre of the shipbuilding industry. It also lies at the northern end of the Kiel Canal *(Nord-Ostsee Kanal)*, which enables large ships to reach the Baltic from the North Sea in a matter

Lübeck: the Holstentor and salt warehouses

of between seven and ten hours instead of having to sail 750 km. round the northern tip of Denmark. The canal was completed in 1895 as a strategic link with the Baltic for the German Navy; when it needed repairs in the 1970s it was also decided to dredge and widen it to take more traffic. Lübeck, the 'town of seven golden towers', was once Queen of the Hanseatic League and the northern end of the old *Salzstraße*, a medieval trade route to central Europe; its prosperity now derives principally from shipbuilding. Travemünde provides one of West Germany's two main shipping links with Scandinavia. The most direct route and the shortest sea-crossing is the *Vogelfluglinie* between Puttgarden and Rødbyhavn in Denmark, which was opened in 1963 when a rail and road bridge across Fehmarn Sound was completed.

The North German Plain east of the Elbe

In the early Middle Ages the Elbe and its tributary the Saale marked the boundary between Teutonic tribes and the Slavs. In the twelfth and thirteenth centuries the Germans colonized the land east of the Elbe almost as far as the Gulf of Finland. They introduced an advanced form of agriculture and built towns and villages of a standard layout; the main feature of the countryside was the *Gut* or large estate, originally occupied by the leader of the colonists. The pattern of settlement was

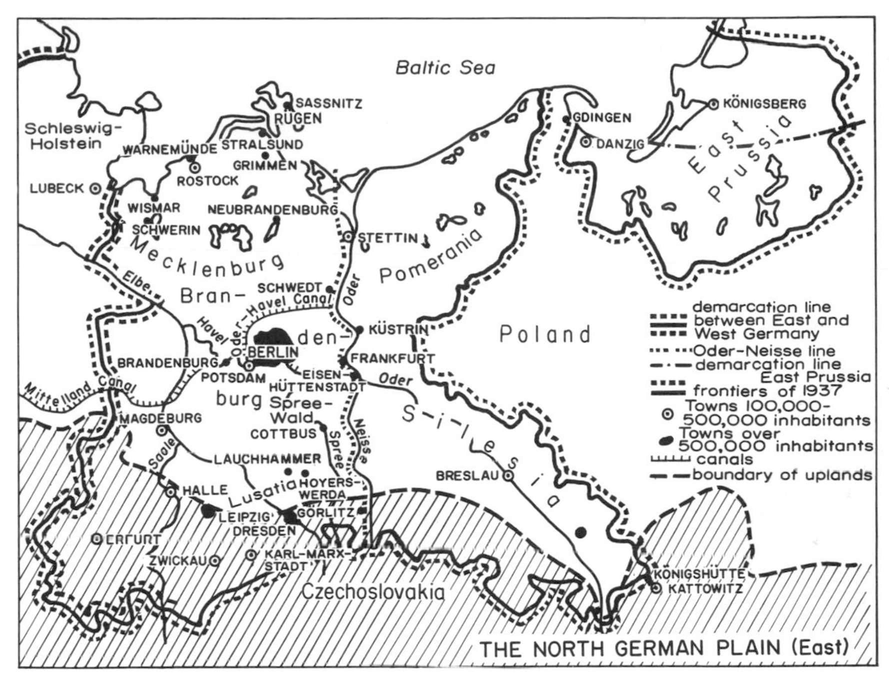

Fig 4

only altered to any great extent by nineteenth century industrialization. The political division of Germany in 1945 has, however, almost re-established the old Elbe–Saale line, while the pattern of farming in the Democratic Republic (GDR) has been changed to eliminate the *Gut* and convert the land to collective farms.

Until recently there were no large ports on the coast of Mecklenburg because the inlets *(Bodden)* are only shallow and are cut off from the sea by banks of sand. Rostock-Warnemünde, Wismar and Stralsund have however been developed by the GDR to replace Hamburg, now in West Germany, and Stettin, now under Polish control. Rostock has become the chief port of the Democratic Republic and the centre of its new fishing and shipbuilding industries. It is the capital of an Administrative District *(Bezirk)* and scene of the 'Baltic Week', the East German counterpart of the 'Kieler Woche'. The port of Saßnitz on the island of Rügen now takes much of the traffic to Scandinavia that went via Travemünde before the division of Germany. Rügen is the largest German island

Rügen : holidaymakers at Sellin

and is famous for its chalk cliffs, unique in the Baltic, which are a valuable source of lime.

Behind the coast there is a fertile belt which extends eastwards from the Holsteinische Schweiz into Mecklenburg, Pomerania and East Prussia. There are many lakes and the region is almost entirely devoted to agriculture; a variety of crops is grown successfully, from rye and potatoes where the soil is poorest to wheat and sugar-beet on the best land. Schwerin is the only important town in the western part of the Mecklenburg Lake Plateau; it is the centre of an Administrative District. Neubrandenburg, an excellent example of the 'planned town' dating from the medieval eastern colonization, has also become an administrative centre.

In the old Province of Brandenburg the countryside changes completely; low-lying plains alternate with wide, marshy valleys *(Urstromtäler)* formed by the melt waters of the vast Ice Age glaciers. The rivers now only partly use these valleys; they have cut new beds through the uplands and flow northwards to the Baltic, whereas the *Urstromtäler* run from south-east to north-west. In the *Urstromtäler* the water-table is high, and before the land can be cultivated it must be drained; the canals dug for this purpose are linked to both the Elbe and the Oder. The river Spree, for example, flows sluggishly through marshland known as the Spreewald, where outdoor life is virtually lived on flat-bottomed boats; houses and haystacks have to be built on stilts because of the dampness. Much of the woodland has been cleared and replaced by market gardens which grow valuable crops to supply nearby Berlin.

The important cities of the Province of Brandenburg were Brandenburg itself, Frankfurt-on-Oder, Potsdam and Berlin. Frankfurt and Potsdam have now become the administrative centres of their own Districts. Potsdam was once the country residence of Prussian rulers; it now has a heavy engineering industry and is the centre of the film industry of the Democratic Republic. Brandenburg has an important steel industry based on scrap; it also produces a large number of tractors. Since 1871 Berlin* has been an important centre of commerce and government; it has a wide variety of industries, in particular those which require few raw materials and a great deal of skilled labour, such as printing, clothing and electrical products. It is linked by canal with the Baltic, the Elbe and the Ruhr, although traffic to the West is now negligible. Despite the political division of 1945 and the uncertain future, the city has continued to prosper. Its cultural and administrative centre has, however, been transformed by the Iron Curtain into a wasteland, and two new focal points have grown up in former suburbs.

South-west of Berlin, at the foot of the Central Uplands is an extremely fertile area of loess called the *Magdeburger*

*For a detailed account, see pp. 179–188

Farmworkers on an agricultural co-operative south-west of Berlin

Börde; the main crops are wheat and sugar beet. The chief marketing centre is Magdeburg on the Elbe, which is also a centre of commerce and industry as well as a District capital. The wide area of loess extends as far west as Brunswick; small pockets of its occur along the whole southern edge of the lowland plain. South-east of Berlin the landscape is largely rural and sparsely populated; new towns are, however, bringing industry to the area. Eisenhüttenstadt was created in 1961 by the merging of Stalinstadt, the new steel town, with the old town of Fürstenberg.

South of the Spreewald is Lusatia *(Lausitz)*, which since 1945 has become an important industrial area because of the extensive deposits of lignite or brown coal, East Germany's most important single source of power. The coal is obtained by open-pit mining, since the seams lie only a few feet below the sandy surface. Near Hoyerswerda a large plant (Schwarze Pumpe) has been built to manufacture electricity, coke and petroleum products from lignite. Cottbus is an important rail and road junction and has a large textile industry. It is a District capital and a centre for the Sorbs, a Slavonic people who have lived for centuries between the rivers Saale and Oder; they are the only national minority group in the Democratic Republic. Whilst they are encouraged to preserve their cultural traditions, politically they are being integrated into the GDR.

The Lusatian industrial area extends into the hills east of Dresden; the only town of importance in Upper Lusatia *(Ober-Lausitz)* is Görlitz, which has engineering, textile and motor-vehicle industries.

The coast of Pomerania is very sandy and is without a port except for Stettin at the mouth of the Oder. Along the coast occur the formations known as *Haffe* and *Nehrungen*; a *Haff* is a sheltered bay cut off from the sea by a narrow strip of land, the *Nehrung*. The water in the bay is so shallow and so liable to silting that the Haffs do not make suitable natural harbours; they do on the other hand provide ideal conditions for holidaymakers. Most of Pomerania, including the old capital Stettin, is now under Polish administration; it was until 1945 an important source of Germany's rye and potatoes. Stettin once handled bulk cargo for Berlin and Upper Silesia; its hinterland was considerably affected by the 'Oder–Neisse line', which cut off access to Berlin. The demarcation line also changed the face of towns such as Küstrin, which were not rebuilt after wartime damage, and altered the aspect of the countryside. For many years after the war, the fine farms, once occupied by the Germans, were neglected, some indeed were turned over to forestry. Little emphasis was placed on agriculture until industry had been rebuilt.

The former free city of Danzig, now also under Polish control, and Gdingen, a new port founded by Poland in the Polish Corridor after the First World War, deal with most of Poland's exports and imports. To the east of Danzig the coast of East Prussia is characterized by *Haffe* and *Nehrungen*. Here the dunes bordering the *Haffe* have in the past been blown forward and engulfed fishing villages; the sand is now retained by specially planted grasses and trees. The beaches here yield quantities of amber. Much of East Prussia is covered by infertile heath, which alternates with groups of lakes. Before the war some agricultural areas were highly developed, producing rye, potatoes and dairy produce. When the Russians and Poles occupied East Prussia they drove out the German farmers and for a number of years neglected agriculture in favour of industry. Königsberg, the old capital, is now under Soviet rule and has been renamed Kaliningrad.

The Central Uplands

The Western Hills

The uplands in the west of Germany are carved into separate massifs by the valleys of the river Rhine and its tributaries. They have therefore not been a barrier to communications.

The Moselle *(Mosel)*, the longest tributary of the Rhine, divides the Hunsrück from the Eifel mountains. The Hunsrück is an exposed, stony plateau, where only such crops as rye and potatoes will grow. There are a few small industries, for example the making of jewellery in Idar-Oberstein, but economically this is one of West Germany's problem areas. Characteristic of the Eifel are some fifty cone-shaped volcanoes, extinct for 10,000 years; circular lakes, the Laacher See being the largest, have formed in some of the craters. Volcanic activity is, however, still evident in the innumerable warm and mineral springs in the area; in Aachen the water temperature reaches 76°C. In the Eifel farming is difficult. The climate in the western part is so wet that farmers concentrate on cattle-rearing; they send their dairy produce and meat into Aachen, a city famous for its textiles and Charlemagne's cathedral. In the Eifel tourism is being encouraged to try to bring prosperity to this picturesque but economically depressed area.

The oldest town on the Moselle is Trier, founded about 15 B.C. by the Romans on the site of an older settlement; among its ancient buildings there are several dating from the Roman occupation. Below Trier the sheltered river banks have grown grapes for 2,000 years; the wines, which take

Fig 5

Eifel: looking towards the Ahr valley

their names from the picturesque villages nestling at the foot of the vineyards, are exported to all parts of the world. The principal marketing centre for all the local wines is Trier. In 1964 the Moselle was made navigable to barges of 1,500 tons in accordance with agreements made with France in 1956 concerning the future of the Saar. Barrages and locks were built at intervals, the bed was dredged and the width made constant. Although the volume of traffic is still lower than was

Vineyards by the Moselle near Zeltingen

hoped, the scheme does provide a potentially valuable link between the Rhine and the industrial areas of the Saar and north-eastern France. Railways and modern main roads do not for the most part follow the river, which has eroded an incredibly tortuous course between steep, high banks.

Koblenz is a market town and a centre of communications because of its position on the Rhine at the mouth of the Moselle and Lahn valleys. There are fruit-canning and artificial building stone industries, the latter being based on extensive local deposits of volcanic ash (pumice).

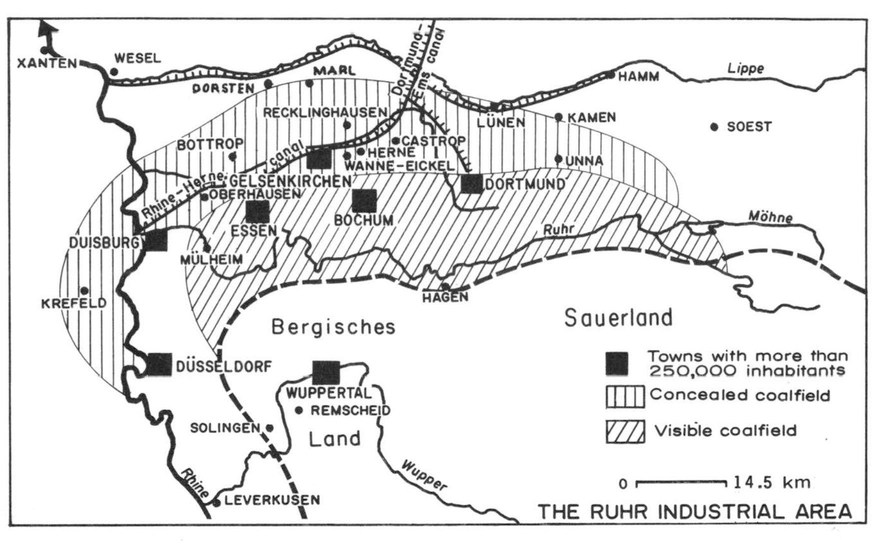

Fig 6

On the right bank of the Rhine the upland massifs are divided by the rivers Wupper, Sieg, Lahn and Main. On the northern fringe of the uplands a large industrial area known as the Ruhr *(Ruhrgebiet)* grew up during the nineteenth century, based on iron ore from the Siegerland and deposits of excellent hard coal in the valley of the river Ruhr. Numerous towns, together having a population of over six millions and still rapidly expanding, are crowded so closely together that they almost constitute a single conurbation 95 km. long and 32 km. wide. The oldest industrial settlements are in the south, where the coal seams are near the surface, but these deposits are almost exhausted and much of the area has returned to rural peace. As industry developed and further resources of coal were needed, mining spread northwards into the concealed coalfield and engulfed the medieval towns of Essen and Dortmund. It is in this region that the giant steel combines of Krupp, Hoesch and Thyssen were founded. Further expansion northwards caused the growth of completely new towns such as Gelsenkirchen and Oberhausen; north of these towns the seams of coal are deep and hence expensive to work. The prosperity of the mining industry declined sharply in the 1950s, when competition from other fuels caused the closure of many mines; in Gelsenkirchen for example 35,000 miners became redundant and had to seek employment in the new light industries which were set up. Of the coal now mined in this area some is made locally into

Dortmund: the blast furnaces of the Hoesch steelworks

Solingen: barber's knives being inspected at a cutlery factory (Henckels Zwillingswerk)

coke; there are extensive industries dependent upon coal, such as the pharmaceutical and chemical industries. Much of the coal is sent south to the furnaces of Duisburg on the Rhine and Dortmund on the Rhine–Herne canal, where the steel and engineering industries are based. Ore is transported to the furnaces by water, and the molten iron passes directly to the steelworks on the same site.

The area is fortunate in having at its disposal cheap water transport not only along the Rhine and its tributaries, but also along a network of modern canals, which is still being improved and extended. Duisburg has the largest inland harbour in Germany. The Ruhr is linked to the port of Emden by the Rhine–Herne and Dortmund–Ems canals; the Mittelland canal links the Dortmund–Ems canal to the rivers Weser and Elbe and also to Berlin. Of recent years oil, brought both by barge and pipeline, has become increasingly important to the industry of the Ruhr; as the refining and petrochemical industries have grown, coal mining has declined.

An extensive network of railways and roads has been built in the Ruhr to cater for the thousands of workers who travel daily to and from their work and for the factories, which need regular supplies of raw materials and an efficient means of despatching their finished products.

Between the rivers Wupper and Sieg rises the Sauerland, with Das Bergische Land to the west and the Rothaargebirge to the east. Das Bergische Land is still largely rural and therefore acts as a lung for the nearby Ruhr. In the valleys, however, industrial development has taken place. Solingen and Remscheid produce cutlery and tools respectively, using steel supplied for the most part by the Ruhr. The largest town is Wuppertal, one of the most important and highly specialized textile-producing towns in West Germany. It lies along the narrow valley of the Wupper, above which the unique suspended railway *(Schwebebahn)* was built in 1900 to solve the problem of difficult communications. South of the Sauerland lies the Siegerland, once Germany's main source of iron ore, but the deposits are now almost exhausted. This was an industrial area long before the Ruhr was developed, but it is now dependent on Ruhr coal and electricity and concentrates on finishing processes for steel products.

To the east of the Sauerland, the Rothaargebirge is dominated by the Kahler Asten (841 metres), one of the highest points in north-west Germany and the site of an important weather station. The Sauerland is a region of high rainfall and it is therefore largely wooded. Several rivers, including the Ruhr, Wupper and Lahn, rise there and the many streams once provided water power for light industry. Some of the valleys have been dammed to form reservoirs which supply water and hydro-electric power to the Ruhr; there are in all 31 such reservoirs. The climate in the Sauerland is so wet that the region has developed a characteristic type of half-timbered house; the west-facing walls are covered with slates in order to protect them from rain-bearing winds.

The Westerwald lies between the rivers Sieg and Lahn. Like the Eifel, the Westerwald is volcanic and provides quantities of basalt used, for example, in road-making and for facing sea dikes. Most of the heights are wooded, but oats, rye and potatoes are grown on the western slopes. The large rural population and the almost complete absence of industry make the Westerwald one of West Germany's problem areas.

The Lahn, navigable only to small craft since its depth in places is merely two feet, is one of the most beautiful rivers in Germany, and is still virtually unspoiled; Marburg is reputedly the prettiest of all the German university towns. Wetzlar, lower down the Lahn, has become a centre of the West

Marburg: the Castle (from the Lutheran Church)

German optical industry; it is the home of the Leitz company, which produces Leica cameras, microscopes and telescopes. Limburg has a moderate amount of light industry, but its fame undoubtedly rests on its picturesquely situated cathedral. Close to the confluence of the rivers Lahn and Rhine lies Bad Ems, a famous spa, which was frequented at the turn of the century by the aristocracy of Europe.

South of the Lahn lies the Taunus, which in general is heavily wooded, although the south-facing slopes along the Rhine (known as the *Rheingau*) grow fruit, notably peaches, apricots and grapes. At several places warm springs, whose medicinal value was known to the Romans, bubble to the surface; the warmest are in Wiesbaden, capital of the State of Hesse *(Hessen)*. Wiesbaden also houses several departments of the Federal Government; it has printing, cement, clothing and film industries. Together with Mainz, situated on the opposite bank of the Rhine, it now forms a single conurbation. Mainz is an important Rhine port, a university and cathedral town and capital of the State Rhineland-Palatinate *(Rheinland-Pfalz)*.

To the south the Taunus is bounded by the river Main, which is usually taken as the dividing line between north and south Germany. On the upper Main lie Bayreuth, famous for the annual Wagner festival, and Bamberg, a fine cathedral city and a market for the surrounding area, which is nicknamed the 'Bavarian kitchen garden'. Bamberg is the limit of navigation on the river Main, but the derelict *Ludwigskanal* cut in the mid-nineteenth century between Bamberg and the Danube is now being enlarged and extended. This canal, the Europa canal, will form the missing link in the waterway which will connect the North Sea to the Black Sea by 1981. It is already open as far as Nuremberg.

Some miles above the university and cathedral city of Würzburg the cultivation of vines on the south-facing river banks becomes possible. The wines produced in this area are sold in unusually-shaped bottles *(Bocksbeutel)*; they are not well-known abroad because they are considered by connoisseurs too good to export. About 40 km. below Würzburg the Main turns abruptly southwards and then flows along three sides of a square, almost enclosing the Spessart, where extensive forests once provided hunting for German kings. There is little space for agriculture, which has remained in a primitive condition, and many farmers find it necessary to augment their income by working in clothing factories in Aschaffenburg or by making up clothes at home.

The largest town on the Main is Frankfurt, at the northern end of the Rhine plain. Frankfurt has been one of the really important towns in Germany since the Middle Ages and has become the great centre of trade and communications in the south-west. It has important motor-car and chemical industries and is a terminal of the oil pipeline from Wilhelmshaven. Other industries in the area are leather, centred in Offenbach, pharmaceutical products in Darmstadt, jewellery and rubber in Hanau.

The Rhine valley, the most important of all the valleys in the western hills, is at its most picturesque between the Hunsrück and the Taunus in the so-called Rhine Gorge. This gorge was eroded along the line of a geological fault which occurred as the Alps were being thrown ever higher by the process of folding. Popular with tourists is the stretch between Bingen and Koblenz, where the Rhine sweeps majestically round bend after bend. The steep, south-facing slopes are terraced and clad with vines; romantic villages squeeze themselves along the banks and forbidding strongholds, now mostly ruined, keep watch over the river traffic. This stretch of the Rhine is particularly dangerous: the many barges and steamers require the services

Frankfurt: the Römer (Town Hall)

of a skilled pilot in order to negotiate the treacherous rapids near Bingen and the narrow bends near St. Goarshausen, where legend has it t' at the beautiful Lorelei lies in wait to entice unwary sailors on to the rocks. The many castles were built as tollhouses by rapacious noblemen, who hung chains across the river to prevent ships passing free of charge, yet they abound in legends of fair maidens, brave knights and fierce dragons. The two tollhouses in mid-stream, the Pfalz and the Mouse Tower *(Mäuseturm)*, are now signal stations, helping navigation in the narrow gorge.

The climate of the Rhine Gorge is extremely favourable; spring comes early and autumn gives way to winter rather later than in the nearby hills. This fact, coupled with the steep, sunny slopes and stony, heat-retaining soil, provides ideal conditions for growing vines. Despite ***Flurbereinigung*** (p. 72) the growers must work long and hard before they can taste the result of their labours The hillsides must be terraced, hoed and cleared of weed, the young vines must be carefully tended (pruned, sprayed and trained) for three years, and the ripe grapes gathered as late as possible in the year. The combined experience of all the growers goes into deciding on the best date for the harvest; if it is too soon, the wine will be sour, if it is too late, the crop will be ruined by frost. The rarest wine

The Rhine Gorge at St. Goarshausen with a castle (Burg Katz) on the right and terraced vineyards on both banks

The Rhine and the Siebengebirge from Bonn

is however 'Eiswein', made from grapes gathered after a fall of snow.

North of Koblenz the river is wider and the banks are neither so high nor so steep. There are a number of attractive towns, such as Andernach, and some industry; the principal occupations in Neuwied, for example, are the manufacture of ceramics and of artificial building-stone. South-east of Bonn is a small group of volcanic mountains known as the *Siebengebirge* ('Seven Hills'). Although they are not very high, the scenic beauty of these hills attracts many tourists; the Drachenfels by the Rhine is the most frequently climbed mountain in Europe, with three million visitors each year.

Bonn became the capital of the Federal Republic in 1949. The arrangement was to be temporary, since it was confidently expected that Berlin would quickly reassume its function as capital. Three decades later the pretty, sleepy university town is learning to live with the army of civil servants, diplomats and politicians which descended upon it.

The Rhine is West Germany's most important inland waterway, being navigable at present to barges of over 2,000 tons as far as Rheinfelden, above Basle. Freight traffic is heaviest between Rotterdam and the Ruhr, tailing off gradually above the Ruhr, where, however, it is joined by passenger steamers and pleasure craft, especially during the summer months. The Rhine valley has for many centuries been an important route between northern and southern Europe; railways and roads follow both banks of the river and in summer almost 300 trains use this route every day.

The Central Hills

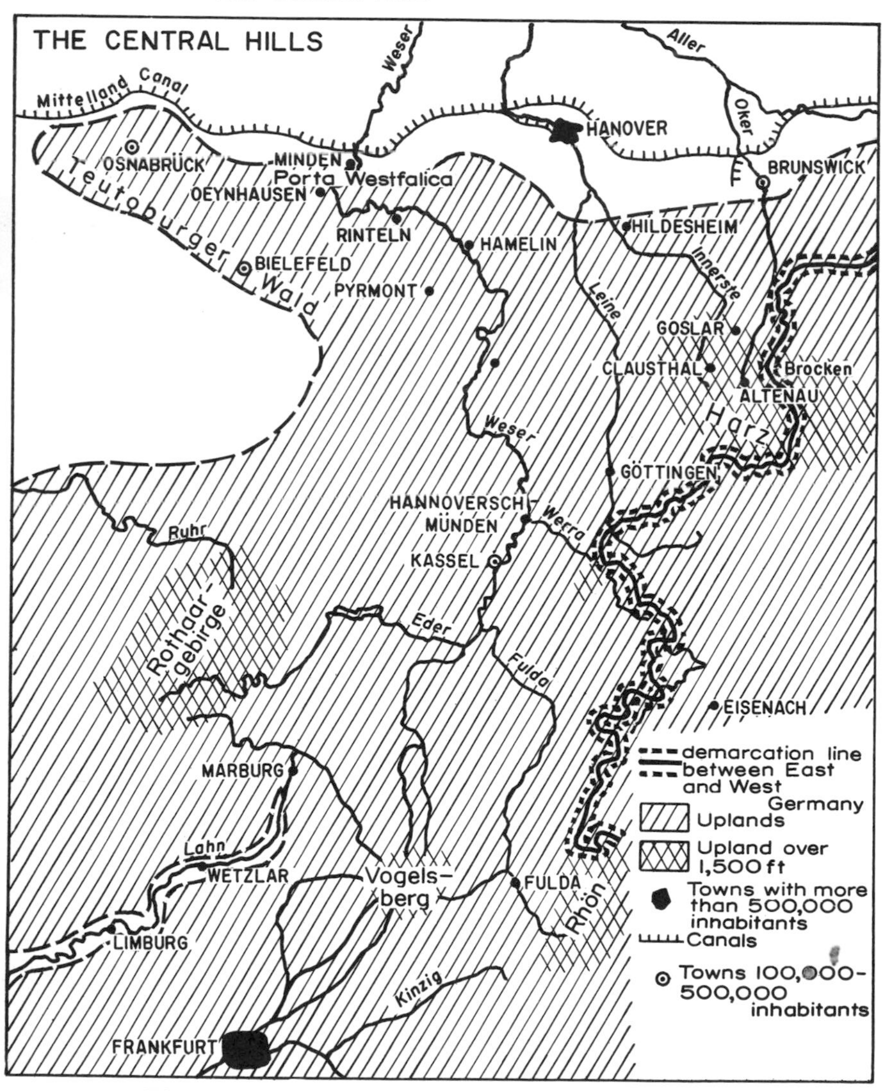

Fig 7

The volcanic uplands in the centre of Germany are dissected by rivers flowing northwards to the Weser, which itself divides the Teutoburger Wald from the Harz mountains. The river Fulda, for example, rises on the Vogelsberg, Germany's highest volcano and an important source of basalt. The high rainfall coupled with the impermeable basalt makes any kind of farming difficult, and small cottage industries based on local skills grew up to provide additional income. The old ecclesiastical city of Fulda grew up on an ancient route along the valley of the river Fulda connecting northern and southern Germany. Lower down the river lies Kassel, an industrial town specializing in heavy engineering and the administrative centre of northern Hesse. The river Fulda joins the Werra at Hannoversch-Münden to form the river Weser.

There is little industry along the upper Weser and the people rely mainly on tourism and farming. Of the many pretty towns and villages Hamelin *(Hameln)* deserves a mention as the place where the Pied Piper is reputed to have charmed away the children. After flowing westwards along a wide, fertile valley, the Weser suddenly turns northwards and breaks through a ridge of mountains in a gap known as the Porta Westfalica. Here the central uplands abruptly end, giving way to the North German Plain. Nearby lies Minden, an industrial city on both the Weser and the Mittelland canal, which is here carried on an aqueduct high above the river. The *Schachtschleuse*, an immensely deep lock, links the canal with

Rinteln on the upper Weser, which once housed a university.

the river Weser, providing an important crossroads for the internal water transport of the Federal Republic.

The Weser is an increasingly important inland waterway; it carries large barges between the North Sea and Minden, and medium-sized barges and pleasure steamers as far as Kassel. Timber, the major raw material in the area, which was once floated down the swift-flowing river in rafts, is now carried either by barge or rail. Much of it is used in the local furniture factories. The upper Weser is not always navigable; it can freeze over for days at a time and in summer there may be insufficient water for heavy barges. The latter problem has to some extent been overcome by a dam on a tributary, the Eder, which, besides providing hydro-electric power and preventing spring flooding, can send a 'wave' downstream big enough to float a flotilla of barges into deeper water. The Weser valley has on account of its winding course been ignored by modern communications, which follow the smaller Leine to Hanover. The university city of Göttingen on the Leine is an important centre of local industry.

On the left bank of the Weser is the Teutoburger Wald, part of which is sheltered and very fertile. The flax grown there is processed in Bielefeld, which, like the important traffic-junction Osnabrück, is situated at the entrance to a valley which provides an easy route through the hills. There are many furniture factories in the area, which draw on the local resources of timber. Spas such as Oeynhausen and Pyrmont have healing mineral springs.

Midway between the Weser and the Elbe lie the Harz mountains, through which the border between East and West Germany runs, illogically splitting what is essentially a single geographic and economic unit. The highest point in the Harz, the Brocken (1,142 metres), is in the Democratic Republic. According to legend this bleak, treeless place is the scene of a witches' gathering on Walpurgis Night (April 30th). The steep northern and western slopes of the Harz are particularly wet, since the rain clouds are forced to rise for the first time since leaving the North Sea, yet Halle to the south-east has the lowest rainfall in Germany. Many rivers rise in the Harz; some of them are dammed to form reservoirs which supply water to distant towns such as Bremen.

Of the two traditional industries, timber and mining, only the former is now of any considerable importance; there is a tradition of fine wood-carving, which is still carried on in Altenau. The skill of the miners, derived from more than six

Stolberg, a delightful little town in the eastern part of the Harz (GDR)

centuries of experience, is, however, passed on at the Mining Academy in Clausthal-Zellerfeld. A certain amount of silver, zinc and lead is still obtained, especially from the 1,000 year-old mines in the Rammelsberg near Goslar. Precious metals from these same mines once helped to swell the treasure chests of the Holy Roman Emperors who from time to time held court in Goslar. The palace and other contemporary buildings are still intact. At Mansfeld on the eastern edge of the Harz there are valuable deposits of copper, which elsewhere in Germany is very rare; the mines have been redeveloped since the partition in 1945.

Nestling amidst the dense forests are countless unspoiled villages, which have been transformed from mining centres into climatic resorts to enable visitors to take advantage of the pure mountain air. In winter the precipitation falls as snow, and so these same resorts have also developed a thriving winter trade, attracting tourists mainly from northern Germany for whom these mountains are the nearest winter sports centre.

The Uplands of the Democratic Republic

The eastern and southern edges of the Harz slope gently towards the Thuringian Basin. This low-lying bowl, flanked

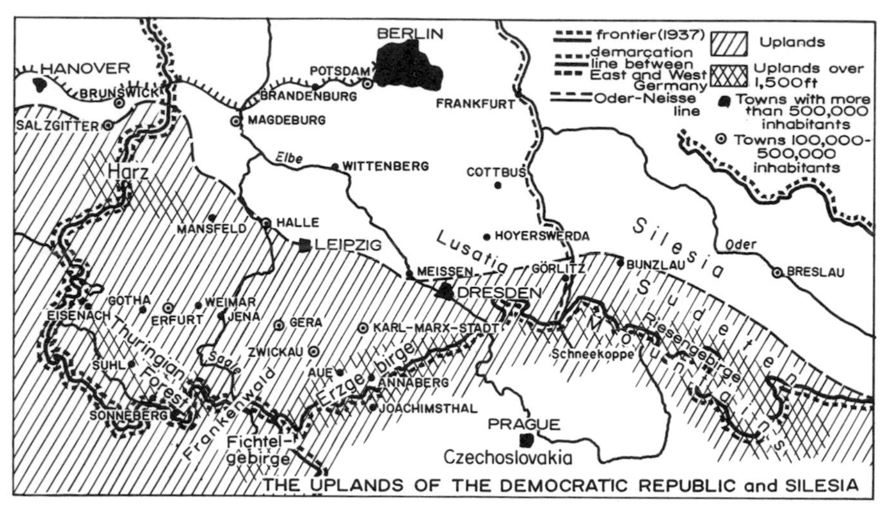

Fig 8

to the south and west by the Thuringian and the Franconian Forests, has been nicknamed 'the green heart of Germany' on account of its fertility. Until recently the area depended almost entirely on its agriculture. Erfurt and Leipzig were the only towns of any size; they are now the capitals of their respective Administrative Districts. Leipzig, scene of great trade fairs each spring and autumn, grew up at the junction of several important routes; it was the centre of Germany's publishing and fur trades and has a long and enviable musical tradition. It is now the second largest town in the GDR, and lies at the heart of the country's south-western industrial area. Weimar, in the nineteenth century the cultural centre of Germany, is now an industrial town producing machinery and footwear. Other industrial towns of importance are Eisenach (motor vehicles), Gotha (engineering and printing), Jena (optics and glassware) and Gera (textiles). Halle is built upon salt deposits; its rise as a railway junction despite the proximity of Leipzig is explained by the fact that it lay in a different State when the railways were built. Both Halle and Gera have since 1952 been capitals of Administrative Districts.

The Thuringian Forest *(Thüringer Wald)* has for many years had a thriving toy-making industry centred on Sonneberg. To some extent this is still a cottage industry in which whole families participate. There is some light engineering, for example in Suhl, the District capital, but glass-blowing has declined since 1945 when many of the workers moved to West Germany. The mineral springs and pure mountain air of the Thuringian Forest attract many tourists.

The Franconian Forest *(Frankenwald)* has the most important slate quarries in Europe and also the largest artificial lake in Germany, 28 km. long, formed by the river Saale. Not only does this dam provide drinking water and hydro-electric power, but it also regulates the level of water in the rivers Saale and Elbe.

The Thuringian Basin is flanked to the south-east by the Erzgebirge, which forms the frontier between Germany and Czechoslovakia. The mountains are high and not easily crossed; the main communication routes avoid them altogether, using the Elbe valley to the east and the gap between the Erzgebirge and the Thuringian Forest to the west. Small industries began in these mountains and eventually spread to the plain as they grew; in this way towns such as Dresden, Karl-Marx-Stadt (formerly Chemnitz) and Zwickau were founded. This industrial area was developed during the nineteenth century on the basis of local raw materials, chiefly brown coal and potash. Supplies of hard coal mined from a small deposit near Zwickau for the foundries and heavy engineering industries of the Democratic Republic will run out by 1980. Textiles and motor vehicles are also produced in the region, chiefly at Karl-Marx-Stadt, a District capital, and at Zwickau. Dresden on the Elbe, the former residence of Saxon kings, was once an elegant town, but many of the fine eighteenth century buildings were destroyed during the war

Meissen: looking across the Elbe to the Gothic Cathedral and the fifteenth-century castle (Albrechtsburg)

and have not been rebuilt; there are however notable exceptions such as the Zwinger Palace. Dresden is an administrative centre and houses several specialized industries, although 'Dresden china' is actually manufactured in Meissen.

Above Dresden the Elbe breaks through the mountains in a narrow deep valley; this is the only place in the Democratic Republic where vines grow. The area, known as 'Saxon Switzerland', is of unusual scenic beauty; tourists come chiefly to see the weird sandstone formations weathered from solid rock by water and frost. The Erzgebirge ('Ore Mountains') derives its name from the rich deposits of silver and lead ores discovered there about 750 years ago. Many towns devoted exclusively to mining grew up, including Annaberg and Joachimsthal; the latter is a German settlement in Bohemia which gave its name to the *Taler* or dollar. Mining, which has been declining since the fifteenth century, was given new impetus by the discovery of uranium ore near Aue. The decline of mining caused the growth of cottage industries depending on local skills and raw materials, notably the making of lace, toys and musical instruments. The old mining towns have more recently been developed as holiday resorts.

Silesia, the most easterly of the former central German provinces, is now for the most part administered by Poland.

Breslau (now Wroclaw), the capital, lies in the heart of Silesia on the banks of the Oder. It was once the economic and cultural centre of the eastern German provinces. The extreme south-eastern tip of Silesia, which boasts Europe's largest deposits of hard coal and also considerable deposits of iron and zinc ores, developed into a large industrial area, part of which, including the towns of Kattowitz (now Katowice) and Königshütte (now Chorzow), was ceded to Poland in 1922.

Toymaking is one of the traditional crafts of the Erzgebirge

Dresden: the Georgi Dimitrov Bridge with the Cathedral (formerly Hofkirche) in the background

The Southern Uplands between Danube and Main

The largest massifs in the southern uplands are the Black Forest and the Swabian Alb in the south-west corner of Germany. To the west of the southern uplands the Rhine flows northwards along a wide plain, sheltered by the Vosges and Pfälzer Wald to the west and by the Black Forest and Odenwald to the east. The Rhine plain is about 300 km. long and more than 35 km. wide; it is a gigantic flood plain within a rift valley which formed when a block of mountains sank between the lines of two faults.

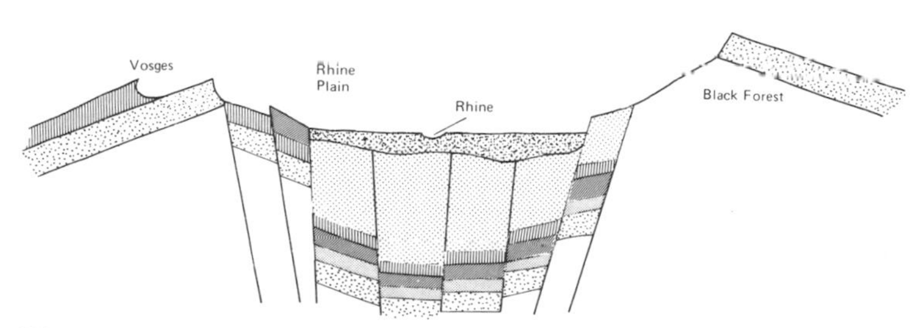

Fig 9: The Upper Rhine rift valley

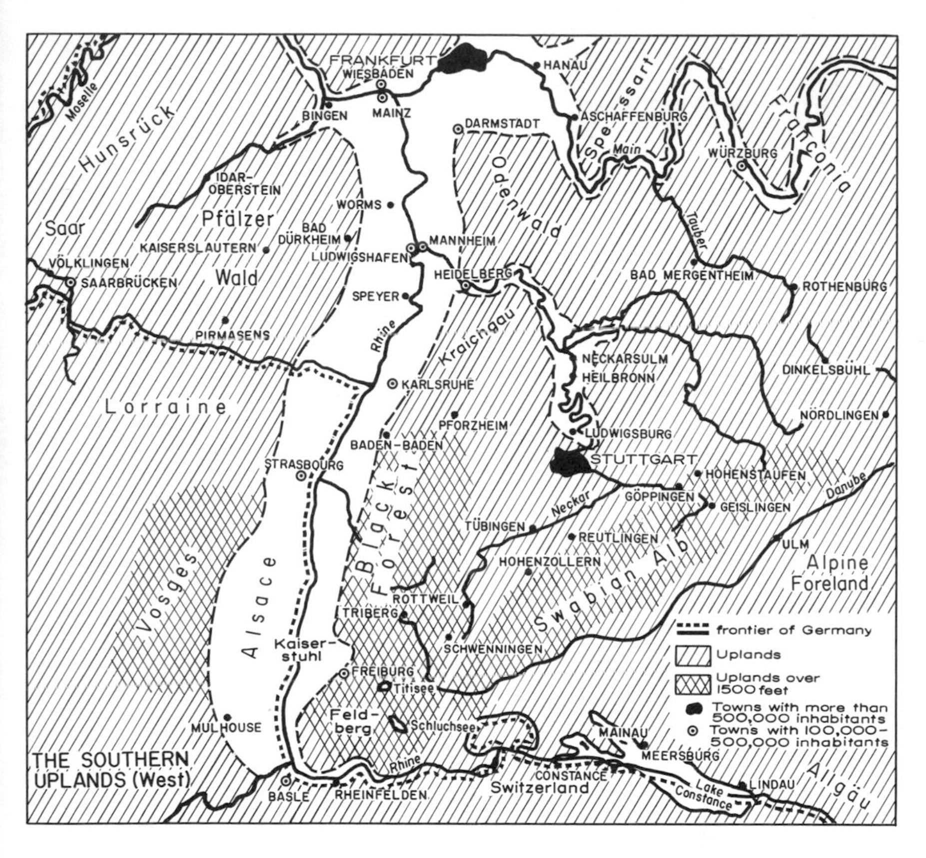

Fig 10

Each spring the river overflowed its banks and frequently changed its course, sweeping away settlements when it was in full spate. In the mid-nineteenth century a straight, deep course was dredged through the plain, bounded on each side by high dikes. Not only did this drain the land and prevent the river flooding, it also made the river navigable to large craft as far as Basle. Harbours were built in Strasbourg to serve France, in Basle to serve Switzerland and in many places on the German banks, notably in Mannheim and Ludwigshafen.

Speyer: the magnificent Romanesque Cathedral (built 1030–1100), burial place of eight Emperors

The climate of the plain is the most favourable in Germany, both unusually warm and dry; spring comes early and the winters are mild, with little frost. The ground is fertile and produces good crops of wheat, tobacco, maize, fruit and vegetables. Grapes are grown and excellent wines made from them in the Kaiserstuhl, an isolated group of volcanic hills near Freiburg, where the climate is warmest of all. The Romans took advantage of the favourable conditions to build many settlements, almost exclusively on the left bank; Germanic settlements on the right bank were built some distance from the river to act as market centres. By the Middle Ages several of the early communities, namely Mainz, Worms, Speyer, Strasbourg and Freiburg, had developed into important towns, a fact demonstrated by the size of their cathedrals. Since the nineteenth century they have however been overshadowed by newer towns such as Karlsruhe and Mannheim. The former was built in the eighteenth century to a distinctive plan with the streets radiating from the Margrave's palace; it is now a river port and houses engineering, electrical and tobacco industries. Mannheim and its sister town Ludwigshafen on the opposite bank together form a major inland port second in Germany only to Duisburg; there is some engineering, but the largest employer of labour is a seven-km.-long chemicals factory in Ludwigshafen

(Badische Anilin- und Sodafabrik, better known by the initials BASF). Oil is supplied to the area by a pipeline from the Mediterranean and also from a small oilfield near Mannheim. Natural gas is fed to the chemical factories from deposits near Darmstadt. Darmstadt itself has a variety of industries, including engineering, electrical goods and paper. The largest town on the Rhine plain is Frankfurt, situated near the confluence of the rivers Rhine and Main (see p. 33).

The Rhine plain extends westwards to the Vosges mountains in France, which are in almost all respects similar to the Black Forest, once part of the same massif. In Lorraine, north of the Vosges, there are considerable deposits of iron ore; further north, near Saarbrücken, is a vast coalfield. The proximity of these two important natural resources has in the past led to disputes between France and Germany over the Saar and Alsace-Lorraine. Since the year 1957 the Saar has been part of the Federal Republic. The European Coal and Steel Community *(Montan-Union)*, which was founded in 1951, has ensured that the industry of the whole region flourished regardless of natural frontiers by providing for the free movement of coal and iron ore. The largest steel-making plant in the Saar is at Völklingen.

East of Saarbrücken lies a group of hills known as the Pfälzer Wald, where some of Germany's most famous wines are produced. The 'Wine Road' *(Weinstraße)* runs along the western edge of the Rhine plain between Bad Dürkheim and the frontier with France. The only towns of any size in the area are Kaiserslautern, which has a small engineering industry, and Pirmasens, home of many factories producing footwear.

The southern part of the Rhine plain extends eastwards to the foothills of the Black Forest. The lower west-facing slopes are even more fertile than the plain, producing wine and tobacco. Some of the steeper slopes are cultivated by contour-ploughing, but where the land is poor and steep, the hills are forested. The Black Forest is highest in the south (Feldberg 1,490 metres), where it was nearest to the effects of Alpine folding. There are spectacular gorges, such as the Höllental, and many lakes, including the beautiful Titisee and the Schluchsee, a source of hydro-electric power. Because of the unfavourable climate and poor soil the mountains are thinly populated. The farmhouses are immense, since the living-quarters, stalls and barn are all under one enormous shingled roof, enabling the farmer to look after his herds even in the most severe weather (see also p. 258). The farmers rely on their sales of timber and on these small herds of cattle which graze clearings in the forest, so tourism provides a welcome source of income. Wood-carving was originally a winter pastime for the farmers; it has now become a profitable trade almost exclusively carried on in small factories. Clock- and watch-making and other precision trades which need few raw materials are the main industries in the towns on the eastern slopes such as Triberg and Schwenningen.

Freiburg, which lies on the edge of the Rhine plain, is the administrative and cultural centre of the southern Black Forest. It has a thriving tourist industry in both winter and summer; the outstanding feature of the town is its magnificent red sandstone Gothic Minster (see p. 142).

The northern Black Forest lacks the abundant lakes and spectacular gorges of the south and bases its tourist industry on the numerous warm and mineral springs around which fashionable spas such as Baden-Baden have grown. Between

The Schluchsee with its dam

Zwingenberg: the castle with barges on the Neckar

the Black Forest and the lower reaches of the Neckar lies the Kraichgau; it is an agricultural region, and is nicknamed 'Swabia's Granary'. Further north the Rhine plain is bounded by the Odenwald, part of an ancient forest where kings once hunted. Along the western edge of the hills between Frankfurt and Heidelberg runs the 'Mountain Road' *(Bergstraße)*, which in spring attracts crowds of tourists since it cuts through mile upon mile of apple, pear, plum, peach and cherry orchards.

South of the Odenwald the river Neckar joins the Rhine at Mannheim. It is now navigable as far as Stuttgart, the capital of Baden-Württemberg, which has a modern harbour in the district of Cannstatt. Stuttgart is an administrative centre and an industrial town specializing in printing and electrical goods; it is also the home of Mercedes-Benz, Porsche and Heinkel. The Neckar valley is both agricultural and industrial; the factories are clean and attractively sited among orchards, vineyards and meadows. Industry in the area ranges from textiles and motor vehicles to musical instruments and toys. Numerous small spas have developed around the mineral springs of the Neckar valley; also popular with tourists are the old university towns of Tübingen (1477) and Heidelberg (1386) and the former royal residence of Ludwigsburg.

The Swabian Alb rises abruptly 400 metres from the upper Neckar and slopes gradually away to the south-east. The hills are chalky and the soil poor and dry, since water drains through the chalk and forms subterranean streams and caverns. The bare hills, which offer no protection against the wind, and the scarcity of water account for the sparse population. Cattle are mostly kept indoors; sheep graze the poor grass where even oats and root-vegetables will not grow. Several hills lie isolated by wide valleys from the steep north-western edge (scarp) of the Alb; of those once crowned by

Heidelberg from the castle

impregnable fortresses, the Hohenzollern alone retains its castle intact. The textile industry has been well-developed throughout the whole region; it is not concentrated in one built-up area, but is distributed in a number of small towns such as Reutlingen and Göppingen. All the raw materials for this and other industries have to be brought into the region and for this reason the factories tend to cluster around the main railway line between Stuttgart and Ulm which crosses the Swabian Alb through a gap known as the *Geislinger Steige*. Ulm, at the eastern end of this pass, has motor vehicle, textile, radio and engineering industries and a Gothic Minster with the tallest spire in Christendom (161 metres).

The plateaus east of the Odenwald are in general extremely fertile; wheat, sugar beet and potatoes are extensively grown. In the valley of the Tauber, which cuts through the plateaus, there are vineyards; at the centre of the wine-growing region lies the well-known spa of Bad Mergentheim.

Ulm: the Minster from the Danube

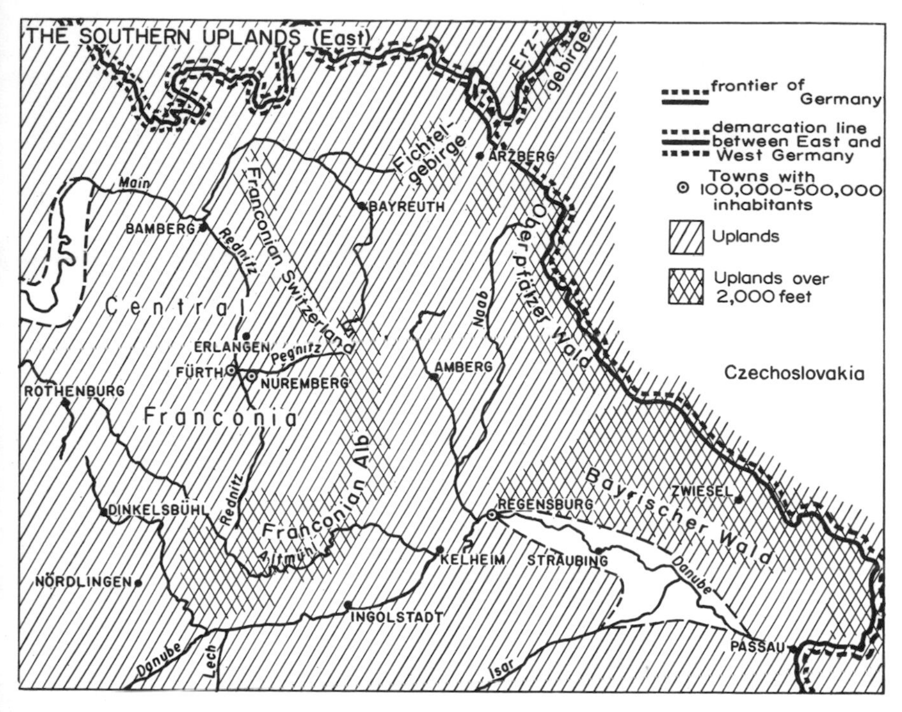

Fig 11

Central Franconia is still largely rural. Most of the villages and towns are very old, and some like Rothenburg and Nördlingen have preserved their medieval appearance. The road from Füssen on the Austrian frontier through Augsburg to Würzburg passes many of these towns and has become known as the 'Romantic Road' *(Romantische Straße)*.

The uplands are sandy and the valleys fertile; in the valley of the Regnitz vegetables and hops are grown. Nuremberg *(Nürnberg)* on the Regnitz was even in the Middle Ages a rich town. It has long been noted for craftsmanship and now specializes in heavy and light engineering and electrical goods; other important products are pencils and toys. The new Europa canal harbour should soon bring increased prosperity. Nearby Fürth, which was in 1835 connected to Nuremberg by Germany's first railway, produces radio and television sets and glassware. North of Nuremberg lies the university town of Erlangen, which since 1945 has benefited greatly from the arrival of refugee firms from the eastern provinces making electrical goods, leather goods and textiles.

The Franconian Alb is neither so high nor so bare as the Swabian Alb. It is dissected by many spectacular river valleys such as those of the Pegnitz and Altmühl; the lower reaches of the latter are to become part of the great Rhine–Main–Danube waterway when the last section between Bamberg and Kelheim is completed. This waterway will enable 1,350 ton barges to sail from the North Sea to the Black Sea and promises to bring new industrial potential to south-eastern Germany. The northernmost hills in Franconia are thinly populated because the soil is poor and water is scarce.

East of the Franconian hills is a low-lying area drained by the river Naab. There is a small amount of industrial development, particularly in Amberg, where southern Germany's sole deposit of iron ore has been discovered.

The lowland area is bounded to the north by the Fichtelgebirge, said to be the heart of the German uplands, since ridges of mountains radiate from it. The Thuringian Forest to the north-west, the Erzgebirge to the north-east and the Franconian Alb to the south-west are mentioned elsewhere. To the south-east, along the frontier with Czechoslovakia, run the thickly forested slopes of the Oberpfälzer Wald and the Bayerischer Wald. This is economically an extremely poor area, completely devoid of modern industrial development. The forests have as yet been only partially exploited. There are no mineral deposits apart from a 100 km. long ridge of hard white quartz, one of the ingredients of glass; on both sides of the frontier with Czechoslovakia there are innumerable small towns such as Zwiesel which concentrate almost entirely on the highly skilled craft of glass-blowing. The industry received a boost after the war when many Sudeten German

Glass-blowers in a factory in the Bayerischer Wald

glass-blowers settled in West Germany. The Fichtelgebirge is rather more prosperous; the industry in the area is at present based upon deposits of china clay, although deposits of uranium ore have recently been discovered. This is the centre of West Germany's pottery industry and is the home of the world-famous firms of Rosenthal and Arzberg. Tourism is being developed intensively throughout these hilly areas.

The Alps and the Alpine Foreland

The Danube rises in the Black Forest, then breaks through the Swabian Alb, where it almost disappears as it passes over the porous chalk; some of its water flows underground to the Rhine. Ulm is the upper limit of navigation for small barges,

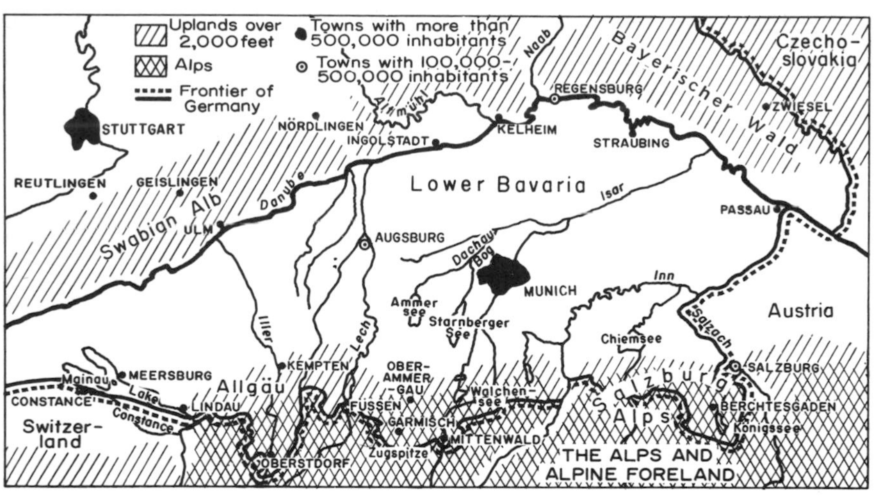

Fig 12

since the flow of water is erratic; large craft can reach Regensburg, where the Danube is already 200 yards wide. Regensburg, known to the Romans as Castra Regina, has now become an industrial city; the old part of the town round the Gothic cathedral with its twin spires has retained its narrow streets and fine old buildings as a reminder of the splendour it enjoyed as a rich trading city in the Middle Ages. The Danube finally leaves Germany at Passau, with only one-fifth of its journey to the Black Sea completed; Passau, a fine cathedral city at the confluence of the Danube, Inn and

Regensburg: the twelfth-century Stone Bridge and Gothic Cathedral

Ilz, has some light industry. Other industrial towns on the Danube are Kelheim (cellulose and rayon), Straubing (breweries and earthenware) and Ingolstadt, which has motor vehicle and engineering factories and an oil refinery, fed by a pipeline from the Mediterranean.

Between the Swabian Alb and Passau the Danube flows along the northern edge of the Alpine Foreland, which extends southwards to the foothills of the Alps. The Alpine Foreland is a wide, gently sloping plain, largely composed of debris carried down from the Alps by the melting glaciers of the Ice Age and by the southern tributaries of the Danube, in particular the Iller, Lech, Isar and Inn. In places the gravel is covered with fertile loess, but elsewhere the land is poor and forested. Oilfields have recently been discovered in the valleys of the Iller and Inn.

The northern part of the plain, known as Lower Bavaria *(Niederbayern)*, is extremely fertile, yielding a variety of good crops including hops for the breweries of Munich. Before crops could be grown, however, the ground had to be drained and protected from annual flooding. A number of bogs still remain where the water-table is high; the Dachau Bog north-west of Munich was the site of a concentration camp during

World War II. The southern part of the plain is rather higher and has a much wetter climate; it is therefore more suited to cattle-rearing than to arable farming. The Allgäu in particular produces many dairy products, which are marketed principally in Kempten and distributed to all parts of the Federal Republic.

There are only two large towns on the plain, Augsburg and Munich *(München)*. The former owes its prosperity to the weaving industry and trans-alpine trade; it was the home of the immensely rich Fugger family, which dominated European banking and commerce in the sixteenth century. Munich, capital of the State of Bavaria, is one of the largest towns in Germany with well over a million inhabitants. It has become the most important centre of communications in southern Germany and the focal point of the cultural and intellectual life of a large area. Its industries include textiles, chemicals, printing, photographic goods (Agfa), motor vehicles and brewing; it is the centre of the West German film industry, the headquarters of many important firms, the home of the famous 'October Festival' *(Oktoberfest)*, and site of the 1972 Olympic Games.

The Alpine foothills consist largely of boulders and moraines left by retreating glaciers. There are many lakes in the depressions, such as the Starnberger See and the Chiem-

Munich : the Hauptplatz or 'Stachus' during the evening rush hour

see; the largest of them is Lake Constance *(Bodensee)*, 60 km. long and 14 km. wide, which is nicknamed the 'Swabian Sea'. The river Rhine rushes down from the mountains into its eastern end and deposits quantities of gravel; the lake acts as a huge reservoir, regulating the Rhine's flood and low-water peaks. There are many beautiful towns, such as Meersburg, Constance *(Konstanz)* itself and the island town of Lindau, but one of the main attractions of the lake is the curious island of Mainau, where sub-tropical plants flourish in the open all the year round. Only in abnormally severe winters does the lake freeze over; the comparative warmth of the water affects the climate, making it ideal for fruit-growing. The warm Föhn wind, which blows throughout the Alpine region during March, keeps frost away from the early blossoms; it quickly melts the mountain snows and often causes avalanches. The favourable climate of Lake Constance attracted early man; traces of Bronze Age lake settlements are still visible after a spell of dry weather.

The German Alps stretch from the eastern end of Lake Constance to the river Salzach, which forms the frontier with Austria. There are three main sections: the Allgäu Alps extending from Lake Constance to the river Lech, the Bavarian Alps from the Lech to the Inn and the Salzburg Alps near Berchtesgaden. Since Roman times the Alpine passes have been important trade routes between northern and southern Europe.

Climate and aspect are important in determining the position of Alpine settlements; direct sunlight does not fall on many north-facing slopes during winter, so farmhouses, villages and pastures are situated on the more favourable south-facing slopes. The north-facing slopes are left forested. The farmers in the Allgäu Alps grow just enough root-crops and soft fruit for their own use and rely for their income on dairy cattle. The farmhouses are invariably huge, with low-pitched roofs weighted down with stones (illustration, p. 259); animals and fodder are kept in the very building where the family lives. This simplifies the farmer's task during the long winter, as it enables him to feed his herds without going out into the snow. Some of the cattle are sent at the beginning of June to the 'alm' (mountain pastures), where they remain until September; hay for the winter is made from the more luscious grass in the valleys, which is dried on poles. The herdsman lives during the summer in a hut high in the mountains in which he prepares butter and cheese and which is also used to

Drying hay in the Alps

shelter the cattle at night. The journeys to and from the 'alm' are the signal for festivities in the villages.

Tourism is a vital secondary source of income to the farmers in the Alps. The region offers many attractions

The famous rococo Wieskirche near Füssen

besides the glorious scenery and pure air; there are picturesque villages, magnificent castles, splendid Baroque churches and monasteries, traditional events such as the Passion Play at Oberammergau and plenty of opportunity for sports both in summer and winter. Some villages such as Oberstdorf now cater principally for tourists, who have proved more profitable and less demanding than farming.

The largest town in the Bavarian Alps, Garmisch-Partenkirchen, scene of many skiing and skating events, lies at the foot of Germany's highest mountain, the Zugspitze (2,950 metres). A funicular railway runs to within 300 metres of the summit; the last stretch, up to the weather station, is accomplished by cable car. Nearby Oberammergau, known mainly for its Passion Play, also has a wood-carving school. Mittenwald has for centuries been the home of violin makers whose products are said to rival those of the Italian masters.

Wood for these and other trades is available in plenty, for almost half the area of the German Alps is forested. Trees are felled all the year round, but most of the timber is actually sent down the mountainside in winter. Mountain torrents swollen with melting snow take over the transport of the logs in spring, carrying them direct to the sawmill; hundreds of timber rafts each year are carried along the Isar to Munich. The roaring Alpine streams and fast-flowing rivers have been harnessed to provide electricity for much of West Germany; the largest power station is at present in the valley below the Walchensee.

Königssee : the Church of St. Bartholomew

The Berchtesgaden Alps are reputedly the most beautiful of all German mountains; Hitler built his personal retreat among the peaks above Berchtesgaden, not far from the idyllic Königssee. The mountains conceal vast deposits of rock salt, which has been mined for centuries. It is dissolved in the heart of the mountain by making a hole and filling it with water. The brine which forms is pumped into the valleys, where it is boiled until only pure salt is left.

Plant life in the mountains is dependent not only on the condition and depth of the soil, but also on altitude. The mixed forests on the lowest slopes give way to conifers at about 1,000 metres, but even they cannot exist above 1,700 metres. Low bushes and grass, studded with gay and often rare flowers characterize the highest slopes where vegetation can exist. Above 2,600 metres the snow never melts, even in summer; Germany has however only one true glacier, the Schneeferner, near Garmisch.

Climate

The climate of north-west Germany is influenced by conditions over the Atlantic. The prevailing winds are from the west and these bring much the same weather conditions as we experience in the British Isles, with cool summers, moderate winters and high rainfall. North-eastern Germany lies further from the moderating influence of the Atlantic; its weather is also affected by the great land-masses to the east, which produce very cold winters and hot summers. Rainfall in the eastern part of the North German Plain is relatively low.

Central Germany is also influenced to some extent by weather conditions over the European continent, which make the summers warmer and the winters colder the further south-east one travels. The Alpine climate is the most severe in Germany; altitude cancels out the beneficial effects of a more southerly position and causes long, cold winters and a high level of precipitation. The short Alpine summers are however warm, since the sun meets the south-facing slopes at a favourable angle. A local influence is the Föhn, an unusually warm wind which blows from the south in spring.

The best climate in Germany is that of the Rhine rift valley; spring comes early, rainfall is light, summers are warm and frost is rare.

II Industry, Trade and Transport

1. Germany before 1945

(a) to 1871

The long tradition of separatism among the German states paralysed trade and postponed the development of the country into an industrial nation because of the protective customs barriers erected by each state. There was no central organization of trade, of finance or of transport, without which it was impossible efficiently to exploit the country's natural resources. The guild system and other medieval institutions continued to exist until 1810, ensuring a high quality of workmanship and fair prices but stifling initiative and progress, so that the Industrial Revolution came to Germany rather later than to most European countries.

At the beginning of the nineteenth century Germany's economy was based essentially on agriculture, yet even this was in a primitive state. Vast tracts of the country were infertile; the North German Plain for example was either too swampy or too sandy to cultivate. There were as yet no scientific aids to increase production; the open-field three-yearly rotational system still persisted. In order to make a living many families ran both a farm and a small business based on some skill such as shoemaking. Urbanization was slow; Berlin was the largest town with a population of 200,000.

Industrialization, deriving principally from the development of steam power, was at this time proceeding extremely slowly. Spinning and weaving were still cottage industries and were only gradually transferred to factories as raw materials began to be imported. Working conditions were atrocious; even by working long hours an able-bodied person could not earn more than a bare living. A considerable population increase made matters worse, since neither industry nor agriculture had sufficient capital to expand quickly. Many were driven to emigrate, particularly between 1847 and 1854, but the rising birthrate still provided a reservoir of manpower for the new factories once industrialization was properly under way. Those who could not work went hungry, yet the upper classes enjoyed many comforts. It was the middle of the century before a social conscience began to awaken; in 1848 the workers were still pleading for the introduction of a twelve-hour working day. In 1869 the Social Democratic Workers' Party *(Sozialdemokratische Arbeiterpartei)*, based on an earlier short-lived Labour Union founded by Ferdinand Lassalle (1825–64), was constituted to represent the workers' interests. The writings of Karl Marx and Friedrich Engels were also beginning to attract attention.

The formation between 1828 and 1844 of the various customs unions such as the *Zollverein,* an economic union of German States led by Prussia, influenced the development of industry, trade and communications, since they reduced protective customs barriers and created larger economic units. The railway and road networks were considerably extended between 1840 and 1870. River transport was facilitated by the abolition in the 1860s of the dues levied by each state through which rivers flowed. Between 1836 and 1845 the Rhine–Main–Danube canal was constructed.

This improvement in communications helped the development of heavy industry and also the exploitation of Germany's natural resources, which lay principally in frontier regions. In 1840 Germany's considerable coal deposits were scarcely being worked, yet by the end of the 1860s Germany had become the leading coal-producing nation of Europe. A similar growth took place in the chemical and metal industries. In the 1860s expansion was rapid; the increased production of machinery benefited other industries, notably textiles.

The growth of trade and better communications were both a material and psychological preparation of the nation for its unification in 1871, which set the stage for further rapid expansion.

(b) 1871–1914

At the time of the foundation of the Empire *(Reich)* (see pp. 113–4) Germany was still able to feed her population, whereas she lagged far behind other nations in terms of industrial output. A major programme of industrialization was therefore needed; the years 1871 to 1873 are known as the '*Grün-*

derjahre' because of the profusion of firms founded at the time. New industrial potential was obtained by the annexation in 1871 of Alsace and Lorraine, where there were deposits of iron ore and a flourishing textile industry. All parts of the new Empire could be reached by rail, and industries were able to settle in places where transport conditions were favourable.

Industrial expansion in the Empire was intensified by an increased flow of capital to industry (much of it French, since France had been forced to pay heavy reparations after the Franco-Prussian War) and by the introduction in 1871–2 of a uniform currency (the Mark), and common metric units of length, volume and weight. Advantage was also taken of the fact that industrialization in Germany was considerably later than in the rest of Europe; the country was therefore spared the cost of experimenting with machinery and different systems of organization. Large enterprises and cartels were characteristic of German industrial expansion after 1873. Cartels were formed to gain tax advantages, to reduce competition and to keep prices uniform. They were supported and encouraged by banking concerns who were usually represented on decision-making bodies, promoting the interests of the company they were financing. These large concerns in the coal and steel industries attracted world-wide notoriety when they turned to producing munitions.

The rapid industrialization and the continuing dramatic increase in population aggravated the already serious social problems; the workers suffered under the authoritarian industrialists and landowners, and their organizations were gaining increasing support. Bismarck saw that this would probably

A Prussian measure, the half-rod (about $2\frac{3}{4}$ yards), in use before the introduction of metric units of length

result in a major uprising of the workers unless they were given better conditions and he accordingly formulated between 1883 and 1889 a system of social security more advanced than in any other country. Additional measures were instituted by enlightened industrialists, notably Alfred Krupp (1812–1887).

As an industrial nation Germany had to compete in order to sell her products. The appalling workmanship of German articles was notorious; in 1887 England insisted that each one should be marked 'Made in Germany'. With characteristic thoroughness the Germans set about improving their products and before long 'Made in Germany' became an indication of good quality.

The distribution of industry has changed little since 1914 except in so far as Germany's frontiers have been altered. The main coalfields were in the Ruhr, Saar, Lorraine and Upper Silesia. Of these the most important was the Ruhr, which supplied fuel for the iron and steel industries. During the years preceding the outbreak of war both the iron and steel industry and the shipbuilding industry based in Stettin, Hamburg and Bremen became increasingly important and successful. The textile industry also flourished as the steel and engineering industries grew; woollen goods came from the eastern provinces and the area around Aachen, cotton goods from the Rhineland, Westphalia and southern Germany. The chemical industry expanded rapidly in the Ruhr and along the Rhine during this period, providing material for the munitions industry and artificial fertilisers. This marked the beginning of the transformation of agriculture into a scientific industry, backed up by research in universities and institutes. A further branch of the chemical industry concentrated on producing by-products from coal, such as dyes and pharmaceutical goods. The electrical industry was founded in the 1880s upon the researches of Werner von Siemens (1816–92). It was concentrated around Berlin and rapidly diversified as new uses for electricity were found. The manufacture of components for lighting, telephones, generators, transport and radio meant that this industry was of considerable importance. By 1914 Germany's economy was strong; she was a leading industrial nation, having 13% of world trade.

A great improvement in communications accompanied increasing industrial output. In 1873 the various State railway systems were unified, though Bismarck failed in his attempt to nationalize them. Inland water transport was expanded; the Dortmund–Ems canal was built to provide cheap transport from the Ruhr to the North Sea without leaving German territory. The Mittelland canal was begun in 1905 to complete the connection of the Ruhr with the Elbe and Berlin. Road transport underwent a transformation with the invention of the internal combustion engine and Benz's patent 'horseless carriage' of 1886. Subsequent improvements came rapidly, principally the invention of pneumatic tyres. Air transport was still in its infancy, but Germany was well to the fore in research and experiment. Graf Zeppelin (1838–1917) developed airships from 1891 (first flight in 1900); by 1910 they were carrying out regular passenger services. Major developments in the field of heavier-than-air flight did not come until the war years.

In 1871 Germany had only a relatively small merchant-shipping fleet, but the need to import raw materials and to export manufactured articles necessitated the building of substantial numbers of ships. Bremen-Bremerhaven and Hamburg were the main ports; transatlantic routes were operated by the HAPAG (Hamburg–Amerika-Linie) and Norddeutsche Lloyd companies, founded in 1847 and 1857 respectively. These two companies led the way in a large-scale development of shipping, so that by 1914 Germany's merchant fleet almost led the world.

Superficially everything seemed to be going well, yet below the surface there were many unsolved problems. After 1900 industrial production exceeded agricultural production and there began to be a shortage of agricultural workers because of the movement of the population into towns; skilled labour was, however, scarce. Women were desperately underpaid and social unrest persisted among the working classes. The principle of collective bargaining was not accepted by the industrial barons, who were afraid of losing their wealth and status. It was these same industrialists who backed the expansionist propaganda leagues, whose aims included the acquisition of colonies as a means of increasing trade and which contributed in no small way to the outbreak of war in 1914.

(c) 1914–1945

The outbreak of war brought to an end the years of plenty in Germany; bread was soon rationed and other commodities such as jam and fat were in short supply. New industries sprang up based on the creation of substitutes for goods which could no longer be imported.

The war proved more expensive than was expected due to its long duration; the state failed to repay money lent by its citizens to finance the war and large sections of the community were reduced to poverty. The industrialists, however, fared better; they were allowed to keep their factories and their main problem lay in obtaining enough orders to maintain full production. They feared that a slump would probably cause a workers' revolution, since the Communists, or 'Spartacists', were already threatening the established order in 1918.

These selfish interests coupled with the impossible conditions imposed by the Treaty of Versailles, in particular the loss of industrial regions and the demands for outrageously high reparations, caused an inflationary situation which the unstable governments of the Weimar Republic were unable to check. The creation of paper money to pay workers refusing to co-operate with the occupation forces finally caused the collapse of the Mark. The banks could not cope with the demand for paper money and many local communities and even industries were permitted to issue 'emergency money', including oddities such as porcelain 'coins' in Stuttgart and Bunzlau. By 1923 the inflation was catastrophic; one dollar was worth 4,200 million Marks (1920: one dollar equalled four Marks) and ordinary people found their savings valueless. Wages and prices spiralled and unemployment increased; the industrialists, however, remained powerful. Germany defaulted in her payment of reparations and France, having occupied Düsseldorf, Duisburg and Ruhrort in 1921, occupied the whole of the Ruhr in 1923.

An attempt was made to save the German currency by the establishment in November 1923 of the Rentenbank, which issued the Rentenmark, based not on the gold-standard but on land-values. It was, however, the currency reform of 1924 which created the Reichsmark that mainly contributed to the stabilization of industry. The railways were improved and combined to form the nationalized Reichsbahn (1920), the airline 'Deutsche Luft Hansa A.G.' was founded in 1926 and the many large new industrial concerns looked forward to a bright future.

By the end of the decade, however, a slump began, unemployment again rose and there were fears of a second inflation. Strict measures were taken to avert the disaster, but they unexpectedly caused a severe deflation when many goods remained unsold and industries failed. Some industrialists at this point began to offer financial assistance to the National Socialist Party in the hope of halting the spread of Communism.

Germany was badly affected by the world economic crisis which began with the Wall Street crash of 1929. German banks crashed two years later, robbing many people of their savings and industry of capital. Cartels were formed and even small firms indulged in price-fixing. The economy became inflexible, so that each slump developed into a crisis before measures were taken to combat it. Unemployment had risen to nearly seven million by the end of 1932 and the State could afford to pay out only token benefits. The workers, reduced to abject misery, did not fail to notice that the upper classes were still living in luxury; the industrialists and landowners feared that this situation would produce increasing support for the Communists. Largely financed by these same industrialists, Adolf Hitler (1889–1945) came to power in 1933 with the slogan 'Arbeit und Brot' ('work and bread').

Hitler began by implementing his plan to create full employment within four years. He set up a vast Party bureaucracy, and from 1935 on drafted young people into the *Arbeitsdienst* ('labour service') or into the armed forces; he began to build the long-planned autobahn network, instigated other projects of public works and began to replace Jews in high office with Germans. He also refused to continue the payment of reparations which he regarded as an unjustifiable burden on the economy. The desired results were achieved; unemployment fell, wages rose and the country recovered from its post-war troubles.

In 1936 a second four-year plan was announced aimed at making Germany as near self-supporting as possible; seen in retrospect this is an obvious preparation for war, but it was not then recognized as such. Industry was working at full capacity; wages, profits and prices were pegged. In general the people were satisfied and they did not pay much attention to Hitler's expansionist policies until it became clear that he was leading them into war.

By 1939 Germany was producing 80% of her food, 40% of her textile needs, 50% of her fuel oil and 30% of her iron ore, but because she lacked other raw materials she was not completely ready for war. There was no properly constructed plan for a wartime economy until 1942, by which time there had been considerable waste. By the end of the war food was running short; the situation was made worse by Hitler's policy of leaving only a waste land for the enemy to occupy ('scorched earth' policy). The war which was to have made Germany great ended with her occupation, the ruin of her towns and factories and the destruction of her transport system.

2. 1945 to the Present Day

When the war ended chaos reigned in Germany. There was social dislocation and a grave shortage of food, clothing and housing. Industry, commerce and agriculture were at a standstill and the people were demoralized. The loss of the Saar, East Prussia, most of Pomerania and Silesia and the division of the remaining part of the country into four Zones of Occupation split up the economic unit that had been the Third Reich.

The Potsdam Agreement reached by the Allies after the cessation of hostilities provided for a central administration to control commerce and industry. It aimed to create a generally balanced economy whilst restricting the production of so-called strategic items such as steel and chemicals to prevent a resurgence of aggressive nationalism. It failed because of a lack of co-operation between the occupying powers.

Between 1945 and 1947 there was economic stagnation; there was no normal foreign trade, transport was poor and even the basic industries were disorganized. Many of the remaining factories had been dismantled by the Allies, strategic industries were forbidden and others were allowed only a limited production, so unemployment was high. A Black Market flourished whilst people were dying of hunger. The British and American Zones merged economically in 1946–7 and later absorbed the French Zone. The currency reform of 1948, which created the D-Mark as the equivalent of 10 Reichsmark, was recognized only in the three western Zones, where it paved the way for political union and industrial reorganization; in the following year these three Zones became the Federal Republic of Germany. The Russians developed their Zone along independent lines and introduced their own currency reform, also in 1948. Soon afterwards the Russian Zone became known as the German Democratic Republic.

(a) The Federal Republic of Germany

The main task facing the newly elected leaders was to restore confidence in the economy and to ensure a rapid industrial recovery. The first step in this direction had already been taken in 1948; the currency reform which created the *Deutsche Mark* (DM) enabled transport and industry to start up and created a firm basis for the Marshall Plan, which made available grants and long-term credits to the value of four billion Marks. The transport system which had been set up by the occupying powers was quite inadequate for the requirements of expanding industry and needed vast investments for reconstruction and modernization. The industries that were functioning by 1949 were handicapped by a lack of capital and for some time still by the Allies' policy of fixing production quotas.

The solution to these problems was proposed by Dr. Ludwig Erhard, then Economics Minister. He discarded the idea of a planned economy and introduced the system of *Freie Marktwirtschaft* to exploit the initiative of free enterprise whilst retaining a measure of State supervision. The free market provided competition and incentives; the workers co-operated, industry boomed, wages rose and prices dropped. The Allies' policy of dismantling large industrial concerns proved to have had a beneficial effect, because the Germans were compelled to build new, modern factories and were thus able to take full advantage of the latest production techniques. New industries were founded by industrialists who were no longer allowed to produce war materials.

The industrial boom marked the beginning of the now legendary 'economic miracle' *(Wirtschaftswunder)*, which took the Federal Republic back to economic stability by 1954. Rationing ended in 1950, luxuries were once more available and new homes were built. By 1959 there was full employment; professional and trade standards rose and soon there was a shortage of labour which was partly relieved by recruiting workers *(Gastarbeiter)* from Italy, Greece and Spain. By 1960 the Federal Republic had become the third largest industrial and trading nation in the world.

Incomes have risen steadily, producing on the one hand general prosperity and on the other increased labour costs in industry. Wage demands remain moderate since most workers prefer not to risk their high standard of living by creating inflation. Fear of inflation was rife in the 1970s when

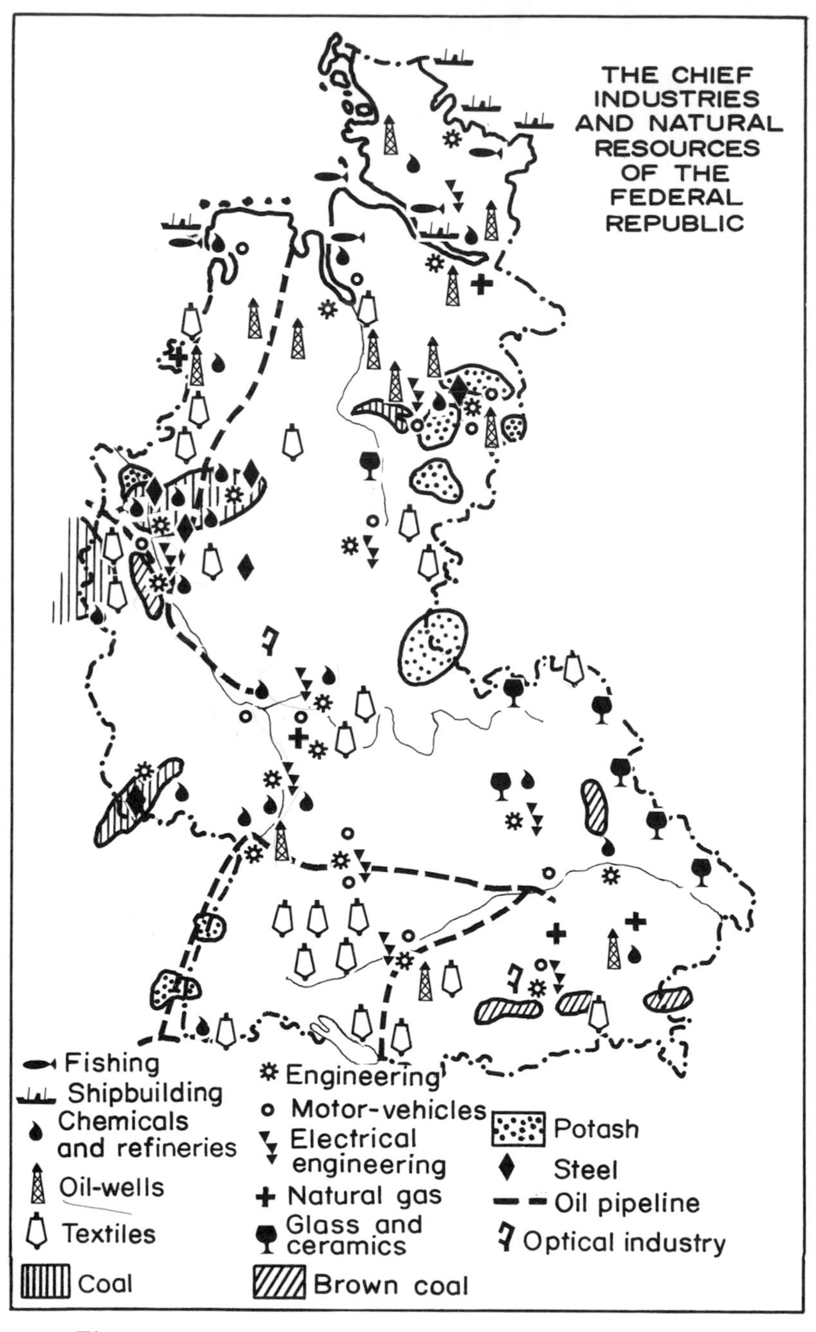
THE CHIEF INDUSTRIES AND NATURAL RESOURCES OF THE FEDERAL REPUBLIC
Fishing
Shipbuilding
Chemicals and refineries
Oil-wells
Textiles
Coal
Engineering
Motor-vehicles
Electrical engineering
Natural gas
Glass and ceramics
Brown coal
Potash
Steel
Oil pipeline
Optical industry

Fig 13

Britain's rate was over 20%; German inflation was hovering around 4½%. A wide cross-section of the people own shares. When some companies (e.g. Volkswagen, Veba) were denationalized low income groups were encouraged to buy shares and have a personal stake in the nation's prosperity. Some of the most important share-prices are given daily at the end of the mid-evening television news bulletin. Savings and home ownership are encouraged by generous tax relief. The highest rate of tax is set at 56% (*c.f.* Britain 83% in 1976) in order to allow the acquisition of wealth and to make available greater funds for investment.

The revaluation in 1961 of the West German Mark so reinforced confidence in it that it became one of the world's most sought-after currencies. It has since risen still further. The Mark's strength and export successes produced regular balance of payments surpluses, which reached a record level in 1974 of 50,000 million Marks. West Germany was thus able to accumulate massive gold and foreign currency reserves which enabled her to weather an economic setback in 1967 and averted the worst consequences of the world recession of 1975–77, despite a trade deficit of 295 million Marks in 1975.

The economic scene in 1977

(i) *Industry*

The largest industrial area is the Ruhr, although almost every sizable town houses industrial concerns of considerable importance. The mining, steel-making and engineering industries in the Ruhr were developed in close association so that production and transport costs could be kept low. This led to the formation of immense concerns such as those of Krupp, Mannesmann and Thyssen. The government keeps a strict watch on the activities of grouped industries to prevent the undesirable effects of price-fixing.

Since cheap fuels became available in the 1950s coal mining has declined. By 1973 55% of Germany's energy came from oil, and even that year's sharp rise in world oil prices failed to boost mining because she could well afford to pay. Home oil exploration had by 1977 discovered no major new fields, so local production remained at roughly 5% of consumption. Natural gas production on the other hand was rapidly expanded

The assembly line at the Volkswagen factory where the bodies are fitted to the chassis

and supplies were also piped in from Czechoslovakia and the Mediterranean; by 1980 it should provide about 17% of Germany's total energy needs. Electricity is produced cheaply in the mountains of southern Germany and by the barrages on canalized rivers, supplemented by electricity produced in the Ruhr from coal and by current imported from Austria. By 1977 some 20 nuclear power stations were already working and several more were under construction. West Germany has uranium deposits in the Black Forest and Fichtelgebirge; she belongs to Euratom, a part of the E.E.C. which provides a common market for nuclear materials and facilities for research and development.

In the mid-1970s West Germany was among the world's leading car producers and exporters, selling 60% of her production abroad. A slump in the motor vehicle industry had brought several firms to the brink of collapse, and much rationalization was undertaken. In the early 1970s the building industry completed many prestige office blocks, sports halls and lavish shopping centres; public works then declined, but the demand for luxury homes kept the industry busy. The electrical and electronics industries are noted for excellent workmanship and export to many countries. The chemical industry, in particular petrochemicals, is booming, as new materials and processes are constantly being exploited. A network of pipelines from the North Sea and the Mediterranean supplies refineries in the Ruhr and southern Germany. Shipbuilding has fared reasonably well despite a world-wide drop in orders, but the steel industry has found its prices undercut by foreign producers; 1976 was a particularly bad year.

Germany's export successes have been achieved because of industry's readiness to invest, its willingness to experiment and its progressive outlook. It is widely admired for its tradition of peaceful industrial relations. However, unemployment, which rose above 5% early in 1976, began to cause unrest among the unions. Recruitment of *Gastarbeiter* was halted and the numbers employed were drastically cut.

(ii) *Agriculture*

Only 65% of the demand can be met by the Federal Republic's own farmers and growers; dairy produce, for example, is imported from Denmark and Holland. Intensive cultivation is widespread and mechanization is generally well advanced. West Germany's farmers are among the more efficient in the EEC and were displeased by the EEC's new policy (1977) of cutting farm prices to keep consumer prices down.

Approximately 58% of the land is used for agricultural purposes. Animal products are of supreme importance; the main herds of cattle are in the Allgäu, where most of the butter and cheese is produced, and in Schleswig-Holstein. Less than half the cattle are reared for meat, since beef is not so popular as pork. Westphalia and Lower Saxony are the chief pig-breeding areas. There are few sheep in the Federal Republic, for mutton is not popular, lamb is almost unknown and it is cheaper to import wool than to rear sheep solely for their fleece. The breeding of horses is a traditional branch of farming in Lower Saxony and Schleswig-Holstein; the animals are exported to many countries and they form a small but valuable source of foreign exchange.

Over half the agricultural land is cultivated. Cereals are the most important crops; rye and wheat are used for bread, oats principally as cattle fodder. Germany is almost self-sufficient in potatoes, sugar (from beet) and certain fruits. Grapes are grown solely for the production of wine, one of West Germany's main agricultural exports. Tobacco is also produced for home consumption.

The acreage of land suitable for agricultural purposes is

being constantly increased by the use of fertilisers, notably potash, which is present in West Germany in such quantities that it can be exported. The formerly barren soils of northern Germany, for example, now make an important contribution to the nation's food supply.

The Federal Government issues annual reports *(Der grüne Bericht)* dealing with a wide range of agricultural problems. These include the availability of labour, the rationalized application of manpower and machines in the face of rural depopulation and the integration of West German agriculture with the agreed policy of the Common Market. An unusual aspect of West German agricultural policy has been the attempt to rationalize the layout of farming land, which had been divided time and again into unenclosed narrow strips as inheritances were split amongst sons. These scattered plots caused much wasted time and land since some were allowed to lie fallow; the use of agricultural machinery was precluded because it can only work efficiently in large fields. The reorganization scheme, known as *Flurbereinigung*, makes grants available to farming communities to reallocate the land in units of at least 25 acres and to resite access roads and footpaths. Wherever the scheme has been carried out yields have increased by up to 30%. A similar scheme in the vineyards along the Rhine has smoothed the hillsides and virtually eliminated the old terraces.

Cultivation in small plots near Minden

The forests of the Federal Republic, amounting to about 29% of agricultural land, were over-exploited after the war. The older forests are entirely coniferous, since conifers are on the whole hardier and swifter-growing than deciduous varieties. More recently mixed forests have been preferred, since conifers were found to be unsuitable for some purposes.

Over half the forests of the Federal Republic are either State- or publicly owned; the largest areas are in the south of the country and it is here that industries such as toy-making, carving, paper-making and the manufacture of musical instruments have flourished.

(iii) *Fishing*

After the war the importance of the fishing industry increased since there was a great shortage of food. Fleets of modern vessels have been built up as quickly as possible, so that West Germany is now the third most important fishing nation in Europe, with Bremerhaven the largest fishing port on the Continent. The main grounds are in the North Sea and in the North Atlantic off Iceland. Catches are now restricted by quota agreements within the EEC and with Iceland.

The fishing ports on the North Sea coast serve the whole of West Germany. Much of the fish is frozen, smoked or canned to facilitate transport to distant regions; some of it is exported.

(iv) *Trade*

West Germany is a founder-member of the European Economic Community (EEC), or Common Market. Her whole pattern of trade has been influenced since 1958 by conditions and concessions operating amongst the member countries, whose ultimate aim is to achieve full economic union, including a free movement of capital and labour. She also trades outside the EEC; her principle exports include machinery, cars, chemical products, precision and optical instruments and electrical goods. The trading partners of the Federal Republic belong mainly to the western world, although the great potential markets in eastern Europe have recently attracted more and more attention. Trade with East Germany has steadily increased since trading agreements were first made in 1950; the Federal Republic imports brown coal, mineral oils, chemicals and textiles in exchange for iron and steel, machinery, chemicals and food.

Almost every year West Germany has achieved a trading surplus so large that other countries have repeatedly pressed

The Hanover Industrial Fair

her to revalue the Mark. The CDU-led governments of the late 1960s, wishing to avoid revaluation, decided to encourage imports. In 1969, however, the new SPD-led government revalued the Mark by 8½% and abolished the CDU's import concessions and export taxes. Further revaluations over the next few years made German exports ever more expensive abroad. Yet such is the reputation of German goods that exports continued to rise, except in 1974. Since West Germany's economic success depends entirely on her ability to export, the sharp drop in orders threw her into a recession. It has been said that this recession was 'imported'.

There is a free movement of capital in and out of the country; because the economy is strong, much foreign capital, in particular from America, has been invested in Germany. Foreign concerns with interests in the Federal Republic include General Motors (Opel), Unilever, British American Tobacco and several petroleum companies.

West Germany stages major trade fairs of international importance. The name *Messe* ('mass') indicates that the modern trade exhibition has developed from the church fairs of medieval times. The Hanover Fair is the most important exhibition of West Germany's industrial products; specialized fairs are also held in other centres such as Cologne and Frankfurt.

From the largest companies down to the 'shop on the corner' internal trade is in the hands of private enterprise. Modern systems of retailing, such as department and self-service stores in town centres, and vast hypermarkets outside the towns are replacing small traders. A consequence of the completely free market is the huge volume of advertising in all the usual mass media. There is a strict code of advertising practice which does not allow misleading statements or comparisons between competing products. The most widely advertised commodities are cosmetics, washing powder, cars and cigarettes.

(v) *Communications*

Good communications are vital to any industrial nation. The Federal Republic is fortunate in having not only extensive railway and road systems, but also many waterways, both natural and man-made, which link industrial areas to ports and consumer centres. After the war the whole emphasis of the transport network changed as a result of the virtual cessation of east–west traffic, now limited to seven crossing points into East Germany. The main axis of road, rail and water transport in the Federal Republic is the Rhine Valley. The autobahn network has been extended to improve north–south communications and also to connect with the motorway systems of other West European countries.

As yet there is no national plan for an integrated transport system, although suggestions have from time to time been made (for example the *Leber-Plan* of 1968) to relieve the congestion on the roads by transferring heavy loads back to the railways and to make increasing use of air transport.

A train headed by an electric locomotive carrying tourists' cars passing through Augsburg station

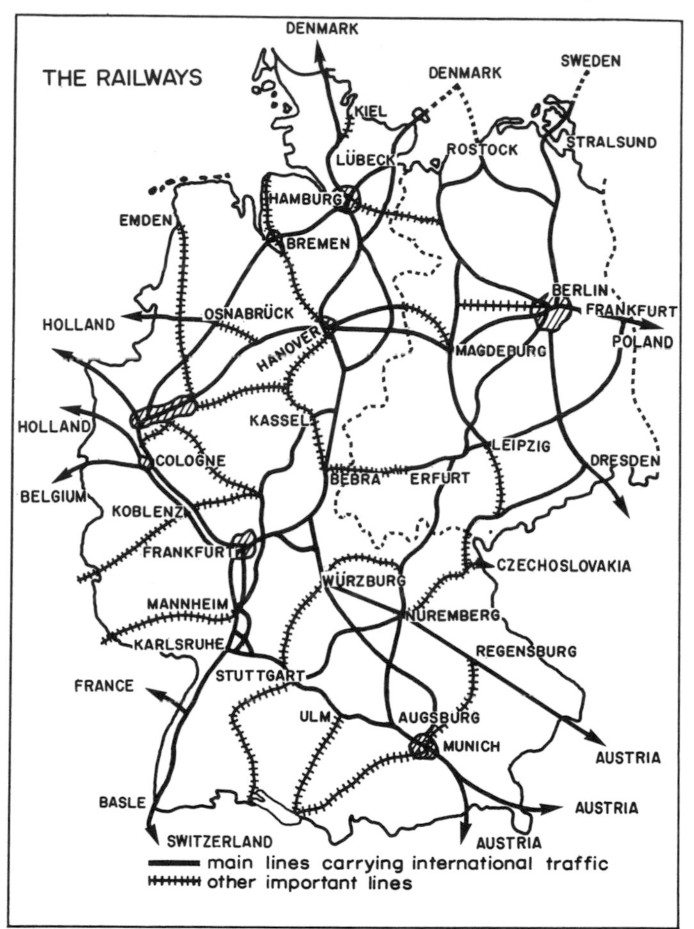

Fig 14

Railways: The nationalized railways of the Federal Republic *(Bundesbahn)* are an integral part of the European railway network. There are some 29,022 km. of track, of which about 9,523 were electrified by 1974. The main routes run from north to south, in particular along the Rhine valley. The network is densest in the Ruhr where it caters extensively for commuters and goods traffic. The *Bundesbahn* also provides commuter services in other large cities, for example the *S-Bahn* in Hamburg, which supplement congested trams and poorly developed bus services.

Like most railway companies the *Bundesbahn* does not

make a profit. Modernization and electrification did not help to reduce the annual deficit, and many branch lines have had to be closed; the introduction of single-carriage diesel trains enables the *Bundesbahn* to serve some that would otherwise be uneconomic.

Waterways: All the navigable waterways, which include over 1,000 km. of canals, are under the control of the Federal Minister of Transport. The most important inland waterway is the Rhine, which carries heavy barge traffic between the

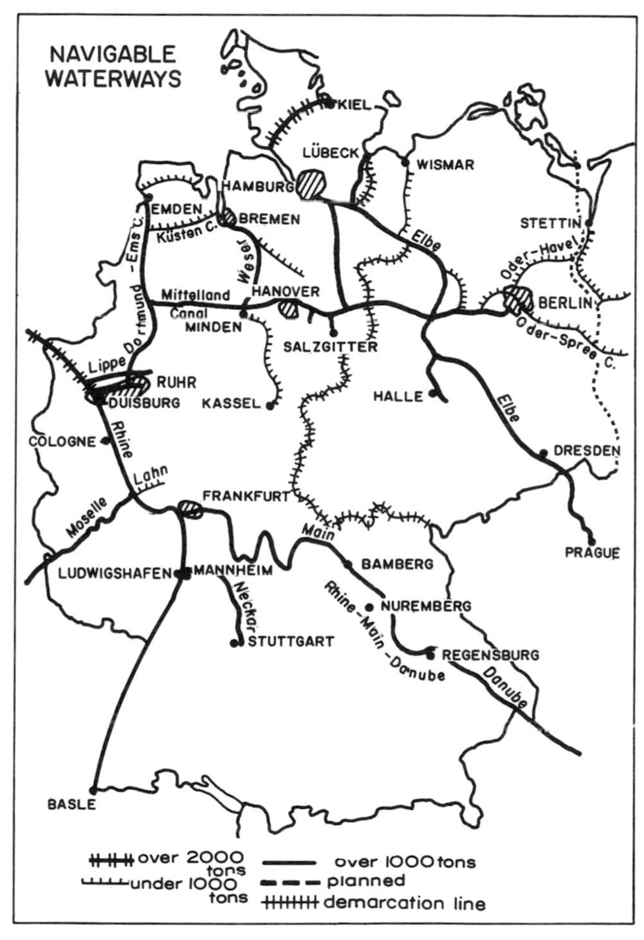

Fig 15

The Mittelland canal (near Osnabrück). The barge carries oil between the Ruhr and Minden

Dutch port of Rotterdam, the Ruhr, the industrial areas of Mannheim and Frankfurt and Switzerland. Duisburg on the Rhine is Europe's largest inland port. Below Duisburg the Rhine carries barges of up to 4,000 tonnes; from Duisburg to Basle the limit is 2,000 tonnes. It is hoped one day to by-pass the Rhine falls at Schaffhausen with a canal which will extend navigation beyond Lake Constance.

The Ruhr industrial area is served by a network of 2,000-ton canals linked to the Rhine; the Dortmund–Ems canal gives access to the North Sea and the Mittelland canal links the Ruhr with the Weser, the Elbe and Berlin. The river Moselle and parts of the Neckar, Main and Weser have been canalized. The Rhine-Main-Danube canal between Bamberg and Kelheim for barges of up to 1,350 tons will be ready by 1981. New canals are planned to bring more trade to Hamburg, whose main supply artery, the river Elbe, was cut by the division of Germany after the war. The Nord-Süd canal is already complete and will carry barges of up to 1,350 tons between the Elbe and Mittelland canal.

West Germany's 6,000 km. of navigable waterway carry over 245 million tonnes of freight per year (370 million tonnes go by rail) for despite its comparative slowness, water transport is cheap; one large barge can, for example, carry as much freight as two or three goods trains.

Roads: The 2,080 km. of motorway bequeathed to the

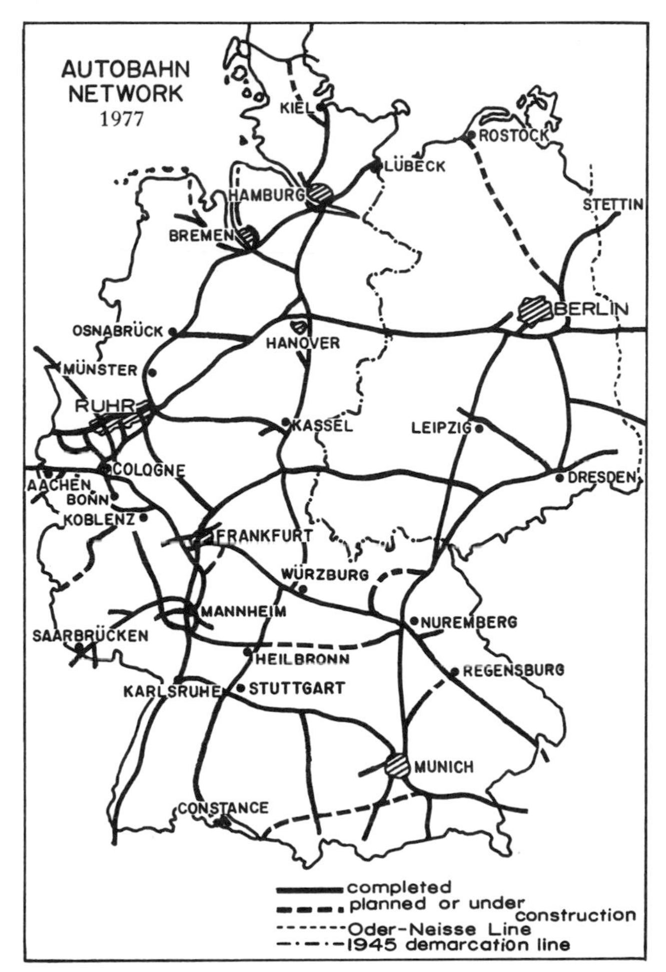

Fig 16

Federal Republic by Hitler soon proved inadequate for the increasing traffic and since 1955 the network has been constantly improved and extended. By 1965 the Federal Republic had 3,360 km. of motorway, by 1975 it had around 6,000 km., and it is hoped eventually to bring the total to some 7,500 km. Political and economic factors have influenced the shape of the network; important new north–south connections include Hanover–Würzburg–Stuttgart–Singen, Bremen–Ruhr and the additional link between the Ruhr and Frankfurt via Wetzlar. These roads form an integral part of the network of European highways *(Europastraßen)* linking the main cities of the Continent. Drivers are aided by motorway information broadcast on special wavelengths by normal radio stations, who warn of hazards ahead, suggest alternative routes, report on the weather and play light music.

Other main roads *(Bundesstraßen)*, which were for some years neglected, are now being generally improved. The removal of basalt sets, steep cambers and sharp bends and the building of by-passes have done much to assist the flow of traffic.

The increasing volume of heavy traffic has choked West German roads, for almost a half of all freight is carried by road. Private cars, too, are on the increase; in 1974 there were more than three cars to every ten people, and in view of the continuing prosperity the numbers will undoubtedly rise in the 1980s. Even now rush-hour traffic jams are common in most sizeable towns and there is a general lack of adequate off-street parking. Some few towns, for example Hanover and Essen, gave priority to motor traffic when replanning their centres after the war. The idea of excluding private vehicles from town centres has been proposed, but the feasibility of the scheme depends on the provision of adequate public transport. In Munich and Hanover, for example, underground railways have been constructed, and it is hoped that they will help to avert a threatened crisis as the number of private vehicles increases. Most cities have tram and omnibus services, run usually by local authorities, plus some additional buses to outlying areas run by the *Bundesbahn* or the Post Office; the town services cater principally for the standing passenger and cannot be described as comfortable especially in the rush-hour, when they are often crammed to capacity, with about 120 passengers in one single-deck tram.

Stone sets are still common, especially in North Germany, and are almost universal in towns and villages

Shipping: After the war less than a quarter of Germany's shipping

Progress on Hanover's new underground railway was slow because every yard of tunnel had to be constructed in an open trench

A typical modern German tram

tonnage remained. Restrictions were imposed by the Allies on the redevelopment of the shipping industry; at first small wrecks could be salvaged and made seaworthy, then the Federal Republic was allowed to buy second-hand foreign ships up to a certain tonnage. In 1951 the last restrictions on shipbuilding were lifted. Gradually shipping increased and eventually surpassed the pre-war proportions; between 1949 and 1962 the registered tonnage of German ships increased seventeen-fold. Regular passenger services have, however, been discontinued.

The late reconstruction of the harbours of the Federal Republic meant a loss of trade to ports in other countries, especially Rotterdam. Hamburg ('The gateway to the World') is West Germany's leading port, but its situation 112 km. from the sea is proving to be an increasing handicap in view of the immense size of new ships, particularly oil tankers. The navigation channel in the Elbe is neither wide nor deep enough to float them even at high tide, so new facilities for discharging oil are being provided on the island of Neuwerk at the mouth of the Elbe. Bremen-Bremerhaven, Wilhelmshaven and Emden are other North Sea ports. Kiel, by virtue of its position at the northern end of the Kiel canal, is a natural centre for trade with Scandinavia and eastern Europe.

Air transport: For some twelve months after the end of the war no civil air traffic was allowed over Germany. Until 1948 only foreign airlines were allowed to operate flights to West German airfields. When the Deutsche Lufthansa A.G. was reconstituted in 1954 it faced keen competition from established companies.

The Federal Republic's central jet airport is the *Rhein-Main Flughafen* near Frankfurt; other major airports are sited in Berlin (Tegel), Hamburg, Hanover, Munich, Bremen, Düsseldorf, Stuttgart and Wahn, which serves Cologne and Bonn. A new airport is planned north of Hamburg. The air link with Berlin is crucial; valuable and perishable cargoes can avoid the frustrating delays suffered from time to time by road and rail users, and passengers are not subject to customs checks. There are three air corridors at the disposal of traffic to West Berlin, linking it with Hamburg, Hanover and Frankfurt; during the blockade of land routes to Berlin in 1948 all the goods needed by the city were flown in along these three routes. The West German airline Lufthansa is not, however, permitted to use these corridors.

The Post Office: The *Bundespost* operates postal and telephone services, provides banking facilities and runs passenger transport. It also gives some technical aid to the regional broadcasting networks and collects radio and television licence fees, retaining 20–25% to pay for its services. In addition the Post Office provides all the facilities needed to run the two national radio stations *Deutschlandfunk* and *Deutsche Welle*, and the second and third television channels. All matters relating to radio communications are the responsibility of the Bundespost.

The telephone service now relies entirely on automatic dialling and has been incorporated into the European and intercontinental telephone networks. Some callboxes are only for local or inland calls; foreign calls can always be made from post offices. There was no direct telephone link between the Federal Republic and East Germany from 1952 until 1971.

Modernization is going ahead quickly; electronic letter-sorting is already in operation and other forms of mechanization such as stamp-vending machines help to offset the shortage of labour. To facilitate the introduction of automated operations the entire country has been divided into 24,000 postal areas, each with a code number *(Postleitzahl)*. There are eight main regions, based on Berlin, Hamburg, Hanover, Düsseldorf, Cologne, Frankfurt, Stuttgart and

Hamburg's television tower. The upper platform is occupied by technical equipment; the lower platforms house a revolving restaurant and cafeteria. The top of the mast is 890 feet from the ground

Munich. These regions are then subdivided; Cologne for example has the code number 5, nearby Bonn is 53, Königswinter across the Rhine is 533 and its tiny neighbour Oberdollendorf 5333. West Germany is co-operating in experiments with both communications satellites and with the use of laser beams to replace overcrowded cables and radio frequencies. The Post Office is responsible for the elegant concrete towers which already grace many German towns. Though they are usually known as 'television towers' *(Fernsehtürme)*, they are also used by the radio and telephone services.

Two other activities of the Bundespost are the organization of a lottery to provide holidays for Berlin children *(Platz an der Sonne)*, and the issue of commemorative postage stamps several times a year. An unusual feature of some series of stamps is the small surcharge payable on each, which goes to charity.

(b) The German Democratic Republic

The economic aftermath of the Second World War affected the provinces of Germany which were under Soviet occupation much more than the western provinces. The east was a predominantly agricultural area, with almost none of the industries such as mining, steel and heavy engineering which are essential to every independent nation. Some processing industries were present, but they had been dependent upon the western provinces for raw materials and components. The situation was already grave when many of the industrial plants which had survived the war were dismantled to satisfy Russian demands for reparations. East Germany thus lost almost half its production potential; West Germany did not even lose a quarter.

Reconstruction work was eventually begun with Russian aid; political and social conditions were imposed on the country quite unlike those in the remaining Zones of Occupation. The division was further emphasized by the West German currency reform of 1948 which was not recognized in the Soviet Zone, although it was intended for the whole of Germany. It was countered by a similar reform in the East, which introduced a Mark of equal value, the *Mark der Deutschen Notenbank* (MDN).

From the outset the declared aim of the leaders was the nationalization of industry, agriculture, transport and trade;

in 1947 the first 'People's Factories' *(Volkseigene Betriebe)* were created. Private enterprise was actively discouraged. The first two-year plan for economic expansion was introduced in 1949. Progress towards the target was, however, slow, since reparations were still being paid.

Every year a National Economic Plan is published by the *Volkswirtschaftsrat,* a department of the State Planning Commission, naming the tasks for the succeeding twelve-month period within the scope of the long-term (5-year) plan. It is up to the individual factories in the Associations of Nationally-owned Enterprises *(Vereinigungen Volkseigener Betriebe)* to work out detailed plans to achieve the aims of productivity, modernization and expansion set by the central planners. The 'New Economic System' of 1963 stressed the necessity of re-investing profits in order to carry out much needed modernization schemes and introduced a competitive element into productivity, rewarding the highest increases with a bonus and public honours. The plan's success produced a dramatic rise in the standard of living – the GDR's economic miracle. By 1974 the GDR led Comecon in the ownership of consumer goods, yet prices remained at 1960 levels. The year had seen a 6·3% growth in national income. The plan for 1976–80 concentrates on high quality optical, electrical and precision goods, mostly for export.

Private industry and retail traders have been almost totally incorporated in 'craft co-operatives' *(Produktionsgenossenschaften des Handwerks),* first founded in 1952. The process has been hastened by the taxation system which places independent firms or individuals at a financial disadvantage. A few private firms do however remain, but most of them have a measure of 'state participation'. Only 3½% of the country's total production is the work of private enterprise.

The economic scene in 1977

(i) *Industry*

The establishment of basic industries in the Soviet Zone was a matter of the utmost importance. Because there were only insignificant deposits of hard coal the mining industry had to be rebuilt around the huge deposits of lignite (brown coal), principally in the south and south-east. These deposits are geologically young; they lie close to the surface and can be mined cheaply in open-pit workings. Lignite is not normally

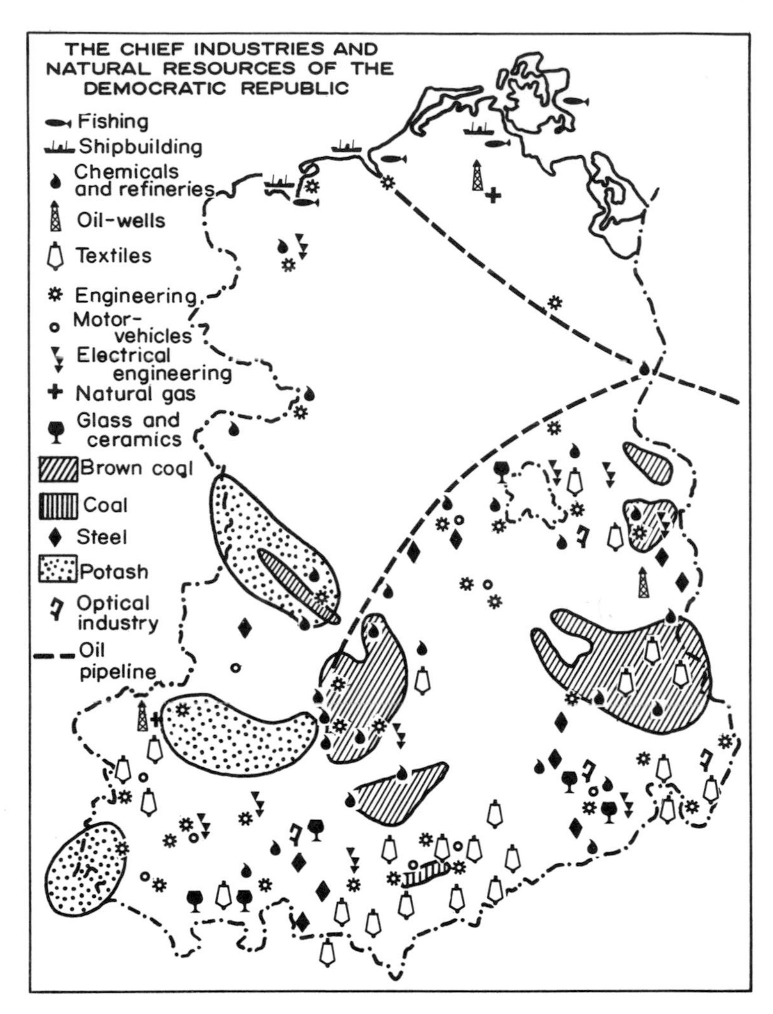

Fig 17

regarded as being particularly suitable for industrial purposes since it contains a high proportion of water and its heating value is about a quarter of that of hard coal, but in the absence of other fuel its use was inevitable. Power stations were built to burn lignite. A method was found of coking it efficiently and a vast plant for this purpose was built at Lauchhammer. Coal gas has been supplemented by natural gas found near Grimmen, but brown coal still supplies 80%

of East Germany's power. So important is brown coal that river beds have been re-routed and whole villages have disappeared before the immense coal-cutters.

Lignite was for many years the basis of the chemical industry, being only recently superseded by the petrochemical industry based at Schwedt, a terminal of the 'Friendship' oil pipeline from Russia and of another from the Baltic port of Rostock. Nuclear power-stations are being assiduously developed; two were already operating by 1976. The Democratic Republic is fortunate in possessing significant amounts of uranium ore in the Erzgebirge and Thuringia, much of which is exported to the Soviet Union. Other rare metals have also been found.

After the war great investments were made in the iron and steel industries. The development was centred partly on the existing industrial areas of Saxony and Lusatia and partly along the eastern frontier, where good communications for importing ore were available. Eisenhüttenstadt near Frankfurt-on-Oder is a new town based on iron-founding and allied industries; by 1974 its population had almost reached 47,000. The policy of building residential neighbourhoods or even whole towns around a certain type of industry has been widely applied; Hoyerswerda for example depends wholly on coal mining and related industries. Heavy and light engineering have been well developed, although both rely heavily on imported raw materials and components. The pre-war shipbuilding industry in Stralsund has been expanded and new centres have been created in Rostock, Warnemünde and Wismar. By 1974 shipbuilding in the GDR had become extremely important to the entire eastern block.

Priority has always been given to those industries producing goods for export; these include the electronics, electrical engineering, optical, and motor industries. The chemical industry in particular is integrated in the economic plans of the East European Council for Mutual Economic Assistance (Comecon). More emphasis is now placed on the manufacture of luxury articles for the home market, but they are relatively expensive and sometimes in short supply. West German economists claim that the Democratic Republic lags ten years behind in the production of consumer goods. Refrigerators and washing machines were freely available only when West Germans were buying deep freezers and coffee machines. Nevertheless, consumer satisfaction with even this progress has produced considerable political stability.

(ii) *Agriculture*

One of the early measures taken in the Soviet-occupied Zone was the 'land reform'. The large estate *(Gut)*, which had long been a feature of eastern Germany, was quite alien to Socialism; estates of over 250 acres were taken over by the State and the land redistributed in units of twelve to twenty-five acres. These farms were too small to become independent and economically sound enterprises, especially as many of the farmers were young and inexperienced; the farmers were therefore organized into co-operatives. Over the next fifteen years conditions were created under which no independent farmer could survive. The collective farms were granted certain tax concessions; they were for example not required to pay purchase tax on equipment nor licence fees for their motor vehicles. Independent farmers were not allowed to buy machinery until the needs of the collective farms were met and they were therefore unable to reach the production targets set by the government. The larger units thus became manifestly more profitable and the government's task of complete collectivization was simplified. By 1960 the private farmer had disappeared.

Collectivization of farms took place in three stages: the first stage included only the available arable land, the second included also the farm machinery and draught animals and

A harvest team on a co-operative farm discussing the use of a combine harvester. Note the number of women workers

the third stage comprised these and all the farm buildings, livestock and other land such as pastures and woods. They all practised crop rotation. All collective farms are run by the members, who draft their own plans to achieve the aims of the national agricultural plan. The farmers in each collective draw on a central pool of equipment; they also have a centralized marketing system for their produce. An unusual feature is the provision of a milk pipeline from Potsdam to Erfurt in the industrial south-west.

Progress on the collective farms is still slow; yields rise by only 1% a year and imports of grain and meat are vital. Food rationing continued until 1958 and even in the mid-1970s certain commodities, for example butter and meat, were rationed by price. Production has been noticeably lower than in West Germany, where the pre-war agricultural output had been exceeded by 1950, whilst East Germany had not equalled it even fifteen years later. The food situation would have become grave had not East Germany lost so many citizens to the West; between 1946 and 1966 the population of the GDR fell by 2½ million.

The quality of the soil in East Germany varies from excellent to very poor. Over a quarter of the countryside is forested and provides 80% of East Germany's timber requirements. It has been found that pines are the trees best suited to the country's sandy soil. Two-thirds of the available land is used for farming, principally for producing rye, potatoes, cereals and sugar beet; the proportion of arable land is high because the climate of winter and summer extremes does not favour lush pasture land. The main agricultural areas lie in the Administrative Districts of Schwerin, Rostock, Neubrandenburg and Magdeburg. A considerable acreage of land has been completely unproductive because the soil is exceedingly poor; more and more attention is being given to reclaiming such land.

(iii) *Fishing*

At the end of the war the demarcation line robbed the eastern part of Germany of direct access to the rich fishing grounds in the North Sea. East Germany had no fishing fleet, harbour facilities were totally inadequate and there was no fish-processing industry. Rebuilding was centred on Rostock-Warnemünde and Saßnitz. Since 1977 her catches have been limited by quotas agreed with the EEC.

Leipzig: the automobile section of the 1969 Autumn Trade Fair

(iv) *Trade*

East Germany trades mainly with other Socialist countries; less than a quarter of her total trading activity is with the western world. The government of the Democratic Republic carries the whole responsibility for organizing imports and exports. These are controlled through trading agreements, usually negotiated by trade delegations attached to an embassy or consulate abroad; payment is made via the GDR government. Individual concerns are not usually allowed to deal directly with clients; the nationalized porcelain factory at Meissen is, however, an exception.

East Germany's trade with the Federal Republic is regulated by agreements which may however be affected by the fluctuating political situation. Despite the difference in the purchasing power of the West German and East German Mark, trade is calculated by the parity 1 DM = 1 M.

The main 'shop window' of the Democratic Republic is the Leipzig Fair, held twice a year in spring and autumn. Once of world importance, this 800-year-old fair does not attract the same interest as in pre-war years. East Germany's chief exports are machinery and chemicals; her chief imports are raw materials of all kinds, food, goods for assembly or further processing and technical equipment. Comprehensive details of industrial output and international trade are not published.

The nationalization of internal trade progressed slowly; even in 1974 almost a fifth of the country's small shops were still run privately. Government marketing organizations, including nation-wide networks of chain stores *(Handelsorganisation* or *HO* and *Konsumgenossenschaft)* are, however, gradually eclipsing the private shopkeeper; in 1974 they handled 97% of total trade. The absence of competition between different firms has eliminated the need for costly advertising and packaging; the latter has been reduced to the production of a simple container for the goods, although most are now rather more attractive than the brown paper bags of twenty years ago.

A number of shops cater exclusively for tourists, who must pay in foreign currency. This 'Intershop' scheme offers for sale goods not normally available on the home market, such as western brands of soap, cosmetics, chocolate and coffee.

(v) *Communications* (see Figs. 14, 15, 16)

Railways: An early task for the East German government was the construction of an adequate railway network to supplement the GDR's relatively poor facilities for water transport. The railways remained a nationalized enterprise, being known as the *Deutsche Reichsbahn.* The centre of the system is still the old capital, Berlin, although a new 'ring-line' has been built to replace the routes through West Berlin. Other important junctions are Leipzig, Halle and Magdeburg. The connections with Rostock and Stralsund have since 1949 assumed a much greater importance, since these are the principal outlets for trade, even from Czechoslovakia and central Europe.

Modernization schemes are in hand to convert the trains from steam to diesel or electric; the electrical equipment installed before 1945 was dismantled by the Russians. By 1974 9% of the total 14,633 kilometres was electrified. Already the railways carry over half the total freight traffic; it is intended that they should eventually carry all long-distance freight.

Inland waterways: East Germany's waterways do not at present offer a satisfactory means of transport between industrial areas and ports, although it is planned to widen the canal between the river Elbe and Wismar to take barges of 1,000 tons. Her network of waterways was created before the war and concentrates on east–west connections. Neither of the main rivers (Elbe and Oder) has its estuary in the Democratic Republic.

Many of the minor rivers are navigable to small craft; they include the Saale, Spree and Havel, which are tributaries of the Elbe. The Oder is linked by canals to both the Spree and the Havel; the latter is also linked by canal to the Elbe. Both the river Elbe and the Mittelland canal have lost much of their significance since the division of Germany, because they offer connections with West Germany which are little used.

Roads: For some years after the war only essential road works could be carried out because there was a shortage of machinery and materials. The condition of most roads has, however, improved, but the autobahns in particular are greatly inferior to West Germany's. Few new stretches have been built and the link with Rostock, planned for so long, was barely begun by 1977.

East Germany does not face the same traffic problems as West Germany. Her roads are not as busy, her towns are not choked by parked vehicles because she places a completely different emphasis on public transport. The aim is to provide an adequate, comfortable and reliable system of public transport. Nevertheless people still want to own cars, though they must save hard and wait several years. There were three times as many private cars on the roads in 1975 as in 1965.

Shipping: The part of Germany which became the Democratic Republic had no major harbour; the area had been served by Hamburg, now in the Federal Republic, and Stettin, now in Poland. New harbours were built at Wismar, Stralsund, Rostock and Warnemünde, once members of the great Hanseatic League. Rostock and nearby Warnemünde together became the GDR's main port, which was later extended to handle Czech trade. The great disadvantage affecting all the East German harbours is their geographical situation off the main trade routes of the world; they do not have easy access to the North Sea.

Air transport: In 1954 a national airline was formed called the *Deutsche Lufthansa V.E.B.* and equipped with Russian aircraft. Because the name was so similar to that of the West German airline *Deutsche Lufthansa A.G.*, many countries in the western world did not recognize the East German airline and would not allow it to use their airports. To overcome this difficulty the *Interflug* company was founded in 1958 and five years later absorbed the *Deutsche Lufthansa V.E.B.* It provides regular services, principally to countries belonging to the eastern bloc.

The main airport is Berlin (Schönefeld). Other cities served by airports are Dresden, Erfurt and Leipzig.

The Post Office: The postal services of the Democratic Republic are similar to those of West Germany, since both countries inherited the same system. The Democratic Republic has also introduced a system of postal codes *(Postleitzahlen)*, which differs only in detail from that used in West Germany. The country is divided into nine main regions, based on the Administrative Districts; region 1 comprises East Berlin, Potsdam and Frankfurt-on-Oder, 2 comprises Rostock, Schwerin and Neubrandenburg, 3 is Magdeburg, 4 is Halle, 5 is Erfurt, 6 includes both Suhl and Gera, 7 is Leipzig and Cottbus, 8 is Dresden and 9 is Karl-Marx-Stadt. The regions are then subdivided into separate postal areas. Letters intended for the GDR which are posted in West Germany carry the letter 'x' before the postal code. In addition to the usual functions the Post Office in the Democratic Republic has the right to sell newspapers and magazines.

III The History of Germany

Summary of Important Events

A.D. 9	*Hermannsschlacht.*
122	Completion of the *limes.*
2nd-8th centuries	European migrations.
453	Death of Attila.
476	End of the Roman Empire.
496	Clovis becomes Christian.
526	Death of Theodoric.
754	Death of Boniface.
800	Charlemagne crowned in Rome.
843	Partition of Charlemagne's Empire—beginning of German history.
926	Otto I crowned.
1076	Heinrich IV begins the quarrel with the Papacy.
1152	Accession of Barbarossa.
12th-13th centuries	Colonization east of the Elbe.
c1250	Formation of the Hanseatic League.
1356	'The Golden Bull.'
c1450	Invention of printing.
1517	Luther's 95 Theses.
1525	Peasants' Revolt.
1555	Religious Peace of Augsburg.
1608	Formation of the Protestant Union.
1609	Formation of the Catholic League.
1618	Outbreak of the Thirty Years' War.
1640	Accession of Friedrich Wilhelm, the Great Elector; beginning of the rise of Prussia.
1648	End of the Thirty Years' War; the Holy Roman Empire becomes a collection of independent States.
1740	Silesia becomes part of Prussia.
1772	West Prussia becomes part of Prussia.
1806	Napoleon defeats Prussia and Austria; end of the Holy Roman Empire.

1807 Prussia loses possessions west of the Elbe.
1815 Congress of Vienna; formation of the German Confederation.
1834 Formation of the Customs Union.
1848 Prussia gains the leading position in the Confederation. Revolution; National Assembly.
1862 Bismarck takes office in Prussia.
1864 Schleswig-Holstein crisis.
1867 Formation of the North German Federation.
1871 End of the Franco-Prussian war; formation of the German Empire. Beginnings of industrialization.
1888 Emperor Wilhelm II.
1890 Bismarck resigns.
1914 Outbreak of World War I.
1918 Defeat of Germany; declaration of a Republic.
1919 Treaty of Versailles. Foundation of the Weimar Republic.
1923 National Socialist putsch in Bavaria. Height of inflation. French occupation of the Ruhr.
1929–33 World slump.
1933 Hitler appointed Chancellor; Reichstag fire; Enabling Act.
1934 Hitler unites the offices of President and Chancellor as Führer.
1936 German troops march into the Rhineland.
1938 *Kristallnacht.* Austria and Sudeten Czechoslovakia taken over. Munich conference.
1939 Invasion of Poland. Outbreak of World War II.
1940 Occupation of Denmark, Norway, Holland, Belgium, Luxembourg and France. Battle of Britain.
1943 First sign of German defeats.
1944 Allied invasion of Europe. Stauffenberg plot.
1945 Germany capitulates. Yalta and Potsdam conferences.
1946 Nuremberg trials.
1948 Separate currency reforms in the Western and Soviet zones. Berlin blockade.
1949 The Federal Republic of Germany and the German Democratic Republic founded.
1950 The GDR becomes a member of Comecon.
1953 The unsuccessful workers' uprising in the GDR.

1955 The Federal Republic becomes a member of NATO. The Democratic Republic becomes a member of the Warsaw Pact.

1958 The Federal Republic is a founder-member of the Common Market.

1961 The Berlin wall.

1970 The first meetings between leaders of the Federal Republic and the GDR; the Federal Republic concludes a non-aggression treaty with the Soviet Union.

1971 Willy Brandt receives the Nobel Peace Prize.

1973 In a treaty with Czechoslovakia, West Germany voids the Munich agreement of 1938. The Basic Treaty *(Grundvertrag)* between East and West Germany comes into force. Both Germanies become members of the United Nations Organization.

1974 Helmut Schmidt becomes Chancellor; Walter Scheel becomes President.

Origins
Germanic tribes can be traced back four thousand years to the Bronze Age in the territory at the western end of the Baltic. From about 1000 B.C. they began to migrate southwards from the Jutland Peninsula and southern Scandinavia into northern and central Europe, colonizing land which they seized from the Celts to support an increasing population. When they met with the Romans, who were still extending their Empire, several great battles took place, for example the *Hermannsschlacht* in A.D. 9, and the Romans found it necessary to build a line of defences *(limes)* along their frontier from Andernach to Regensburg to halt the advancing tribes. Almost the whole course of this 340-mile long earthen rampart and some of the forts and castles (such as the reconstructed Saalburg in the Taunus) can still be seen today. South and west of the *limes* there exist many relics of Roman civilization, notably in Trier, which between A.D. 285 and 400 was the Imperial summer residence. Little of contemporary

A.D. 122

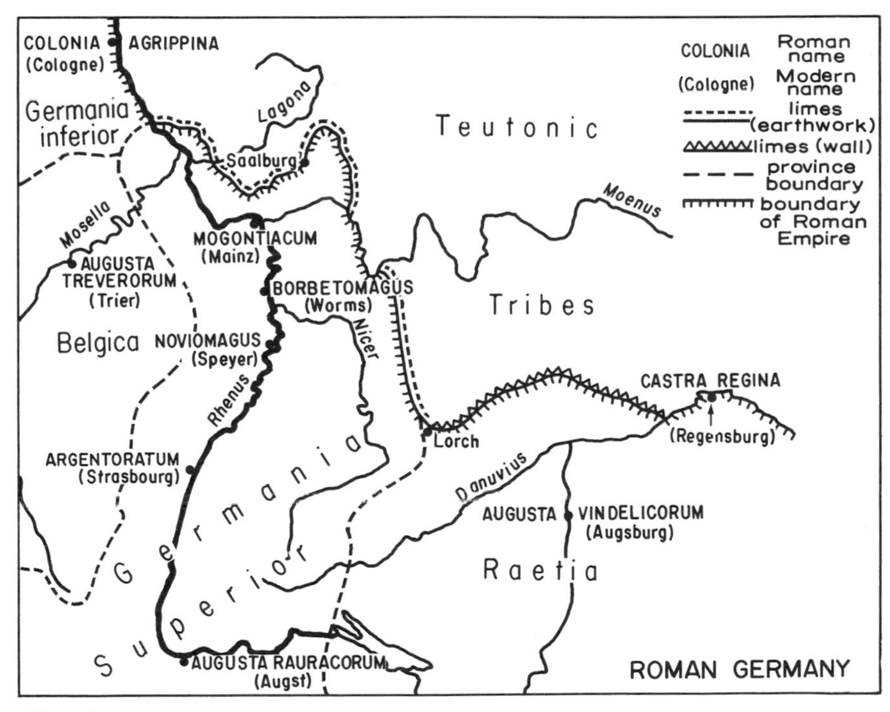

Fig 18

Germanic civilization remains, because they built only insubstantial wood and wattle houses.

The Migrations

Some of the land settled by the Germanic tribes proved inhospitable; the North Sea coast for example was often hit by great storms which drove the sea far inland. The Saxons who had colonized the area wanted to move southwards away from their ruined farms, but found the land occupied by the Franks; the latter were however soon able to take advantage of the recall of the Roman soldiers and occupied former Roman territory. The mass migration of European peoples (*Völkerwanderungen*) had begun. The Alemanni penetrated

375 the *limes* and reached northern Italy, the Angles and Saxons sailed across to Britain and the Goths migrated from southern Sweden to the Black Sea and eastern Mediterranean and became divided into two rival groups, the Ostrogoths (Eastern Goths) and the Visigoths (Western Goths). The Vandals moved westwards from the Oder valley to Spain and eventually conquered the North African coast.

The Germanic migrations were interrupted by the ferocious Huns who stormed westwards from Asia. They conquered the Ostrogoths in about 375 and forced them to serve in their

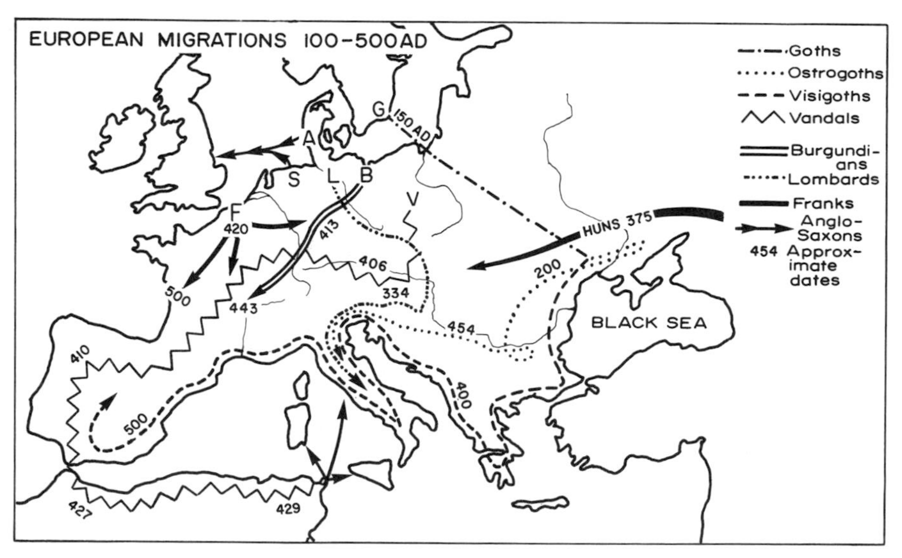

Fig 19

army. The Visigoths retreated westwards before the advancing Huns and, led by Alaric, captured Rome and occupied much of southern France (lost to the Franks in the sixth century) and most of Spain (which they held until the arrival of the Arabs in 711). Under Attila the Huns penetrated far into Gaul before being beaten by the Gauls, Romans and Visigoths; the Empire of the Huns disintegrated after the death of Attila in 453 and they retreated eastwards beyond the Volga. Once they were free of their bondage to the Huns, the Ostrogoths led by Theodoric conquered Rome in about 492 and he became ruler of the western part of what had been the Roman Empire. After his death in 526, the Ostrogoths were defeated by the Romans and driven back to the Alps, where they eventually dispersed.

500

The arrival of Christianity

Christianity was spreading throughout Europe with the migrating tribes, who learned of the new faith as they colonized parts of the former Roman Empire. The Franks, who lived near the Rhine, Main and Moselle, followed the example of their king Clovis *(Chlodwig)* and became converted to Christianity in 496. Further conversions among the Germanic tribes were accomplished by the Celtic saints Kilian (died 689) and Columbanus (died 615) and by the Anglo-Saxon missionary Wynfrith, renamed Boniface by the Pope (died 754). He is sometimes spoken of as the Apostle of Germany. The Islamic religion, founded in the seventh century, was carried into Europe by the Arabs, who in 711 conquered the Visigoths in the Iberian peninsula. A further advance of the Arabs into southern France was halted by Charles Martell in 732.

The first German Empire

By the beginning of the eighth century the Franks had conquered all the Germanic tribes except the Saxons and had imposed Christianity on them. In 751 close co-operation between the papacy and the king of the Franks began. The Pope placed himself under the protection of the king in return for his support in the theological dispute with Byzantium, and conditions were created for the fusion of the new Christian and old Germanic traditions. This took place in the reign of Charlemagne *(Karl der Große)* (768–814), who was crowned Emperor by the Pope in Rome on Christmas Day, 800. Charlemagne chose Aachen (Aix-la-Chapelle) as the centre of his Empire, which he extended until it comprised present-day

800

West Germany, Holland, Belgium, France, Switzerland and most of Italy; the last of the Germanic tribes, the Saxons, was conquered in 805 and forcibly converted to Christianity. Although he could not write he is said to have been a learned man. His reputation as a humble and wise leader spread beyond the farthest outposts of his Empire; Eastern potentates showered him with rich gifts and mourned with Christians when he died in 814.

Within thirty years of his death Charlemagne's great Frankish Empire was broken up into three kingdoms. This partition may be said to mark the beginning of truly German history, since the Germanic-speaking Kingdom of the East

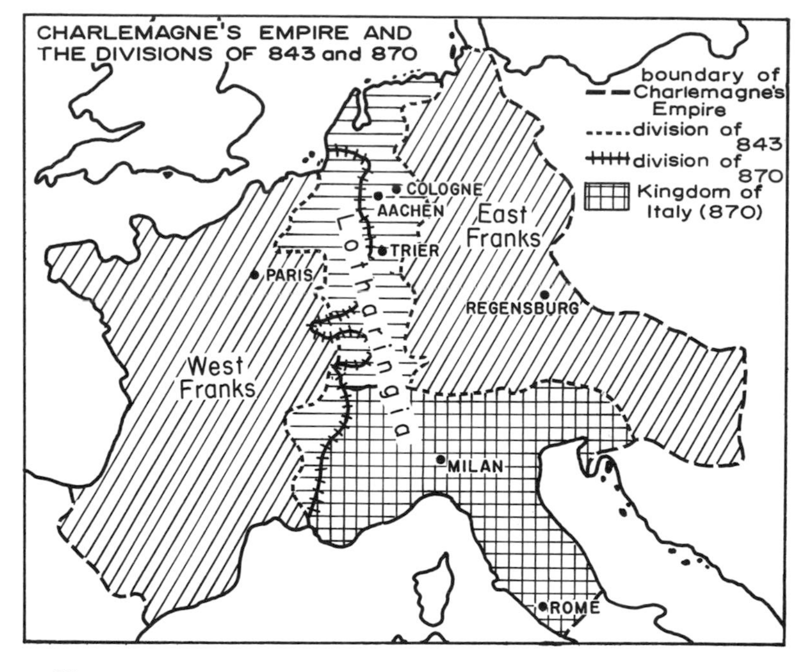

Fig 20

Franks, which was given to Ludwig the German (843–76) eventually became modern Germany. The Kingdom of the West Franks, where a language derived from Latin was spoken, eventually became France; the lands between the two kingdoms were apportioned to Lothar, who gave his name to Lorraine (Lotharingia, *Lothringen*). Lothar's dynasty died out in 870 and his kingdom was divided into three parts: one part joined France, one joined Germany and the third, comprising Burgundy, the Rhône delta and northern Italy, became independent. This division was not final, but marks the beginning of the struggle for supremacy in Alsace-Lorraine which has persisted for over 1,000 years. **870**

East Francia, the Kingdom of the East Franks, was a loose association of hostile tribes including the Saxons, Franks, Bavarians and Swabians, who engaged constantly in local feuds. Neither King Ludwig nor his successors proved able to unify them and it was left to Heinrich I, Duke of Saxony, who was elected king in 919, to bring about the necessary reconciliation. Saxon kings and emperors then reigned for over a century, during which the land experienced one of its greatest periods. Under the leadership of Heinrich I attacks by the Northmen and Magyars were repulsed; Heinrich's son Otto I (936–73) inflicted a final defeat on the latter in 955. It was also Otto who reconquered northern Italy; he was crowned Holy Roman Emperor by the Pope in 962, thus securing for himself the secular headship of Christendom. He later became known as Otto the Great. **962**

The Investiture controversy

The young Heinrich IV (1056–1106), second in a new line of Frankish kings, began a dispute with the Pope over the right to appoint Bishops *(Investiturstreit)*. Pope Gregory wished to see the Church free of simony and worldly influence; Heinrich bestowed bishoprics upon loyal priests and gave them land and wealth in order to ensure their future allegiance. The bishops demanded that the Pope resign; instead he dismissed them and excommunicated the king (1076). In the following year Heinrich, in order to preserve his throne, went to Canossa and humbly besought the Pope to readmit him to the Church. The request was granted, but a second excommunication caused Heinrich to march to Rome at the head of an army, drive out Pope Gregory and replace him with a German Bishop, who immediately annulled the excommunication and crowned Heinrich Emperor (1084). **1077**

The inability of the Pope and the Emperor to resolve the disagreement about which of them should be the leader in a Christian Empire caused its disintegration. The dispute encouraged the rise of powerful local rulers especially in areas near the frontiers, who resented all attempts to create an effective central government. This dislike of centralization coloured German history for the next 800 years. The *Investiturstreit* was finally settled in the reign of Heinrich V (1106–25) at the Concordat of Worms in 1122, which determined that the Emperor's gift of worldly possessions should precede the consecration of the bishops, but even so relations between the Papacy and the Empire continued to be strained throughout the twelfth century.

1122

The Hohenstaufen dynasty

The Hohenstaufen dynasty provided a succession of Emperors between the years 1138 and 1254. The best known is probably Friedrich I (1152–90), called Barbarossa on account of his red beard. Friedrich wished to emulate the greatness of Charlemagne and to revive the Empire. He repeatedly attacked the cities of northern Italy and finally succeeded in re-establishing the former power of the Holy Roman Empire over the Papacy. During the last of his Italian campaigns he quarrelled with his cousin Heinrich der Löwe, Duke of Saxony and Bavaria, whom he later punished by taking from him both these dukedoms and by sending him into exile. Barbarossa now reigned supreme in Germany and Italy, although the Pope still claimed superiority on account of his spiritual leadership. The Pope also claimed a measure of temporal power in Italy and became embroiled in political disputes, which led to demands from many quarters that he should restrict himself to his spiritual duties. Barbarossa's great reign culminated in a Crusade to free Jerusalem from the Turks. He was drowned crossing a river in Asia Minor.

1190

Barbarossa was succeeded by his son Heinrich VI (1190–97), who proved to be another great ruler, but he died young. His son, Friedrich II (1212–50), spent most of his life in Italy and made only a half-hearted attempt to restore some semblance of order to Germany, which was fast becoming a conglomeration of semi-independent princedoms. The Hohenstaufen dynasty died out in 1254; with it died the splendour of courtly life, which had existed since about 1150.

1254

Eastern colonization

In the twelfth and thirteenth centuries there was considerable Germanic colonization of the territories east of the Elbe and Saale. The local people in Bohemia, Silesia and Hungary welcomed the colonizing Germans, from whom they learned new crafts and improved methods of cultivating the land. Most of the Slavs were still heathen and many were converted to Christianity by monks and priests who accompanied the Germans. Further north the people were forced to accept the new faith by religious orders of knights, whose campaigns were organized on the lines of a Crusade. By 1346 these Teutonic Knights ruled most of the Baltic coastlands as far as the Gulf of Finland.

The rise of the towns

In all the Germanic areas towns were established as centres of crafts and trade and there appeared alongside the knights, clerics and peasants a new class of citizen, the burgher, or town-dweller. Local rulers granted charters to the new towns, fixed market days and made the people responsible for keeping law and order and for organizing crafts and trade. Senior members of patrician families came together to govern the towns, admitting at first no representatives from the guilds until the latter rose up and finally gained their objective by force of arms. Trade between the towns flourished and they became rich, yet they found that individually they were no longer strong enough to resist the influence of local rulers and to protect their traders so many of them joined together in leagues. The great Rhine League stretching from Cologne to Basle was founded in 1254 and soon numbered seventy towns. By far the most important of these alliances was the Hanseatic League which had over eighty members, including all the important towns on the North Sea and Baltic coasts and some inland towns such as Cologne, Lüneburg and Cracow. The members made common laws, set up warehouses throughout their trading area and agreed to come to each other's help whenever one of them was in difficulties. In the fourteenth century the Hanseatic League became so strong that it was an influential political force, even declaring war on and defeating Denmark.

The decay of the Empire

Since the death of Friedrich II in 1250 Germany had been without an Emperor (Interregnum) and anarchy had spread throughout the land. In 1273 Rudolf of Hapsburg (1273–91), a hitherto unknown man, was elected king by a body of men, the Electors, appointed for the purpose in 1257. He set about restoring law and order by punishing wrongdoers and destroying the strongholds of robber-knights who had flourished in the Interregnum. He added a great deal of present-day Austria to his kingdom.

1273

The approval of the Pope was necessary before a German king could become Emperor; the election of Ludwig IV (1314–47) was not ratified and he was excommunicated for acting as ruler of the Empire without Papal legitimation. Ludwig set up a rival puppet-pope, but he received no great support and Ludwig had to admit failure. It was decided in

1338 1338 that the Pope's approval should no longer be necessary; from this point Empire and Papacy went their separate ways.

On the death of Ludwig, Karl IV of Luxembourg (1347–78) was elected king. He was dismayed at the state of the country when he took over the throne; he encouraged the development of trade and crafts and turned his capital Prague into a cultural centre. His court had a considerable influence on the rest of Germany in the establishment of a unified language; the first German university was founded in Prague in 1348. Karl also fixed the composition and the rights and duties of

1356 the body of Electors in the 'Golden Bull' of 1356. There were to be seven Electors *(Kurfürsten)*, three spiritual and four temporal 'princes', the Archbishops of Mainz, Cologne and Trier, the Duke of Saxony, the King of Bohemia, the Margrave of Brandenburg and the Count Palatine of the Rhine. One of the main provisions stated that the lands of the Electors were to be passed intact from generation to generation. The 'Golden Bull' was intended to strengthen the position of the Electors in the belief that this would encourage them to govern responsibly and use their power wisely, but in fact the Electors chose weak men, since they did not wish to be subjected to the rule of a strong king. The king himself was in an impossible position; he knew that he could easily be deposed if he took unpopular action. The Empire was too large to be run efficiently, there was no fixed capital, no central administration. The Diet (parliament) was usually poorly attended, and then only by people determined to further their own interests; anarchy seemed the likely outcome.

Even the establishment on the throne in 1438 of the strong Hapsburg dynasty did not prevent the disintegration of the Empire; the religious differences of the sixteenth century caused a split which never completely healed. The Hapsburgs were an Austrian family and so Austria became the leading power in the Empire, losing the position to Prussia only in the eighteenth century.

The Renaissance

The great advances in learning and the spread of literacy to the middle classes of Europe during the fifteenth century culminated in a wide movement known as the Renaissance.

The invention of printing in about 1450 assisted the dissemination of knowledge, and the use throughout Europe of the Latin language as the chief medium of instruction produced an intellectual unity in which new ideas and cultures could easily spread. The invention of gunpowder hastened the decline of the knighthood, and further inventions (compass, watch, quadrant) helped explorers on their hazardous journeys. The turn of the century saw the beginnings of modern astronomy with the discoveries of Copernicus and Kepler. As knowledge of the physical world began to be assembled, superstitions, alchemy and astrology gradually lost favour. The humanists accepted nothing at its face value, challenging everything from the truth of the scriptures to the class system within society. **1450**

The Peasant's Revolt

As trade increased, more goods became available; money became extremely important, bringing power and position to those who possessed enough of it. The one section of the community that had no part in this financial growth was the peasants, who even lost many of the rights, for example of common pasture, that they had formerly enjoyed. They were taxed more and more heavily and those who could not afford to own land were being pressed by the prosperous nobles into helpless serfdom. The Black Death, which had begun to spread across Europe in the middle of the fourteenth century, added to their suffering. The peasants no longer meekly accepted their lot; they joined together in groups to try to gain their freedom and by 1524 they were ready to rebel throughout the whole of Germany. There was however no real organization behind the revolt and the landowners had little difficulty in putting down the individual rebellions, often with the utmost cruelty. After the fighting the peasants found themselves worse off than ever before, since they were forced to pay for the damage they had done. **1524**

The religious upheaval

The sixteenth century was also a time of religious upheaval. Many people both inside and outside the Church were dissatisfied with the worldliness and corruption of many leading clerics and also with certain of the beliefs that they were ordered to accept. A learned monk, Martin Luther, found himself unable to accept the doctrine of salvation by 'good works' and began in 1514 to preach salvation by faith alone. He declared himself against the common practice of buying indulgences, since less emphasis was being placed on penitence than on the need to raise vast sums of money for the building of St. Peter's Church in Rome. In 1517 Luther nailed 95 'theses' (statements about religious belief intended as topics for discussion) on the door of the church in Wittenberg, which found approval with a great many people. In 1520 the Pope sent Johannes Eck, a personal enemy of Luther, to Germany with a Papal Bull condemning many of Luther's assertions as heretical and calling upon him to recant or suffer excommunication. Luther publicly burned the Bull in Wittenberg. He was summoned by the Emperor Karl V (1519–56) to appear before the Diet in Worms, but his conscience would not permit him to recant and he was outlawed. Safe with a friendly prince in the Wartburg, Luther translated first the New Testament (1522) and then the whole Bible (1534) into German. Printed copies of his translation and of his various treatises quickly circulated amongst the people, on whom their influence has been of considerable and lasting importance.

1517

Luther's reforms appealed to a world ready for change. The Reformation, as it has become known, spread quickly, especially in northern Germany. The Catholic Emperor Karl V tried to put down the new beliefs by force of arms, but although he was victorious on the battlefield he failed to reconvert the people to Catholicism. In 1545 the Catholic Church was reformed by the Council of Trent and the powerful Jesuit order was founded. In 1555 agreement was reached at Augsburg that both the Catholic and Protestant religions should be equally acceptable in Germany; the ruling Prince was to decide which faith would be adopted in his land and dissenters were to leave. About half the population, principally in southern Germany, now belonged to the Church of Rome.

1555

The Thirty Years' War

The once powerful German Empire was now no more than a loose confederation of principalities and towns, divided into two main groups according to their religious beliefs. Several times war threatened to break out between the League of Catholic States and the Union of Protestant States. When in 1618 the Protestants of Bohemia were denied some of their

1618

rights, they withdrew their allegiance from the Emperor, who sent an army under General Tilly to crush the rebellion. Tilly extended his successful campaign into northern Germany, much of which he laid waste. In 1623 the Protestant King of Denmark entered the battle with an eye to winning Schleswig-Holstein for his realm. He formed an alliance with England and Holland, so that what had begun as an internal dispute blossomed into a European war which was to last thirty years (1618–48). A second army raised by the Emperor under Wallenstein was successful in all its campaigns, outlasting that of Tilly, who was defeated near Leipzig in 1631 by King Gustavus Adolphus of Sweden. Wallenstein, who enjoyed a reputation for terrible cruelty, was himself defeated by the Swedes at Lützen in 1632; he subsequently came to terms with his enemies, and as a result was dismissed by the Emperor and later murdered. France now joined Sweden in the war, which had developed out of a religious war into a

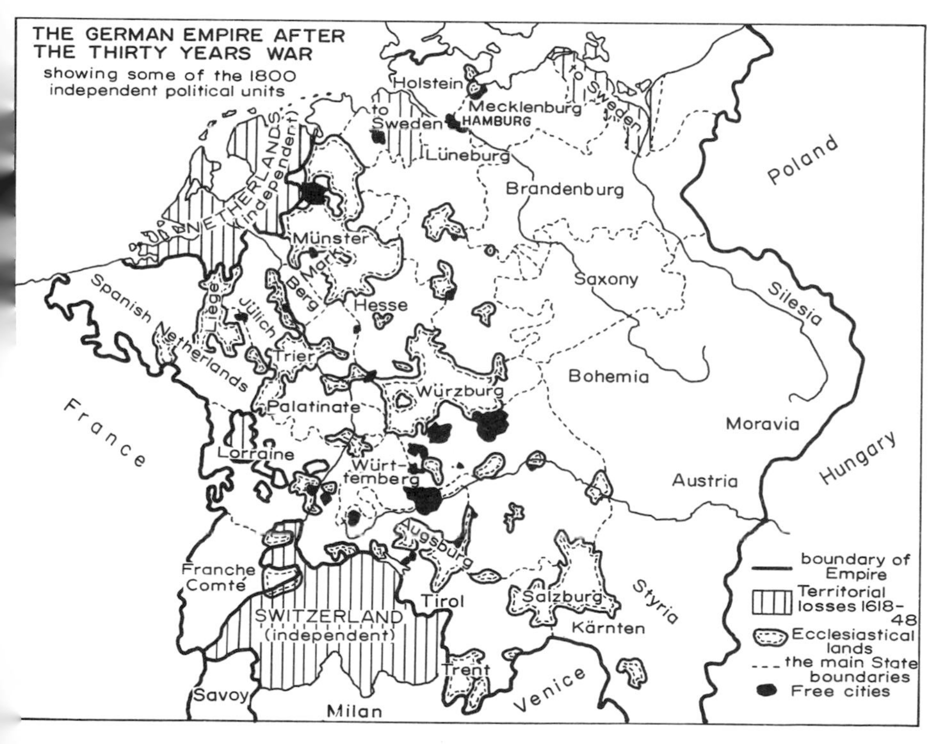

Fig 21

battle for superiority in Europe. It ended with the Treaty of **1648** Westphalia of 1648 which restored the *status quo* of 1624 and reaffirmed the right of a ruler to determine the religion of his state. The Treaty also gave independence to the Netherlands and Switzerland and ceded parts of Germany to France and Sweden. Vast expanses of Germany had been devastated by the war, famine and plague, and almost half the population had been killed. The religious division of Germany still existed, the power of the Emperor had been broken and that of the Princes increased. Germany consisted of more than 1,800 independent political entities; the Holy Roman Empire now existed only on paper.

The emergence of Brandenburg–Prussia

After the Thirty Years' War the Electorate of Brandenburg emerged as the most important of the Protestant States. Brandenburg had been created in 1134 to act as a buffer state between Germanic tribes and the Slavs. In 1356 its ruler was chosen to be one of the Electors. From 1415 it was ruled by the Hohenzollern dynasty, in whose hands it remained until 1918. It was Friedrich Wilhelm, the Great Elector (1648–88), who turned Brandenburg into a force to be reckoned with; from his capital Berlin he encouraged agriculture and industry and raised an army out of all proportion to the size and wealth of his lands, making sure that it was organized efficiently. He succeeded in creating an absolute monarchy on the model furnished by his contemporary Louis XIV of France. His son, Friedrich III (1688–1713), renamed the Electorate of **1701** Brandenburg the Kingdom of Prussia in 1701 and made himself King under the title Friedrich I. He was succeeded by his son Friedrich Wilhelm (1713–40), an austere character obsessed with creating a large, perfectly disciplined army, which he was able to hand over to his better-known son Friedrich II (1740–86), called 'der Große' (Frederick the Great), together with vast resources of gold which he had amassed by practising extreme economy in the government of his lands. Prussia *(Preußen)* was now ready to challenge Austria's supremacy.

The expansion of Prussia

Soon after the accession of Friedrich II, the Emperor Karl V (1711–40) of Austria died without a male heir for the House of Hapsburg. Karl had taken the precaution of securing promises from various other countries that they would recognize his daughter Maria Theresa as his heir, but scarcely had her reign begun when her greedy neighbours prepared to seize her lands. The Austrian province of Silesia was coveted by Friedrich II of Prussia. In 1740 he marched his armies into Silesia and defeated the Austrians, but before long both parties found themselves embroiled in wider conflicts. The peace treaty of 1763 which ended the Seven Years' War finally gave Silesia to Prussia. Friedrich now turned his attention to making his subjects happier and more prosperous by draining and colonizing swamps, encouraging industry and drawing up a new and fairer code of laws. He found time to revive his youthful interest in literature and music and gathered a number of French intellectuals, notably Voltaire, at his court in Sanssouci near Potsdam.

1740

In 1772 Prussia, Russia and Austria decided to divide amongst themselves the Kingdom of Poland, which had long had a system of government that was so inadequate as to create anarchy. Friedrich was anxious to secure a stretch of Poland known as West Prussia which separated the central provinces of his kingdom (Brandenburg, Silesia and Pomerania) from East Prussia. The Partition of Poland enabled him to add this valuable territory to his realm, and when he died in 1786 Prussia was a formidable European power with a large and well-organized army.

Apart from Prussia and Austria, there were at this time no large or powerful states in Germany. The diversity of independent estates, towns and abbeys, each trying to outdo the other, produced an extremely varied cultural life which encouraged outstanding composers, writers, philosophers and scientists and brought a period of considerable architectural interest.

The end of the Holy Roman Empire

Three years after the death of Friedrich, revolution broke out in France. After the execution of Louis XVI in 1793 and the establishment of the Reign of Terror, many European monarchies allied themselves against France because they feared that the revolutionary ideals of freedom and equality would take root in their own lands. At this time Napoleon Bonaparte was making a name for himself in military campaigns against Austria which gained the left bank of the Rhine for France. He was a ruthless leader and had such considerable success that he was hailed as a national hero and given complete control of the state. He had himself crowned Emperor of

France in 1804 and dreamed of one day becoming Emperor of Europe. In the Napoleonic Wars Austria and Prussia, now fighting together to preserve their independence from France, were defeated at Austerlitz and Jena. Napoleon forced the Emperor Franz II to abdicate, bringing to an end the Holy **1806** Roman Empire. Austria severed her connections with the German Empire and Franz took the title of Emperor of Austria. Prussia lost all her possessions west of the Elbe in the Treaty of Tilsit (1807) and was to pay a vast sum of money in reparations. The greatness created by Friedrich II was at an end.

A period of social revolution now began in Prussia; up to the defeat at Jena she had been much more backward than most of the neighbouring lands. Great changes, including the abolition in principle of serfdom, were introduced by Stein, Hardenberg and Scharnhorst. Prussia's citizens now began to take a real interest in what they could justifiably regard as their own country; a feeling of nationalism started to grow, fanned by the compelling speeches of the philosopher Fichte in 1807–8 and by the songs and poems of Arndt and Körner.

The German Confederation

Napoleon's hopes of becoming Emperor of Europe had meanwhile been dashed; after the spectacular entry into

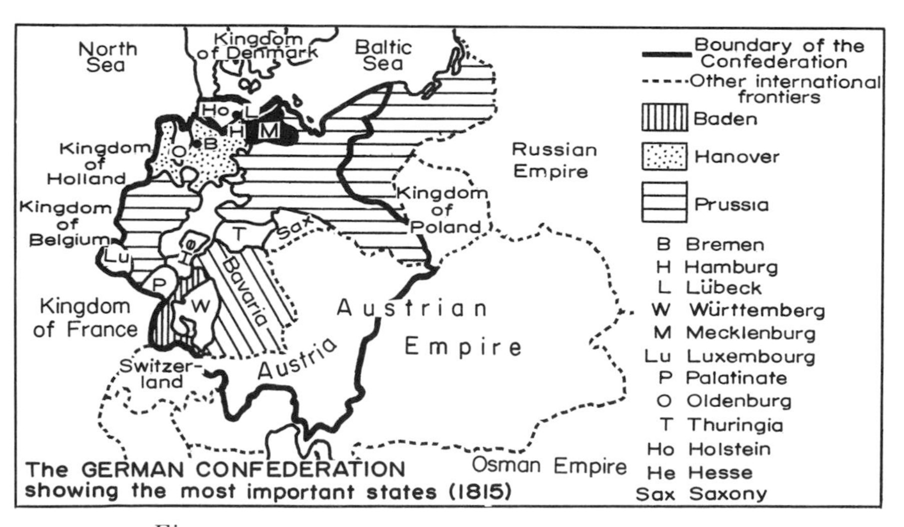

Fig 22

Moscow his armies had suffered one defeat after another, until they were finally conquered on French soil. Napoleon was forced to abdicate in 1814. A year later he attempted to regain control of France, but he was beaten by the English and Prussian armies under Wellington and Blücher at Waterloo and was banished to St. Helena. The Congress of Vienna which ended the Napoleonic Wars in 1815 redetermined the frontiers of all European states. The German Empire was not restored; instead a federal union of independent states with a central Parliament in Frankfurt-on-Main was created. To this German Confederation of 1815 belonged 35 Sovereign Princes and four Free Cities under the Presidency of Austria. The ordinary people were not represented in the government, which had no power to raise money or an army and hence could not implement such decisions as were reached. Nevertheless this Confederation managed to exist for half a century, although it was clear that it could never form the basis of a truly united German state.

1815

Liberal elements within the Confederation were disappointed that the Congress of Vienna had failed to weld Germany into a true nation, and angered by the failure of most of the Princes to give their States the promised new constitutions. The nobility was largely against the formation of a single democratic nation because they saw that such a step would reduce their own power. The people were not in general prepared to challenge the *status quo*, since the tradition of submission to authority was deeply rooted in their way of life. The Austrian Chief Minister Metternich, who had played a prominent part in the Congress of Vienna, met the German Princes at Carlsbad in 1819 and instigated measures to suppress all talk of national unity; censorship was introduced and intellectuals were to be watched by the police. Although these measures outraged the liberals, there was no general protest for another thirty years. This era of tacit acceptance has become known as the 'Biedermeier' era, after a character invented to personify the politically apathetic, respectable middle-class citizen.

1819

The National Assembly of 1848

The first half of the nineteenth century was a time of great inventions which were to change the people's lives far more profoundly than any purely political measure. Industrialization was getting under way, and the middle and upper classes grew richer and more powerful. Customs unions were formed in 1828 and 1834, which lowered economic barriers and promoted trade, but they failed to produce political unity. News of the 1848 revolution in France encouraged the German people to rise up in support of their own demands for democracy. Metternich was overthrown and the social reforms, which he had opposed, quickly introduced. Austria was robbed of her leading position within the German Confederation by Friedrich Wilhelm IV, King of Prussia. He gave way to the demands of his people and summoned an elected assembly to draw up a State constitution. A National Assembly, composed of many of the most dis-

1848 tinguished Germans of the day, was convoked in 1848 in Frankfurt to draft a national constitution, but before this could be done the question of what form a united Germany should take had to be settled. The delegates argued for months whether to restrict the new nation to purely Germanic peoples *(Kleindeutschland)* or whether to admit Austria with its multiplicity of different subject peoples *(Großdeutschland)*. The former solution was finally agreed and the crown was offered to Friedrich Wilhelm IV of Prussia; he refused it. This decision rendered the deliberations of the National Assembly fruitless and its members gradually dispersed; power remained with the petty monarchs.

The rise of Prussia

With the accession of Wilhelm I in 1858, Prussia gained an ambitious king whose aim it was to expel Austria from the Confederation and to construct from the remaining states a firm union under the domination of Prussia. He saw that war was bound to come and determined to have at the ready a large, efficient army, but his parliament refused to vote him

1862 the necessary money. In 1862 the King called upon Otto von Bismarck (1815–1898) to help him carry out his plan, threatening to abdicate if Bismarck refused. Bismarck had taken part in the Frankfurt parliament of 1848 and realized that nothing would ever be gained by talking. Once in office he did not hesitate to overrule parliament if his wishes were ignored. In doing so he became extremely unpopular, but he did not permit himself to be deflected from his avowed aim, hoping that time would prove him right. Bismarck allied himself with Austria against Denmark to win the provinces of Schleswig and Holstein; he then provoked a crisis with Austria and forced her into a war in 1866. Austria was quickly defeated. She did not lose any of her territory to Prussia, but she was expelled from the Confederation, which was now replaced by a North German Federation of all 22 states north of the Main. Prussia itself absorbed the States of Hanover, Nassau and Schleswig-Holstein, the Electorate of Hesse and the Free City of Frankfurt-on-Main; it now extended from the present Dutch and Belgian frontiers to Silesia and East Prussia. The King of Prussia was made President of the new Federation; Bismarck became Chancellor.

1867

The new German Empire

France saw her superiority in Europe threatened by this new power and sought to prevent the unification of the southern German states with the North German Federation. Bismarck was eager to wage war on France, believing that the southern states would be more willing to join Prussia if they were fighting a common enemy. In 1870 the Franco-Prussian War began. Prussia emerged victorious and, as expected, the southern states joined the North German Federation. Alsace and Lorraine were annexed from France in the peace treaty, which also demanded that France should pay considerable reparations. The terms of the treaty were indeed so harsh that they provoked a desire for revenge on the part of France which was only fulfilled by the First World War. Wilhelm, King of Prussia, was proclaimed Emperor *(Kaiser)* of the new German Empire and Bismarck became the first Chancellor.

1871

The Empire was a federation of 20 states and three free cities; the states were ruled by Princes, who sent representatives to form the upper house of Parliament, the *Bundesrat,* in which Prussia had an absolute veto. The lower house, or *Reichstag,* was elected by the people every five years. Each state had its own Parliament, which dealt with internal matters, but foreign policy, laws, communications and finance were organized on the national level. Bismarck assured himself of a position of power in the Empire by being Imperial Chancellor, Minister-President of Prussia and President of the Federal Council, responsible not to the government but to the Kaiser. Whilst this arrangement worked admirably so long as Wilhelm I was on the throne, it was destined to collapse in 1890, two years after his death. The new system did however enable Germany to progress far towards actual unity and uniformity. An imperial currency replaced in 1873 the bewildering variety of coins and paper

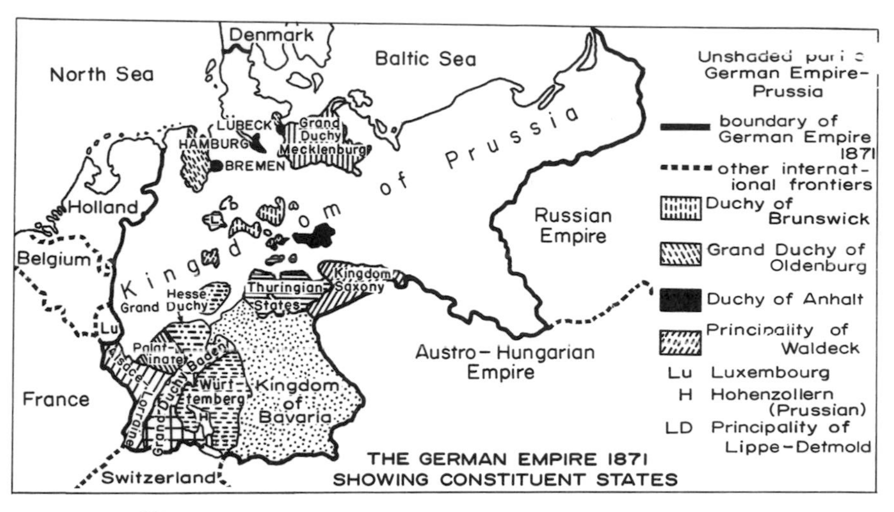

Fig 23

money of the individual states and the metric units of length, weight and liquid measure were introduced, speeding trade and financial transactions. Postal services were integrated and it was proposed that the various rail networks should be united to form a national system, but this plan was only realized in 1919.

Bismarck's achievements satisfied the majority of Germans, yet the newly formed Empire had both internal and external problems. Bismarck at first wished to assert the supremacy of the state over the Catholic Church, especially in Prussia. A series of laws passed from the year 1873 placed education, even of priests, under government supervision, expelled certain religious orders, including the Jesuits, from the Empire and deprived the Church of the sole right to marry. The Pope's protests went unheeded, but the effect of these new laws was to drive the Catholics into a solid political party *(Zentrumspartei)*. Bismarck eventually realized that he would gain nothing by using force to apply these laws, and saw that it would be to his advantage to win the support of the *Zentrumspartei* against the Socialists, who by this time were seen to be a new and disturbing force in the country. He repealed almost all the laws which had offended the Catholics in 1880, retaining however state supervision of education and the institution of civil marriage, which to this day must precede a religious marriage in Germany. Bismarck's treatment of national minorities—the Danes in North Schleswig, the French in Alsace-Lorraine and several million Poles in the eastern provinces—was characterized by injustice and a marked lack of tact. He provoked, instead of allegiance to the Empire, an even greater awareness amongst these peoples of their own separateness. The rapid industrialization of the 1870s and the resulting social upheaval presented Bismarck with further problems. The working classes felt themselves in need of protection from the power of the new factory owners and formed themselves into groups, out of which grew the Social Democratic Party. Bismarck attempted to suppress the Party and indeed succeeded in driving it underground for about twelve years. He eventually realized that he could never abolish it and tried instead to placate the workers with an exemplary programme of social insurance, passed in the years 1883–5. The Socialists rejected these plans, and the newly formed unions pressed instead for more thorough-going reforms such as the abolition of child labour and the introduction of an eight-hour working day.

1883

The basic aim of Bismarck's foreign policy was to protect his own position by making alliances with the powerful Austrian and Russian Empires and securing the isolation of France. However he lost the friendship of Russia, due to his part in the Congress of Berlin in 1878, but regained it for a time through the secret Re-insurance Treaty of 1887, which contained mutual promises of neutrality for three years.

Bismarck had at first little interest in acquiring colonies, seeing Germany's role rather as an influential power within Europe, but the obvious trading advantages caused him to change his views. The German colonial Empire, mainly in Africa, was largely formed during the last six years before Bismarck's fall.

The isolation of Germany

With the accession of Wilhelm II in 1888 began a conflict which ended with Bismarck's resignation in 1890. There was a difference of opinion on policy and on where the supreme power was to lie, with the Kaiser or with the Chancellor. Bismarck's departure left the young, inexperienced and temperamentally unstable Kaiser in charge, who began by pursuing a liberal policy at home, thus displeasing the land-owners and the nobility. This unpopularity caused him to change course and go along with the industrial magnates, who had risen to prominence with the growth of industry after

1890

1871. His foreign policy, too, was inconsistent, and some six years after he came to the throne Germany found herself faced by just the situation Bismarck had feared: an alliance between Russia and France, which was later extended to include England. By 1906 Germany was completely encircled by hostile powers, and the conflicting interests of European states were leading to crises which became increasingly difficult to contain. The assassination of Archduke Franz Ferdinand, heir to the throne of Austria-Hungary, on

1914

June 28th 1914 by Serbian extremists precipitated the outbreak of a war which involved most of the nations of Europe.

The First World War

Austria, supported by Germany, invaded Serbia. The Serbs had the support of Russia, who was seeking to extend her sphere of influence in the Balkans. France promised to come to the aid of her ally, Russia; Germany declared war on both of them and invaded France through Belgian territory, so violating Belgium's neutrality. England intervened to defend Belgium. On the western front the fighting settled down into trench warfare and continued until mid-1918 with no decisive result and immense loss of life on both sides. On the eastern front Germany had considerable successes, conquering Rumania by the end of 1916. In 1917 the German U-boat campaign brought America into the war, although the vast reinforcements she provided did not have any marked effect until early 1918.

Later that year the German leaders Ludendorff and Hindenburg, perturbed about the shortage of food and materials and about internal political and social tensions, saw that they could not hope to emerge victorious and decided to seek an armistice. Ludendorff, who had led Germany

1918

as a military dictator throughout most of the war, recognized that Germany would get better terms from the armistice if she had a democratic government and it was at his instigation that a parliamentary system was adopted. Shortly before the armistice was signed on November 11th 1918 a group of sailors in Kiel mutinied; they were supported by army units and by a large section of the working population, which came out on strike. This revolution caused the breakdown of the old order; all the ruling Princes and the Kaiser abdicated and on November 9th a Republic was declared. The last Hohenzollern ruler spent the rest of his life in exile.

The Treaty of Versailles

The Treaty of Versailles which ended the war declared that Germany and her allies must bear the whole responsibility for its outbreak and for making good the damage they had caused. The former German Empire was reduced in size; Alsace-Lorraine was returned to France, West Prussia and part of the industrial area of Upper Silesia were given to

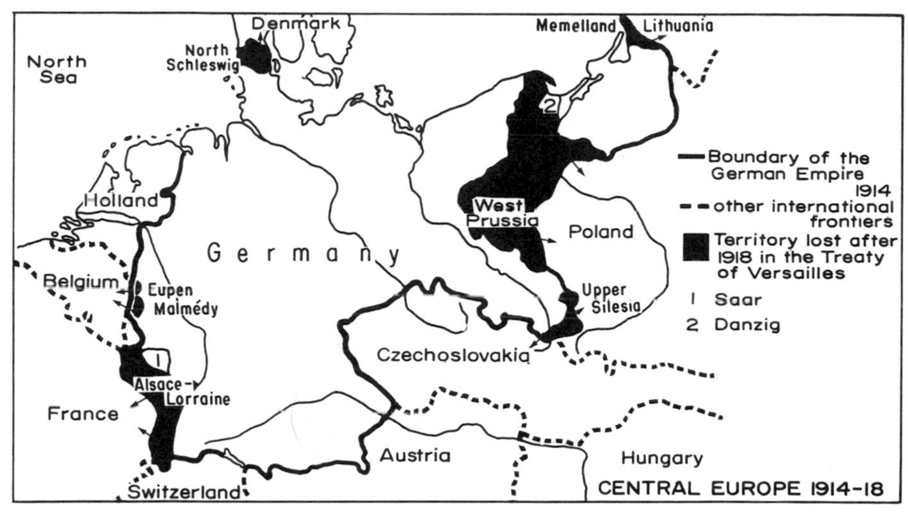

Fig 24

Poland, North Schleswig to Denmark and Eupen-Malmédy to Belgium. The Polish Corridor was created and Danzig became a Free City. The Austro-Hungarian Empire of the Hapsburgs was split up and the new countries of Czechoslovakia and Jugoslavia were formed. South Tirol was given to Italy, Galicia to Poland, Transylvania to Rumania and what remained of Austria was declared a Republic and ordered to remain independent of Germany. Three million Germans now lived beyond the frontiers of Germany. The Treaty of Versailles demanded that Germany should reduce the strength of her army to a nominal 100,000, surrender most of her fleet and pay a fantastic sum in reparations over a period of 70 years. In addition to this she was deprived of all her colonies and had to consent to the occupation of the Rhineland.

Friedrich Ebert, leader of the Social Democrats, was given the task of rebuilding Germany. He announced that a National Assembly would be elected to draw up a new constitution.

Communist-inspired disturbances were taking place in Berlin, where in January 1919 the leaders of the Spartacists, Karl Liebknecht and Rosa Luxemburg, were murdered, so the National Assembly met at Weimar. Weimar gave its name to **1919** the new constitution adopted in August 1919, in which the basic rights of a democratic nation were secured; it provided for a government elected by universal suffrage. Ebert became the first President of the Republic. The Weimar constitution sought to create an ideal democratic state, but it failed to create a stable government because of the large number of political parties which grew up, necessitating the formation of coalitions. The German people were unused to democratic government, and in the post-war years when crises followed quickly one upon the other, they found themselves unable to manage their new-found freedom. Various vested interests such as the landowners, military leaders and the industrialists undermined the constitution, encouraging extreme nationalist and anti-republican groups in the hope of gaining power and wealth for themselves.

Post-war problems

There was a series of crises between 1919 and 1924 over the payment of reparations. In 1923, when it had become apparent that Germany could not keep pace with her commitments, French and Belgian troops occupied the Ruhr in an attempt to make the Germans work harder; the government ordered the workers to offer passive resistance to the occupation forces and many came out on strike. To provide the vast sums of money needed to support the strikers paper money was printed; inflation followed, destroying savings and causing the German economy to collapse. Meat which in 1914 had cost 90 Pfennigs per pound soared in 1923 to 3,200 milliard **1923** Marks per pound. By the end of 1923 one dollar could buy 4,200,000,000 Marks.

The climate of the twenties proved ideal for the growth of extremist political parties; both the Communists and right-wing Nationalists gained widespread support because they opposed the Treaty of Versailles and supported the view that Germany had been betrayed by its government in 1918. The supporters of rival political parties often clashed in the streets; the Nationalists murdered Matthias Erzberger (1921) and Walter Rathenau (1922), who were both government ministers, because of their support of the armistice and the Treaty of Versailles respectively. Stresemann, a moderate politician, became Chancellor in August 1923 and made great efforts to subdue the extremist elements, but in November 1923 the National Socialists, under the leadership of Adolf Hitler, tried to take over the Bavarian government. The attempt failed and Hitler spent twelve months in prison for his part in the *Putsch*. Stresemann managed to fix a more reasonable sum for the reparations and obtained loans from America to rebuild German industry, but the effects of the inflation did not immediately disappear, since the real sufferers were not the industrialists but the middle and working classes. Meanwhile attempts were being made to circumvent the disarmament clause of the Treaty of Versailles. It was said that 100,000 men were not enough to defend Germany's frontiers, and secret formations were raised, being disguised as labour battalions. The co-operation of industry was enlisted to equip these forces, bringing several years of comparative economic prosperity.

However nationalism still flourished, although it was not until 1929 that there was any widespread support for the National Socialist (Nazi) Party (NSDAP). The world slump of 1929 created almost 7 million unemployed workers by 1932 and brought fears of a second inflation in Germany and a lack of confidence in the government. As a result the National Socialists, who had gained only twelve seats in the 1928 election, increased their representation to 107 in 1930; by July 1932 they held 230 of the 608 seats. Support had come in particular from the rich industrialists and land-owning classes, who saw in National Socialism the only hope of avoiding Communism. The picture of patriotic Germans working together for the glory and prosperity of the Fatherland was calculated to appeal especially to the young, who became Hitler's most fanatical and devoted followers.

Hitler gains power; the Third Reich

The government under von Papen found it impossible to rule democratically, since they could not command a majority even for important legislation, and the Chancellor had to make use of emergency powers. Parliament was dissolved and in the elections of November 1932 the National Socialists again emerged as the strongest party. President Hindenburg did not however invite Hitler to become Chancellor until January 1933, when it had become clear that no one else could command the support of a majority of the house.

1933

A fire which extensively damaged the Parliament building *(Reichstag)* some four weeks after Hitler took office gave him an excuse for banning the Communist Party, whom he blamed for the blaze, and for arresting many of its members. Elections held shortly after the incident gave Hitler a two-thirds majority in the Reichstag. The 'Enabling Act' passed by the Reichstag in March 1933 in effect suspended the constitution; it gave Hitler the power to make laws for the next four years without consulting his parliament. Rival political parties were quickly suppressed, trade unions abolished and Party control extended to cover every sphere of life. The purge of all anti-Nazis began.

1934 On the death of Hindenburg in 1934 Hitler proclaimed himself leader *(Führer)* of Germany, uniting the offices of President and Chancellor. He began systematically to eliminate his opponents, sending them to concentration camps or having them murdered. He felt, for instance, that Röhm, leader of the S.A. *(Sturmabteilung,* 'storm-troops') was challenging his leadership and a purge of the S.A. was organized, known as 'the night of the long knives'. The purge was carried out by the S.S. *(Schutzstaffel* or 'blackshirts') under Himmler. The removal of Jews from public office signalled the beginning of Hitler's campaign to get them out of the way. All this and more was tolerated by the German people, who for the most part believed in Hitler's promise of an imminent millenium. Hitler recognized the importance of mass media and in his propaganda minister Goebbels he found a man who had no scruples in using the press, films and radio to indoctrinate the people.

Anti-semitism

The attempt to avoid an open conflict with the Churches was at first successful, since the National Socialists advocated regular attendance at church, but the racial theories and power politics of the Party did not long deceive true believers. In his youth Hitler had developed certain racial theories which he now expanded and imposed on the people. He aimed to create a pure-blooded German super-race. The most outstanding aspect of this policy was the systematic attempt to make the Jews outcasts of society; in 1936 they were deprived of all rights: they could no longer vote, visit places of entertainment or marry non-Jews. In the *Kristallnacht* of November

1938 1938 many Jewish dwellings, shops and synagogues were burned down. As Hitler's empire increased he was able to attempt a total extinction of Judaism throughout Europe; millions of Jews perished in the ghettos and gas chambers and Hitler's 'final solution' of 1942 came very close to complete success.

When Hitler took office, unemployment was a serious problem. By employing men on State projects such as the building of an extensive motorway network, introducing compulsory labour service and expanding the armaments industry full employment was eventually achieved. In formulating his policies Hitler ignored the Treaty of Versailles, and presented Germany's former enemies with *faits accomplis* about which they chose to do nothing in the hope of maintaining peace. He created an air force, introduced compulsory military service and declared that Germany would cease paying reparations. In 1935 the Saar voted to return to Germany. A year later Hitler marched his troops into the demilitarized Rhineland; had the Allies objected, he was prepared to withdraw.

The Anschluss

Hitler aimed to annex the countries bordering on Germany which had a German population, to provide more 'living space' *(Lebensraum)* for an enlarged German race. He began by marching into Austria in 1938. At a meeting in Munich he convinced the British, French and Italians that peace could be preserved only by allowing German troops to occupy the Czech frontier lands immediately and without resistance, claiming that this was his final territorial demand. The British Prime Minister Neville Chamberlain believed in the policy of appeasement; he persuaded the other two powers to agree to Hitler's suggestion and they put their names to the famous Munich agreement. A few months later the world witnessed the extent of Hitler's deception; German forces marched into Prague and Hitler declared that Bohemia and Moravia, the Czech provinces of Czechoslovakia, were henceforth to be a German protectorate. The rest of Europe continued to look on with little more than a murmur of disapproval. Only when Hitler demanded the return of the Polish Corridor and Danzig and signed a non-aggression treaty with the Soviet Union did France and Britain issue a strong warning that no further territorial gains would be tolerated. On September 1st 1939 the German army marched into Poland. On September 3rd France and Britain declared war on Germany; the Second World War had begun.

1939

The Second World War

The war against Poland lasted only 18 days, then the country was divided between Germany and Russia; France and Britain were insufficiently armed to fulfil their promise to help Poland. In March 1940 Hitler secured the active co-operation of Italy's Fascist dictator Mussolini; in April he occupied Denmark and Norway in order to secure his supplies of iron ore and to provide unhindered access from the Baltic to the North Sea. A month later Germany attacked Luxembourg, Belgium and Holland, whose neutrality he had earlier promised to respect, and penetrated to the Channel coast, forcing the British army back to Dunkirk, from where they were able to organize a retreat. By the end of May Holland and Belgium had surrendered, and when the French government followed suit in June, most of France was quickly occupied by the Germans. Italy now entered the war on Hitler's side, attacking Greece and Egypt, leaving Hitler free to plan the invasion of Britain. The loss of 1,000 aeroplanes in the Battle of Britain and Italian defeats in Greece caused the Germans to postpone the invasion until the following spring.

1940

In the summer of 1941, in flagrant violation of the non-aggression pact signed in 1939, German troops marched into Russia. Surprise was Hitler's key weapon, since he aimed to defeat the Russian army before the onset of winter, but delayed by the poor roads and Hitler's failure to concentrate on one objective at a time, his forces did not quite reach Moscow before the weather changed, catching them unprepared for the biting cold. Russian troops, equipped for winter and without a long campaign behind them, were able to regain much ground. In December 1941 Japan attacked the American Pacific Fleet in Pearl Harbour, Hawaii, and captured Hong Kong, Singapore and the Dutch East Indies. America was already supporting Britain in the European war and so Hitler and Mussolini joined Japan in the fight against her, completely underestimating her strength and her ability to help decisively in Europe.

1941

The summer of 1942 at first brought German successes in North Africa and in Russia, but German forces were now too thinly spread over the various fronts. In the autumn British and American forces landed in North Africa and within a few months had defeated the Germans under Rommel, after Hitler refused to permit a withdrawal. The Russians meanwhile encircled the German army at Stalingrad and Hitler's refusal to withdraw led to the loss of almost 275,000 men. The Allied invasion of Italy in July 1943 was followed a few weeks later by the fall of Mussolini and the capitulation of the new Italian government. Italy now joined forces with the Allies; Hitler retaliated by occupying Rome. The Germans held their positions until the middle of 1944, when they were forced back to northern Italy. Meanwhile the German fleet was beginning to lose the battle at sea and German cities were crumbling in the bombing raids by the British and American Air Forces.

1943

There were many dissenters in Germany, especially in the Churches, but most were effectively silenced. There was also opposition to Hitler's plans among the Generals, whose advice he increasingly ignored. In July 1944 an attempt on Hitler's life organized by Stauffenberg narrowly failed; Hitler told the people that his life had been saved by 'Providence'. In the summer of 1944 a Russian offensive almost obliterated the German line in the east, whilst America and Britain landed in Normandy to create a 'second front'. By the end of the year American and British forces had liberated France and reached the German frontier despite a desperate German counter-attack. By March 1945 Allied troops had reached the Rhine, but Hitler would not concede defeat. He had illusions that mythical armies were marching to his aid, whereas in reality his only reinforcements were fourteen-year-old boys armed with sticks and the vague instruction to fight. Meanwhile the Allied advance continued and Hitler determined that Germany should not again suffer a humiliating defeat, but should rather disappear in smoke and ashes: he ordered that only 'scorched earth' was to be left for the advancing enemy. In April the British and Americans reached the Elbe and Berlin fell to the Russians. Hitler shot himself rather than surrender; his forces soon gave up the unequal struggle and capitulated on May 8th. Germany was in chaos; the future lay once more in the hands of her conquerors.

1944

1945

The defeat in 1945 had brought life in Germany to a standstill; morale was low, the proud nationalism of a few years before had turned into an immense national shame. Hitler's dream of an empire that was to last a thousand years had disintegrated in a shattering trauma.

'Das Jahr Null'

Only when the Allied forces penetrated deep into Germany was the full horror of the concentration camps revealed.

Even a large section of the German population had remained ignorant of their grim existence and they were deeply shocked at what had been done there in their name. Many of the camps such as Belsen were immediately razed to the ground, others such as Dachau have been preserved as documents of the past.

Those responsible for these and other atrocities were brought to trial at Nuremberg in 1946. Eleven of the accused were executed and seven received prison sentences ranging from ten years to life. Others had already committed suicide or managed to flee, but many were relentlessly pursued and later brought to justice. The whole population had to undergo a process of denazification; everyone was to be categorized according to the degree of responsibility he bore for the events of the war.

The Occupation

The four Allies, Russia, the United States, Britain and France, took over complete control of Germany; they were determined to eradicate all trace of Hitler's Greater German Empire *(Großdeutsches Reich)* and to prevent Germany from ever waging another war. Prussia with its militaristic tradition was wiped from the map and four zones of occupation were created, covering the whole of Germany west of the Oder–Neisse line except for Berlin, which was divided into four sectors. The German territory east of the Oder–Neisse line (within the frontiers of 1937) was already temporarily under Polish and Russian control. It was Allied policy to permit Poland, partitioned in 1939 by Hitler and Stalin, to rise again, but Stalin insisted on retaining that part of Poland (more than one third) granted to him by Hitler; in return Poland received the southern part of East Prussia, Silesia and part of Pomerania. This was at the time considered to be a temporary arrangement, but in fact it has already persisted for a quarter of a century. The Saar was lost to Germany in 1946 when it became linked to France.

At the end of the war a stream of refugees began pouring into Germany from the former German communities in Poland, Czechoslovakia, Hungary, Rumania and Jugoslavia, whence they had been forcibly evicted; they came to join the thousands of Germans who had fled before the advancing Red Army. This influx of people aggravated an already catastrophic lack of food; the majority of people were allotted rations on the basis of 800 calories per day against a minimum

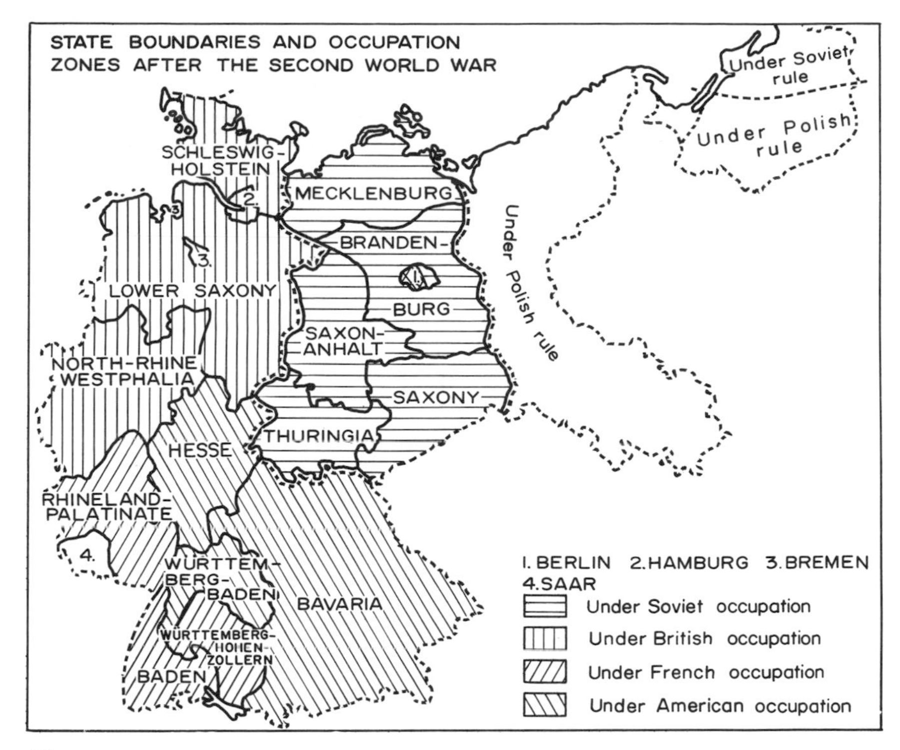

Fig 25

need of 2,000, and a Black Market flourished for three years. All habitable accommodation, about half the pre-war amount, was commandeered and divided up so as to shelter as many people as possible. The refugees continued to arrive for more than ten years; between 1955 and 1957 the officially recognized German minority group in Poland shrank from 150,000 to 65,000.

It was intended at the time of the Potsdam Agreements that the four occupation zones should one day be reunited, once safeguards had been made against a resurgence of German militarism. By 1947 however, a physical barrier had appeared along the frontiers of the Russian Zone, indicating that co-operation between the zones' leaders was already failing. In 1948 the currency reform, necessary in order to permit the expansion of industry, was not accepted in the Soviet Zone, which retaliated a few days later with an independent reform. The Soviet authorities also refused to accept Marshall Aid, which from 1948 to 1952 enabled the western part of Germany to accomplish a remarkable industrial recovery *(Wirtschaftswunder)*. Berlin became the focus of a series of crises, the most serious of which was the year-long blockade (1948–9) by the Russians of all land routes to the city; the blockade was relieved by the Allied air-lift.

Two German States

1949

The western zones were united in 1949 to form first a Tri-Zone and then the Federal Republic of Germany. Free elections were held, as a result of which the first *Bundestag* met in the temporary capital Bonn; local government had been gradually returned to the German people over the previous three years. The first Federal Chancellor *(Bundeskanzler)* was Konrad Adenauer (CDU*); its first President was Theodor Heuss. Meanwhile the Russian Zone was being transformed into the German Democratic Republic without the aid of free elections to ascertain the will of the people. The first Prime Minister *(Ministerpräsident)* was Otto Grotewohl; the first President was Wilhelm Pieck. Pankow, in the Russian sector of Berlin, was chosen as the seat of government. Berlin itself retained four-power status.

In 1950 the citizens of the GDR elected the first 'People's Chamber' *(Volkskammer)* from a single list of candidates. The year also saw the recognition by the government of the GDR of the Oder–Neisse line as the permanent western frontier of Poland, and the acceptance of the GDR as a member of Comecon, the eastern European economic association. The Federal Republic joined the European Coal and Steel Community in 1951.

The GDR finally broke with the political past in 1952 when it abolished the old States *(Länder)* and their governments and introduced instead 14 Districts *(Bezirke)*, each with a Council strictly subordinate to the central government. Thus two quite distinct types of government, the one completely centralized, the other largely decentralized, came into existence on German soil. In the GDR collectivization of agriculture, begun with the land reform of 1945, continued with the introduction of LPGs *(Landwirtschaftliche Produktionsgenossenschaften)*. These reforms, together with the raising of industrial norms, aggravated an already tense situation amongst the citizens of the GDR and on June 17th

*See p. 160

1953 they rose up in all the main cities. The revolt was put down with Russian aid. **1953**

The years 1954 and 1955 consolidated the position of the GDR within the eastern bloc. Not only was the country officially recognized by Russia; it began to raise armed forces and was a signatory of the Warsaw Pact, and became a member of two organizations offering respectively economic and atomic aid to eastern European countries. The Federal Republic also began to raise armed forces in 1954 and in 1955 she became a member of NATO; in this same year full sovereignty was returned to the West German people. A plebiscite held in the Saar in 1955 resulted in the decision that the Saar should once again become German; it became a State of the Federal Republic on 1.1.1957. West Germany became a founder member of the European Economic Community. The GDR was meanwhile pursuing its policy of converting industry and agriculture into socialist enterprises; a new planning policy introduced in 1958 brought the first 'People's Factories' *(Volkseigene Betriebe)*.

In 1959 Heinrich Lübke replaced Heuss as President of the Federal Republic. In 1960 the post of President of the Democratic Republic was abolished on the death of Pieck and its place taken by the newly formed Council of State *(Staatsrat)*; Walter Ulbricht, leader of the SED,* became its chairman.

The Berlin Wall

The flow of refugees into West Germany still continued; from time to time the steady stream became a flood, especially when there were strong rumours of tighter frontier controls. Ever since 1947 the Russian and East German authorities had been strengthening the frontier with the Federal Republic, so that by 1960 it had become almost impenetrable. The flow of refugees was therefore concentrated in Berlin, where controls were relatively lax. The tremendous loss of skilled manpower was ruining hopes of industrial progress in the GDR and was causing the gradual financial ruin of the country. By contrast, industry in the Federal Republic was booming, and the economy was so strong that in 1961 the West German Mark was revalued upwards. On August 13th, 1961, the government of the GDR acted; overnight a wall was built along the whole length of the sector boundary in Berlin and the remaining frontier defences were strengthened, severing virtually all the remaining contacts between the people of **1961**

*See p. 188

the GDR and West Germany. By 1963, however, industry in the GDR had still not reached its full potential and its leaders were forced to consider the principles of profit and profitability and to introduce bonus schemes. By 1974 East Germany had become one of the world's industrial giants.

The Treaty of Friendship between the Federal Republic and France, concluded in 1963 by Konrad Adenauer shortly before his resignation, marked a new phase in Franco-German relations. It was answered in 1964 by a similar Friendship Treaty between the GDR and the Soviet Union. Adenauer's successor as Chancellor was Ludwig Erhard (CDU), chief architect of the economic miracle. His term of office ended in 1966, when the coalition government between the CDU/CSU* and the FDP* was dissolved and replaced by a coalition of CDU/CSU and SPD,* led by Kurt Georg Kiesinger (CDU). On the death of Grotewohl in 1964 Willi Stoph became Prime Minister *(Ministerpräsident)* of the GDR.

In 1968 the GDR adopted a new constitution, which reflected the trend towards a reduction of personal liberty and towards increased alignment with the countries of Eastern Europe. In the same year the Federal Republic passed controversial legislation governing a state of emergency *(Notstandsgesetze)*; the laws were interpreted in the GDR as providing evidence of the militaristic ambitions of the Federal Government.

1969 In 1969 the SPD and FDP were able to form a coalition government with Willy Brandt as the first socialist Chancellor in the history of the Federal Republic. In 1970 he had talks with Willi Stoph of the GDR, this being the first time in the history of the two Germanies that their leaders had met. Brandt's government also concluded a non-aggression treaty with the USSR and a pact with Poland recognizing the Oder-Neisse line as her western frontier.

1973 1973 was a highly significant year for Germany. The future policy of East and West Germany towards each other was enshrined in a Basic Treaty signed by them both; Ulbricht, for so long the undisputed leader of the GDR, died and was succeeded by the team of Willi Stoph and Erich Honecker. Both Germanies were admitted to the United Nations. In 1974 Brandt resigned over the discovery of an East German spy among his advisers, and Helmut Schmidt became Chancellor.

---

*See p. 160.

The Arts through the Ages

DATE	LITERATURE	MUSIC
Eighth and ninth centuries	Old High German heroic poetry (e.g. *Hildebrandslied* *c.* 800) Translations, mainly of religious texts Religious epics: *Wessobrunner Gebet* (creation story), *Muspilli* (Last Judgement), *Heliand* (life of Christ)	Gregorian chant
Tenth and eleventh centuries	Religious drama develops out of the liturgy Charms and spells (e.g. *Merseburger Zaubersprüche*) Most written poetry in Latin, composed by monks Traditional epics recited by wandering troubadours	Part-music
Twelfth and thirteenth centuries	Middle High German poetry: Heroic Epic (e.g. *Nibelungenlied* *c.* 1200) Courtly Epic (e.g. Wolfram von Eschenbach *Parzival* *c.* 1200–1210) Minnesang (e.g. Walther von der Vogelweide *c.* 1170–1230) Passion plays and religious drama *(Osterspiel von Muri* *c.* 1250)	
Fourteenth and fifteenth centuries	Mysticism (e.g. Meister Eckhart *c.* 1260–1327) Love poetry (Oswald von Wolkenstein 1377–1445) Satire (Sebastian Brant *Das Narrenschiff* 1494)	Polyphony evolving (Heinrich Isaak *c.* 1450–1517)

ARCHITECTURE	PAINTING AND SCULPTURE	CONTEMPORARY EVENTS
;arolingian style Kaiserpfalz at Goslar, ;harlemagne's chapel in \achen Cathedral, Corvey nonastery church p. 140)	Art almost exclusively religious: Ivory reliefs Murals Manuscript illustration	800 Charlemagne crowned 750–1100 Old High German
:omanesque—at its height ı the eleventh century 5peyer p. 45, Worms p. 40 and Mainz Cathedrals)	Reichenau school (painting) Bronze sculpture (West doors of Hildesheim Cathedral p. 141)	936 Beginning of the Ottonian period
omanesque gradually ves way to Early Gothic Aagdeburg Cathedral egun 1209) 250 onwards igh Gothic (Cologne athedral begun 1248) ıd Brick Gothic in orth Germany Aarienkirche in Lübeck, gun 1260 p. 142)	Murals Manuscript illustration Stone carving (e.g. statues in Bamberg Cathedral and Naumburg Cathedral p. 141)	1096–1291 Crusades 1100–1500 Middle High German 1138–1254 Hohenstaufens *c.* 1250 Hanseatic League
ıte Gothic (e.g. auenkirche in ıremberg, Ulm thedral p. 49) te Brick Gothic own Halls in Lübeck d Stralsund)	Stone and wood carving (Michael Pacher *c.* 1435–1498) Religious painting (Stefan Lochner *c.* 1410–1451 p. 144; Martin Schongauer 1445–1491)	1200–1400 Eastern colonization 1420 Italian Renaissance 1450 Printing invented 1492 America discovered

DATE	LITERATURE	MUSIC
Sixteenth century	Renaissance Humanism (Melanchthon 1497–1560) Luther (1483–1546) translates the Bible Meistersinger (Hans Sachs 1494–1576; also wrote many *Schwänke* or short comedies) *Volksbücher* or chap-books (e.g. *Dr. Faust* 1587)	Polyphony (Orlando di Lasso 1532–1594) Lutheran chorale Secular songs and dances (Hans Leo Hassler 1564–1612)
Seventeenth century	Martin Opitz 1597–1639: influential theoretical writings on poetry Hymns and chorales (Paul Gerhardt 1607–1676) Mystical religious poetry (Angelus Silesius 1624–1677) Baroque drama (Andreas Gryphius (1616–1664) tragedies, often about martyrs; also comedies) Picaresque novel (*Simplicius Simplicissimus* by Grimmelshausen, 1622–1676)	Protestant composers Michael Praetorius (1571–1621) Heinrich Schütz (1585–1672) antiphonal effects, the first German opera *(Daphne)*, settings of the Passion story Opera
Eighteenth century	Enlightenment 1720–85: Rationalism, tolerance, optimism. J. C. Gottsched 1700–1766 (championed French classical drama) G. E. Lessing 1729–1781 (advocated the English style of drama)	Late Baroque: J. S. Bach 1685–1750 (Cantatas, organ and instrumental music, master of polyphony) G. F. Händel 1685–1759 (oratorios, operas, instrumental music) C. W. Gluck 1714–1787 (operatic reform)

ARCHITECTURE	PAINTING AND SCULPTURE	CONTEMPORARY EVENTS
Continuation of Late Gothic (Augsburg, St. Ulrich p. 143) Renaissance: mainly secular buildings (Bremen Town Hall p. 143) and decorative additions to existing ones. Weserrenaissance (*e.g.* Hamelin, Rinteln p. 37) *Schloß* replaces *Burg* Heidelberg Castle, Ottheinrichsbau 1556–66)	Sculpture (*e.g.* Tilman Riemenschneider *c.* 1460–1531 p. 144) Intense religious painting (Lukas Cranach 1472–1553 p. 145; Matthias Grünewald *c.* 1475–1528) More realistic painting (portraits by Holbein 1497–1544 p. 147, engravings and paintings by Dürer 1471–1528 p. 146)	1465–1536 Erasmus 1500 New High German 1517 Luther's theses 1534 Society of Jesus 1564–1616 Shakespeare
arly Baroque (originally nickname, meaning alformed, strange, antastic) (Munich: Michaelskirche 1583–97, heatinerkirche 1663 ff nd Nymphenburg alace 1663 ff p. 148)	Ecclesiastical art, mainly lavish decoration for splendid Baroque buildings	1618–48 Thirty Years' War Descartes, Racine, Corneille, Molière 1643–1715 Louis XIV
ate Baroque to 1750: er increasing grandeur Vürzburg Residenz 720–44 by Neumann, ttobeuren Abbey 748–66 by J. M. Fischer 148)	Portraiture; idealised 'arcadian' painting, frequently in frescoes	1724–1804 Kant Voltaire, Rousseau

DATE	LITERATURE	MUSIC
Eighteenth century (continued)	1767–85 Sturm und Drang: rejection of rationalism, worship of genius Young Goethe and Schiller J. M. Lenz 1751–1792 Classicism 1786–1832: objective, humanitarian idealism J. W. Goethe 1749–1832 *(Iphigenie, Tasso, Faust II)* F. Schiller 1759–1805 *(Maria Stuart, Wilhelm Tell)* F. Hölderlin 1770–1843 (poetry)	Joseph Haydn 1732–1809 (developed the symphony and string quartet) W. A. Mozart 1756–1791 (operas, symphonies, concertos, chamber music) Ludwig van Beethoven 1770–1827 (gave a new scale to music of all kinds)
Nineteenth century	Romanticism 1800–30: subjective, introspective; interest in nationalism, history and the supernatural Collections of folksongs (Arnim and Brentano *Des Knaben Wunderhorn* 1808) and of fairy-tales (*Grimms Märchen* 1812 ff) Lyric poetry (Joseph von Eichendorff 1788–1857; Eduard Mörike 1804–1875) Grotesque Novellen E. T. A. Hoffmann 1776–1822 Post-Classical drama 1800–1850 1. Classical verse form, but pessimistic: H. W. von Kleist 1777–1811; Franz Grillparzer 1791–1872; Friedrich Hebbel 1813–1863 2. Realism: Georg Büchner 1813–1837	Romanticism: Franz Schubert 1797–1828 (chamber-music, symphonies, developed the 'Lied') Carl Maria von Weber 1786–1826 (pioneered German Romantic opera: *Der Freischütz* 1821) Felix Mendelssohn 1809–1847 and Robert Schumann 1810–1856 (piano and chamber music, lieder, symphonies)

ARCHITECTURE	PAINTING AND SCULPTURE	CONTEMPORARY EVENTS
oco 1730–80: iter intimacy, more orative (Wieskirche 5–54 by Zimmermann 6; Sanssouci, Potsdam Knobelsdorff 1745–7) ssicism 1780–1805 hloß Wilhelmshöhe, sel 1786–98; ndenburg Gate, in 1788–91)	Porcelain: Dresden china (made in Meissen)	1789 French Revolution 1762–1814 Fichte
val of earlier styles, cially Classical (*e.g.*, otothek 1816–30 and Pinakothek 1826–30 Iunich by Leopold Klenze) and Gothic pletion of Ulm, gne and Regensburg edrals, ich New Town Hall) Romanesque, iissance, Rococo etc. antic reconstructions edieval castles ienschwangau p. 149)	Romanticism C. D. Friedrich 1774–1840 (landscapes) p. 149 Nazarenes: P. Cornelius 1783–1867 (religious paintings)	1788–1860 Schopenhauer 1812 Climax of Napoleon's campaign

DATE	LITERATURE	MUSIC
Nineteenth century (continued)	Biedermeier: solid middle class morality, realistically portrayed Junges Deutschland 1835–50: anti-Romantic, political movement Heinrich Heine 1797–1856 (lyric poetry, satire) Poetic Realism 1840–90: a precise but generally optimistic portrayal of life Gottfried Keller 1819–1890 and Theodor Storm 1817–88 (Novellen and poetry) Naturalism 1889–1915: humble characters; accurate reproduction of speech and milieu Gerhart Hauptmann 1862–1946 (*Die Weber* 1892)	Richard Wagner 1813–1883 (large-scale music-drama as in the cycle of operas *The Ring of the Nibelung)* Johannes Brahms 1833–1897 (his music retains a Classical element) Anton Bruckner 1824–1896 and Gustav Mahler 1860–1911 (expanded the symphonic form)
Twentieth century: 1900–1933	Symbolist poetry: Stefan George 1868–1933; Rainer Maria Rilke 1875–1926 Expressionism 1891–1925: surrealist elements; attack on bourgeois morals Drama: Frank Wedekind 1864–1918 *(Frühlings Erwachen* 1891); Georg Kaiser 1878–1945 (*Gas* 1917–20) Poetry: Georg Trakl 1880–1914; Georg Heym 1887–1912 Novel: Franz Kafka 1883–1924 *(Das Schloß*)	Richard Strauss 1864–1949 (opulent orchestration, symphonic poems, operas, including *Der Rosenkavalier,* 1911) New Viennese school: Arnold Schönberg 1874 1951 (developed the twelve-note technique) Alban Berg 1885–1935 (free atonality, expressionist features, opera *Wozzeck*)

ARCHITECTURE	PAINTING AND SCULPTURE	CONTEMPORARY EVENTS
	Biedermeier (to 1850): middle class realistic, sentimental painting Neo-Classicism Anselm Feuerbach 1829–1880 Realism Hans Thoma 1839–1924 (country scenes) Impressionism: Max Liebermann 1847–1935 (dappled light effects, portraits) Lovis Corinth 1858–1925 (landscapes, portraits)	1847 Marx-Engels manifesto 1848–9 Frankfurt Assembly 1844–1900 Nietzsche 1859 Darwin's *Origin of species* 1860 Beginning of large-scale industrialization 1871 Germany united
unctionalism: Bauhaus 919–34 (directed 919–28 by Walter ropius 1883–1969)	Expressionism: *'Die Brücke'* group founded 1905; Emil Nolde 1867–1956 (non-realistic use of brilliant colours) *'Der Blaue Reiter'* group founded 1911 W. Kandinsky 1866–1944 (abstract paintings) Franz Marc 1880–1916 (animals) Paul Klee 1879–1940 (delicate, semi-abstract paintings)	1914–18 World War I

DATE	LITERATURE	MUSIC
Twentieth century (continued)	Neo-Romanticism: Hugo von Hofmannsthal 1874–1929 (verse, drama, poetry)	
	Epic Novel: Thomas Mann 1875–1955 (*Zauberberg* 1924) Hermann Hesse 1877–1962 (*Das Glasperlenspiel* 1943) Epic Theatre: Bertolt Brecht 1898–1956 (*Dreigroschenoper* 1928, *Mutter Courage* 1939)	Carl Orff *b.* 1895 (operas, choral and instrumental music in a tuneful but percussive sty Paul Hindemith 1895–1963 (early works lively and satirical, later works more severe, philosophical)
1933–45	Nazi period Writers in exile (Thomas Mann, Brecht, Zuckmayer etc.)	
1945–70 *(West Germany)*	Hörspiel (radio play): Günther Eich *b.* 1907 Satirical novel and short story: Heinrich Böll *b.* 1917 (*Doktor Murkes gesammeltes Schweigen* 1957); Günther Grass *b.* 1927 (*Die Blechtrommel* 1959) Drama: Max Frisch *b.* 1911 Friedrich Dürrenmatt *b.* 1921 (*Die Physiker* 1962) Carl Zuckmayer *b.* 1896 (*Des Teufels General* 1946)	Karlheinz Stockhausen *b.* 1928 (serial and electronic music) Hans Werner Henze *b.* 1926 (operas, cantatas, instrumental music for conventional media)
1945–70 *(East Germany)*	All types of writing show heavy political committedness, but some writers are critical of the regime. Novel: Anna Seghers *b.* 1900, Christa Wolf *b.* 1929 (*Nachdenken über Christa T.* 1968) Poetry: Johannes Bobrowski 1917–1965; Wolf Biermann *b.* 1936 (satirical ballads). Drama: Peter Hacks *b.* 1928 (strong influence of Brecht)	Patriotic compositions for conventional media, especially songs and cantatas (Paul Dessau *b.* 1894, Hanns Eisler 1898–1962)

ARCHITECTURE	PAINTING AND SCULPTURE	CONTEMPORARY EVENTS
	Sculpture: Ernst Barlach 1870–1938 (simplified expressive forms)	1919–1933 Weimar Republic
zi; imposing (massive crete structures *e.g.*, lin Sports Centre— ue for 1936 Olympic nes)	Realistic, propagandist painting and sculpture	1933 Hitler assumes power 1939–45 World War II
ernational style (*e.g.*, nsaviertel, Congress l p. 183 and harmonic Hall in st Berlin)	Abstract painting and sculpture; experimental techniques	1949 Formation of the Federal Republic
ssive, imposing style 5–60 (*e.g.*, Frankfurter e, former Stalin Allee, ast Berlin) rnational style (*e.g.*, T.V. er p. 184, and Berolina el in East Berlin)	Socialist Realism (largely propagandist art)	1949 Formation of the Democratic Republic 1961 Berlin Wall

Wall paintings at Idensen near Hanover (c. 1131) showing the baptism of Christ

Romanesque *(see also p. 45)*

Corvey: the ninth century west end of the monastery church

Worms Cathedral: the west end (late twelfth century)

The 'twin chapel' at Schwarz-Rheindorf (twelfth century)

Hildesheim Cathedral: Bernward's bronze doors (early eleventh century)

Naumburg Cathedral: one of the thirteenth century statues of benefactors (Uta von Meissen)

Brick Gothic: The Marienkirche, Lübeck (1260–1350)

Late Gothic: the choir of Aachen Cathedral (1355)

Gothic *(see also p. 49)*

Freiburg Minster: (i) the choir (1354 ff.)

(ii) the High Gothic nave (1250 ff.) with Late Gothic pulpit

Münster Town Hall: Late Gothic façade (1350)

St. Ulrich, Augsburg: the very late Gothic choir with Renaissance altars (1604)

Bremen Town Hall: Renaissance façade (1610)

A Gothic painting of St. Martin in the Liebfrauenkirche, Oberwesel

Stefan Lochner : The Madonna in the Rose Arbour (detail) (Wallraf-Richartz Museum, Cologne)

Tilman Riemenschneider : part of the Heiligblutaltar in Rothenburg (1499–1505)

Lukas Cranach: Adam and Eve (Courtauld Institute Galleries, London)

Albrecht Dürer : Christ bearing the Cross (woodcut) from the Great Passion (1

Hans Holbein: Sir Thomas More (1527) (National Portrait Gallery, London)

Ottobeuren Abbey (1748–66):
(i) West Front

(ii) view towards the High Altar

Baroque

Nymphenburg Palace, Munich dating in its present form from 1716–28

C. D. Friedrich: Trees in the Dusk (Wallraf-Richartz Museum, Cologne)

Romanticism

Hohenschwangau Castle (1833–7)

Franz Marc: The Tiger (1912) (Staatliche Graphische Sammlung, Munich)

Expressionism

Ernst Barlach: Scholar reading (1930)

IV Post-war Germany

At the end of the Second World War Germany automatically forfeited all the territory she had not possessed in 1937. In addition the Saar *(Saargebiet)* was placed under a predominantly French government and economically attached to France. With the agreement of the Allies Russia occupied the northern part of East Prussia, including Königsberg, which was renamed Kaliningrad, and Poland occupied the remainder of East Prussia and a considerable area of Germany east of the Oder-Neisse line together with the port of Stettin on the western side of the Oder estuary. Whilst the Saar returned to Germany in 1957 (economically in 1959), the territories in the East are still occupied and have increasingly become incorporated into Russia and Poland respectively. The German population was driven out in the early years of the occupation, often with great suffering. The Germans had to leave behind almost all their possessions and created a considerable problem when they arrived in such great numbers (12 million before 1950) in the western provinces, which had themselves scarcely begun to recover from the war.

At the Potsdam conference of 1945 the occupation of East Prussia and Silesia was confirmed and the remainder of Germany was divided into four Zones of Occupation, to be administered separately by Britain, France, the United States and the Soviet Union. The Allies forced upon these Zones a complete political reorganisation in order to break down the old power-structure. There had been a completely centralized government under the National Socialists, and even prior to 1933 there had been a marked domination by one State, Prussia. The States had differed greatly in area and population, and some, such as Hesse and Brunswick, had been fragmented. It was therefore decided to ignore all previous political boundaries and to divide what remained of Germany into 17 autonomous States *(Länder)*.

The Russians occupied the States of Mecklenburg, Saxon-Anhalt, Brandenburg, Thuringia and Saxony. The Western Allies occupied Schleswig-Holstein, Lower Saxony, Hamburg, Bremen, North-Rhine Westphalia, Hesse, Rhineland-Palatinate, Bavaria, Baden, Württemberg-Baden and Württemberg-Hohenzollern. Berlin was subdivided into four Sectors and likewise occupied by the Allies.

1. West Germany—the Federal Republic

By 1948 the Germans were allowed to take over local administration in the eleven States occupied by the Western Allies and State Parliaments had been elected. The leaders of these eleven Parliaments were invited by the Allies to form a committee *(Parlamentarischer Rat)* to draw up a constitution for a national government in which they would all participate. This constitution, described as 'temporary', created a federal republic based on democratic principles and on the provisions of the Declaration of Human Rights of 1776; details are contained in the Basic Law *(Grundgesetz)*.

In accordance with the constitution which came into force on May 24, 1949 free elections were held for a Federal Parliament *(Bundestag)*, which met in Bonn, the temporary capital. The Federal Republic of Germany *(die Bundesrepublik Deutschland)* came into existence in September 1949 and finally achieved full sovereignty in May 1955, exactly 10 years after the end of the Second World War. Its official flag is horizontally striped in black, red and gold; the arms are a black eagle on a gold ground. The anthem "Deutschland, Deutschland über alles" is played on official occasions.

Since 1951 the States of Baden, Württemberg-Baden and Württemberg-Hohenzollern have been united under the name Baden-Württemberg; the Saar became part of the Federal Republic on January 1st, 1957 after a plebiscite, making ten States in all. West Berlin is still partially controlled by the Occupying Powers and does not legally belong to the Federal Republic; the Federal Constitution is not fully enforceable in the city. For many purposes, however, it is regarded as the eleventh State and it is still considered by the West German government to be the real capital of Germany; from time to time official business is conducted there.

The States (Länder) of the Federal Republic

Baden-Württemberg (capital: Stuttgart)
The State was formed in 1951 from the former States of Baden, Württemberg-Baden and Württemberg-Hohenzollern. By 1974 its population had reached $9\frac{1}{4}$ millions; this figure includes a high proportion of refugees, who were attracted by the prospect of employment in its expanding industries. Baden-Württemberg is governed by a state parliament *(Landtag)* with 127 seats.

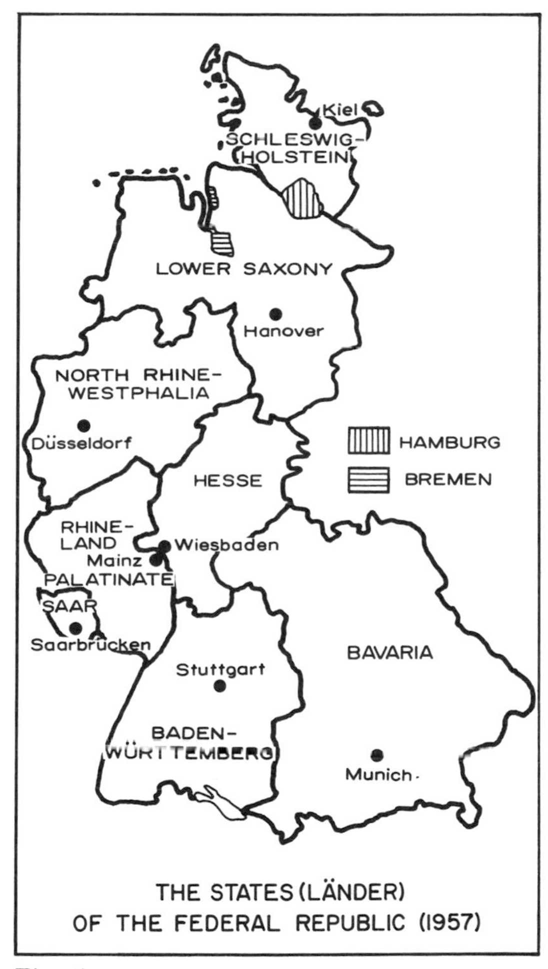

Fig 26

Bavaria *(Bayern)* **(capital: Munich** *(München)***)**
Bavaria is the largest State in the Federal Republic; its boundaries have not changed since 1937. Although comparatively neglected by industrial development, Bavaria had to absorb many refugees, who chose to settle in the State because it was nearest to their home. By 1974 its population was over 10¾ millions. Bavaria has a *Landtag* with 204 seats.

Bremen—city-state
Bremen is the smallest State in the Federal Republic; its population in 1974 was three-quarters of a million. Its history as a free city dates back to the days of the Hanseatic League; it is however no longer a compact unit, since it also comprises its outport of Bremerhaven. Bremen is ruled by the *Bremische Bürgerschaft* with 100 seats.

Hamburg—city-state
Hamburg's independence dates back to the Hanseatic League. Its population in 1974 was about 1¾ millions, making it the most densely populated State. The increase in population since the war has been significantly less than in other States because new residential development is taking place outside the city boundary. Hamburg is governed by the *Bürgerschaft* with 120 seats.

Hesse *(Hessen)* **(capital: Wiesbaden)**
Hesse was formed in 1946 by the amalgamation of Hessen-Darmstadt and Hessen-Nassau; its boundary with the Rhineland-Palatinate formed by the Rhine illogically divides the economic unit of Wiesbaden-Mainz. In 1975 its population was over 5½ million. Hesse is governed by a *Landtag* with 96 seats.

Lower Saxony *(Niedersachsen)* **(capital: Hanover** *(Hannover)***)**
The present State dates from 1946, when Lower Saxony was constituted from the former Prussian Province of Hanover and the States of Brunswick and Oldenburg. In 1974 the State had a population of 7¼ millions. For the most part it consists of the lowland plain. It is a predominantly agricultural State; the main industrial area is the Brunswick-Salzgitter complex. Lower Saxony is governed by a *Landtag* with 149 seats.

North-Rhine Westphalia *(Nordrhein-Westfalen)* **(capital: Düsseldorf)**

This state was formed in 1946 from part of the Rhine Province and the Province of Westphalia and the County of Lippe. It is the most populous of all the States, with over seventeen million people (1974). The population is still increasing as more and more people are attracted by the variety of employment offered, especially in the Ruhr. North-Rhine Westphalia is governed by a *Landtag* with 200 seats.

Rhineland-Palatinate *(Rheinland-Pfalz)* **(capital: Mainz)**

The Rhineland-Palatinate was formed in 1946 from the southern part of the Rhine Province, the Bavarian Palatinate and part of Hesse known as Rheinhessen. It was part of the French Zone of Occupation and was expected to be divided at some later date amongst the neighbouring States. The river Rhine forms the boundary between Rhineland-Palatinate and Baden-Württemberg, splitting the economic unit of Mannheim—Ludwigshafen. In 1974 the population of the State was well over three and a half millions. The Rhineland-Palatinate is governed by a *Landtag* with 100 seats.

The Saar *(Saarland)* **(capital: Saarbrücken)**

The *Saargebiet*, as it was then known, was attached to France after the war and was only returned to Germany in 1957 after a plebiscite; it retained economic connections with France until 1959. When the Saar became the tenth State of the Federal Republic, it was renamed *Saarland*. By 1975 its population was well over the million mark. The long history of dispute over the sovereignty of this region indicates that its natural resources and industry are of immense importance. The Saar is governed by a *Landtag* with 50 seats.

Schleswig-Holstein (capital: Kiel)

Schleswig-Holstein was formed in 1946 mainly from the old Prussian Province of the same name, when Prussia was dissolved after the war. Its population in 1975 was more than 2½ million, including a high proportion of refugees. It is predominantly agricultural. Schleswig-Holstein is governed by a *Landtag* with 69 seats.

The Constitution

Great care was taken as the constitution was being formulated to create a document which would prevent a repetition of the events of 1939–1945. The freedom of the individual, equality before the law, freedom of belief, religion and speech and the right to challenge apparent injustice were accorded supreme importance and declared to be inviolable.

The constitutional head of the Federal Republic is the President *(Bundespräsident)*, elected for a 5-year period by the Federal Assembly *(Bundesversammlung)*, composed of all the members of the *Bundestag* and an equal number of representatives of the States; it traditionally meets in Berlin. The President is the official representative of the Federal Republic; he signs treaties and agreements, appoints the Heads of Germany's diplomatic missions abroad, receives the Ambassadors of other nations and entertains visiting Heads of State. His official residence is the Villa Hammerschmidt in Bonn. The President also appoints the Federal Chancellor chosen by the *Bundestag*, and approves the appointment and dismissal of government ministers, judges, officers and high-ranking civil servants. He has the right to pardon a criminal. In order to safeguard his neutrality, the constitution states that he must not have any role in party politics at any level whilst in office, neither may he accept any other position, even if it is unpaid. He may also be re-elected for a second term of office. His deputy is the President of the *Bundesrat*.

The West German parliament consists of two houses: the *Bundestag* and the *Bundesrat*. The *Bundestag* is elected by the citizens of the Federal Republic every four years. All the members belong to a major political party and vote according to the directions of that party's leaders. Rather less than half are elected directly from the constituencies and the rest are nominated by the parties according to the system of proportional representation. About 20 delegates come from West Berlin; they do not have the right to vote. The function of the *Bundestag* is to examine and approve legislation. From within the *Bundestag* a Chancellor is elected *(Bundeskanzler)* to lead a Cabinet of Ministers which forms the government; a Chancellor may also be dismissed by the *Bundestag*, but only if a new candidate is available who can command the support of a majority of the delegates. This precaution, the '*konstruktives Mißtrauensvotum*', was written into the con-

Bonn: the Bundeshaus (Parliament Building) by the Rhine

stitution to avoid a crisis occurring if no one could be found to form a new government. The Chancellor determines the policies which his government will adopt and decides what legislation he will put before the *Bundestag*; he assumes control of the armed forces in war. He is helped by a team of about twenty Ministers of his own choice *(Bundesregierung)*, who advise him on new legislation and who are individually responsible for ensuring that existing laws are properly applied.

The *Bundesrat* consists entirely of delegates nominated by the State governments. Since the States can at any time change their representatives, it never becomes necessary to dissolve the Bundesrat. There are 45 members, including four from West Berlin, who attend purely in an advisory capacity, since the constitution does not at present allow them to vote. The President of the *Bundesrat* is elected annually from amongst the Presidents of the ten States. Seats are allocated to the States as follows:

Baden-Württemberg, Bavaria, Lower Saxony and North-Rhine Westphalia: 5

Hesse, Rhineland-Palatinate and Schleswig-Holstein: 4

Bremen, Hamburg and Saar: 3

The function of the *Bundesrat* is to represent the State governments' views; all business which comes before it must first be discussed by the Cabinet of Ministers in each State, which then directs its delegates how to vote in the *Bundesrat*. The delegates from any one State are required to vote as a block. Certain measures, such as finance bills and those which affect the sovereignty of the States, need the express consent of the *Bundesrat* before they can become law.

The *Bundesrat* may initiate legislation. It may become the law-making body for a period of six months in the unlikely event of the *Bundestag* withdrawing support from the Chancellor without agreeing on his successor *(Gesetzgebungsnotstand)*.

All the laws which affect the whole country must be passed by the *Bundestag*. They may originate from both the *Bundesrat* and the *Bundestag*, but by far the majority are formulated by the governing body of Ministers in the *Bundestag*. Planned legislation is first presented to the *Bundesrat*, which can consider it over a period of three weeks. It then goes to the *Bundestag*, where it is discussed both in committee and in the full assembly *(Plenum)*. Most laws need a simple majority of the *Plenum* to be accepted, but those which make any change to the constitution must receive the vote of two-thirds of the members both in the *Bundestag* and in the *Bundesrat*. Legislation which has been passed by the *Bundestag* is returned to the *Bundesrat*, which has the right to convene a committee to consider any measures which it cannot approve. This committee can make recommendations to both Houses when the legislation is considered, but since many bills do not need the consent of the *Bundesrat*, the latter's influence is limited.

Once a law has been passed through Parliament, it is engrossed (formulated) by the *Bundespräsident* and is published in the Federal Law Journal *(Bundesgesetzblatt)*. It becomes law fourteen days after publication, unless it explicitly states otherwise. Laws passed in this way are binding on all States and may if necessary be enforced by the central government *(Bundeszwang)*.

The *Bundestag* and the *Bundesrat* appoint an equal number of judges to the Federal Constitutional Court *(Bundesverfassungsgericht)* in Karlsruhe. Both the *Bundesrat* and individual State Parliaments may appeal to the Federal Constitutional Court if they feel that the Federal Government or the President is exceeding their constitutional role. The same court also examines new legislation passed by both the Federal and State Parliaments and investigates reports of organizations such as extremist political parties alleged to be endangering the nation. It is, in other words, the guardian of the constitution.

Since West Germany is a federal nation, it is necessary to define exactly the functions of the State and central governments. The Parliament in Bonn has full responsibility for defence, foreign policy, the postal services, the railways, air transport, currency, trade, tariffs and the issue of passports and for all other matters which must be decided at national level. It issues to the States outline regulations in matters concerning the press, the cinema and the registration of people and of personal movements. In matters of taxation, responsibility is shared with the States.

Regional Government

Each State *(Land)* within the Federal Republic has its own government and parliament elected for a term of four years. The political composition of the parliaments differs in many cases from that of the Federal parliament; it is quite normal for the party in opposition at national level to form the government within a State.

As the duties of the central government have increased, so those of the State parliaments *(Landtage)*, in particular with regard to finance, have decreased. The States still retain, however, complete authority over their own health and education services and broadcasting systems; they also have the duty to raise a police force to maintain law and order, to control traffic and to enforce Federal laws within their boundaries. They organize their own systems of administration and have the right to award among their own citizens a quota of 'Federal Orders of Merit' *(Bundesverdienstkreuze)* allocated by the central government.

Much of the administrative work within the States is carried out by *Kreisregierungen* and *Gemeinden*, small units corresponding in function roughly to the new English District and Town or Parish Councils respectively. Some of the larger States also have Administrative Divisions *(Regierungsbezirke)*, which comprise several *Kreise*. The local councils have charge of road-building and maintenance, hospital and school building programmes; they provide education, welfare, youth and transport services, gas, electricity and water and subsidise municipal theatres and orchestras. To raise money the *Kreise* are allowed to levy charges for the use of public sewers and for garbage collection; the water supply is metered in the same way as gas and electricity.

Neither the *Kreise* nor the *Gemeinden* are represented in the State government in the way that the States are represented by the *Bundesrat* in the Federal government, and there is a widespread feeling that they in fact enjoy little of the independence that is theoretically theirs. They are at present asking to play a greater role in formulating the laws they must administer and for a greater share of public money.

Elections

Every citizen (male or female) of the Federal Republic who has reached the age of 18 may vote in all elections unless a court has for some reason (insanity, serious crime, illegal political activity) deprived him of his civic rights *(Bürgerliche Ehrenrechte)*. Candidates for election must be at least 21 years old. In elections for the *Bundestag*, which take place every four years, each elector has two votes. One vote is a direct vote for a specific candidate; the other goes to a political party, which will be allotted seats in the *Bundestag* in proportion to the number of votes polled in each State. Seats which fall vacant during a parliament's term of office are not filled; it is therefore important that any government should have a comfortable working majority.

Elections for State parliaments *(Landtagswahlen)* and for local authorities *(Kommunalwahlen)* are also held every four years, but they do not coincide with a general election. There is no compulsion on anyone to cast his vote in any election, and no check is kept on the names of voters or of the way they voted. However the population is aware of its political role and even in local elections some 75% of the electorate usually votes; at the Bundestag election of 1976 the figure was well over 90%.

Political Parties

Since 1945 there has been a marked tendency towards large political parties, which contrasts strongly with the multiplicity of tiny parties after the First World War, none of which could command enough support to govern the country until the National Socialists came to power. The main political parties are the conservative CDU *(Christlich-Demokratische Union*—'Christian Democratic Union'), the socialist SPD *(Sozialdemokratische Partei Deutschlands*—'Social Democratic Party') and the FDP *(Freie Demokratische Partei*—'Free Democratic Party'), which is slightly right of centre. The CDU and its Bavarian sister-party, the CSU *(Christlich-Soziale Union*—'Christian Social Union'), played a leading part in every government between 1949 and 1969; for many years it was led by Konrad Adenauer. The CDU/CSU formed several coalitions with the FDP; in 1966 began the 'grand coalition' between the CDU/CSU and SPD, with Kurt Georg Kiesinger (CDU) as Chancellor.

Posters advertising political parties contesting the 1969 Bundestag election

In 1969 the CDU/CSU failed to achieve an overall majority and were sent into opposition by a coalition between the SPD and FDP. The Socialists retained power in 1972 and 1976.

To prevent a recurrence of the situation as it was between 1918 and 1933, measures were written into the constitution to exclude from State and Federal governments any party polling less than 5% of the total votes (10% in Bavaria) or obtaining less than three mandates by direct election. This does not, of course, prevent anyone from forming a political party, which he is permitted to do so long as that party is based on democratic principles. Nor does it prevent small groups of people (500 are necessary) from proposing a candidate for election; this practice is most useful at *Kreis* and *Gemeinde* level. It has, however, hitherto prevented extremist parties such as the right-wing NPD (*National-demokratische Partei Deutschlands*—'National Democratic Party'), in so far as they have not been banned, from gaining seats in the *Bundestag*, although they have had some successes in local elections; in the 1969 general election 94·69% of votes cast went to the three major parties. The Communist Party (KPD or *Kommunistische Partei Deutschlands*) was banned in the Federal Republic in 1956 although it continued to exist in West Berlin; it was reconstituted in the Federal Republic in 1968 as the DKP *(Deutsche Kommunistische Partei)*.

The past experience of older members of the population has taught them to be very wary of holding strong political views and the young seem to have little enthusiasm for the present form of government, so actual party membership is low. The ordinary citizen feels that in casting a vote he has done his duty and he is more than willing to leave the function of government to '*Vater Staat*'. The existence of a coalition government reduced still further the interest in party politics and favoured the rise of pressure groups representing people with common interests, such as industrialists, refugees, farmers and students. Of recent years extremist groups have figured prominently in the news, although in fact they represent only small minorities. Among the most active of these have been the left-wing anarchist APO *(Außerparlamentarische Opposition)*, the radical student organization SDS *(Sozialistischer Deutscher Studentenbund)*, the New Left *(Neue Linken)*, the Youth Wing of the SPD *(Jungsozialisten)* and the Baader-Meinhof gang of urban guerillas. Right-wing groups outside the NPD and CSU are rare.

Currency

Since 1948 the currency in use in the western part of Germany has been the *Deutsche Mark*, created when the *Reichsmark* was devalued by some 90% to cure post-war inflation. The central bank was until 1957 the *Bank Deutscher Länder*; since 1957 it has been the *Deutsche Bundesbank*. Each State has its own bank, which operates as a branch of the *Bundesbank*. The functions of the central bank are to issue money and set the official bank rate (1977: 3½%) to maintain the stability of the currency. (Since 1967 the bank rate (Diskontsatz) has never risen above 7½%. The British rate in 1977 was 12½%; in 1976 it had exceeded 14%.)

In 1949 the *Deutsche Mark* was devalued along with other European currencies, but since then it has become one of the strongest and most desired currencies in the world; in 1961 it was revalued upwards. In 1968 the Federal Republic's balance of payments was showing such a considerable surplus that it threatened the stability of world trade and the value of many currencies. To avoid revaluing the mark, the Kiesinger government temporarily placed a 4% duty on exports and gave a 4% bonus to imports, in the hope of increasing the flow of foreign goods into the country. The socialist-led government which came to power in 1969 chose to adopt a different policy however, and the Mark was revalued by 8½%. There have been subsequent revaluations of the Mark coupled with devaluations of other currencies. Their combined effect was to raise the value of the Mark between 1972 and 1977 by 33% against the US dollar and by 91% against sterling.

The *Deutsche Bundesbank* has in recent years been called upon to support weaker currencies, including sterling, with large loans. It also gives financial aid to some developing countries and offers credit facilities to the GDR.

Policy

When the SPD/FDP coalition led by Willy Brandt came to power in October 1969 the policy of the Federal Government towards Eastern European countries changed considerably. The Governments led by the Christian Democrats (CDU) had always insisted that both the Oder-Neisse line that separates the German Democratic Republic from Poland and the border between the Federal Republic and the German Democratic Republic were to be provisional until a peace treaty was concluded as laid down by the Allied Powers in the Potsdam Agreement of 1945. The Federal Government laid claim to all the territory that had been part of the German Reich in 1937, although it always emphasized that it would never use force to change the *status quo*. It also claimed that it spoke for the whole of Germany because the population in the GDR had not been given the right to elect freely the government it wanted.

The CDU-led Governments had no dealings with the GDR at government level, the only link being the *Interzonenhandelsabkommen* ('interzonal trade agreement'), in which the GDR was granted certain concessions not allowed to foreign trading partners. In all schoolbooks, broadcasts and official papers, various euphemisms for the German Democratic Republic and its Government were used as a form of propaganda in order to avoid recognizing its existence even by implication; these included the abbreviation SBZ ('Soviet-occupied Zone'), Pankow (seat of the Government of the GDR; a suburb of East Berlin), and *Mitteldeutschland* ('Central Germany'). The description 'East Germany' *(Ostdeutschland)* was officially reserved for the German territories beyond the Oder-Neisse line, although outside Government circles it was often used as a term for the GDR. The term 'abroad' was interpreted as meaning outside the frontiers of 1937.

Another aspect of the tough line pursued by successive CDU-led Governments was the Hallstein Doctrine, named after Professor Walter Hallstein, who was a Secretary of State at the Federal Republic's Foreign Office at the time of its formulation. It stipulated that the Federal Government was to have no diplomatic relations with any country that recognized the GDR Government diplomatically. If diplomatic relations existed with countries that later recognized the GDR, they were to be broken off, as indeed happened with Jugoslavia in 1957. The Grand Coalition between the Christian Democrats and the Social Democrats (1966–1969) relaxed the Hallstein Doctrine to the extent that it was no longer applied to countries that had had no choice but to recognize the GDR, such as the East European Communist countries. This was done with Rumania in mind, with whom diplomatic relations were then established on this basis; the Federal Government relaxed its attitude even further when ambassadors were exchanged with Jugoslavia once again. The Brandt Government abandoned the Hallstein Doctrine; it also concluded non-aggression treaties with the USSR and Poland; in the latter the Oder-Neisse line was recognized as the inviolable western frontier of Poland, and West Germany renounced all claim to the former Reich territories.

During the years of the Grand Coalition, letters sent from the GDR Government to the Federal Government were for the first time no longer ignored but accepted and answered, although in rather general terms. Brandt's contribution, for which he later received the Nobel Peace Prize, was to begin talks with the GDR at the highest levels. At an early stage his Government recognized the GDR as a second German state *(Staat)* whilst insisting that there could be only one German nation *(Volk)*. Within West Germany his policies, known as *Ostpolitik*, met with considerable opposition, but they removed much of the tension from East–West relations and led eventually to the signing of the Basic Treaty in 1973. In this the Federal Republic gave up her claim to speak for the whole of Germany in return for concessions on travel and communications. Both countries recognized each other's existence and the permanence of all their frontiers; diplomatic representatives were exchanged. The mutual recognition of the two German states was soon followed by wide international recognition and the admission of both to the United Nations. The benefits of *Ostpolitik* are real enough, but there is much still to be done before the Iron Curtain is flung open and the Berlin Wall torn down.

The changed atmosphere in the relations between the Federal Government and all East European countries should continue at least as long as Socialist governments are in power, although among the refugees and their sympathizers, united in so-called *Landsmannschaften*, there are still some who uncompromisingly insist that the former German territories east of the Oder-Neisse line must again be part of Germany one day; it was they who put up posters proclaiming "*Dreigeteilt?—Niemals!*" ('Divided into three?—Never!'). Similar organizations erect road signs throughout the Federal Republic giving the distances to Breslau, Danzig, Königsberg and Stettin. In other cases road signs have not been removed; in the Harz mountains, for example, conventional road signs

Dreigeteilt? Niemals!

still direct the traveller to places now inaccessible behind the Iron Curtain. Even postage stamps have been used as vehicles of propaganda; one issue used pictures of Dresden, Königsberg, Neubrandenburg and Stettin. The East German postal authorities refused to deliver mail bearing such stamps.

The Ministry for German Internal Relations *(Ministerium für innerdeutsche Beziehungen)*, formerly the Ministry for All-German Affairs *(Ministerium für gesamtdeutsche Fragen)*, is responsible for keeping the West German public informed about the GDR. A number of private organizations exist to keep alive the idea of a united Germany; one, *Unteilbares Deutschland* ('Indivisible Germany'), denies by its very name that Germany has ever been divided.

The Federal Republic has since 1955 been a member of NATO (North Atlantic Treaty Organization). She belongs to the Council of Europe and was a founder-member of the Common Market. Since 1949 the Federal Republic has pursued a policy of reconciliation with France; the conclusion of the Franco-German Treaty of Friendship in 1963 marked the climax of the career of Konrad Adenauer. The Federal Republic has been a member of the United Nations Organization since 1973.

The Legal System

It was obvious that the new Germany which was to rise from the ashes of war would have to reform the legal system of the Third Reich in order to restore confidence in its trustworthiness. It was decided to retain whatever seemed valuable and to take as a basis for new laws the nineteenth century books of law, which had been a compromise between 'popular' law and Roman law. The fundamental rights of the individual expressed in the constitution were protected by the *Generalklausel im Verwaltungsprozeß*, which gives to the individual the right of appeal to an independent court if he feels that he has been unjustly treated. In addition the law-making bodies (the *Bundestag* and the *Landtage*) are quite separate from the executive and judicial bodies to eliminate the possibility that at some future date they might collaborate against the best interests of the German people, as happened under Hitler.

The highest court in the Federal Republic is the *Bundesverfassungsgericht* ('Federal Constitutional Court') in Karlsruhe, which amongst other things ensures that new legislation conforms to the principles laid down in the constitution. The *Bundesgerichtshof* ('Federal Supreme Court'), also in Karlsruhe, is the highest court for civil and criminal cases *(Zivil- und Strafrecht)*. Each State has its own High Court *(Oberes Landesgericht)*, which hears cases referred from the subsidiary *Landgericht*, occasionally from an *Amtsgericht*, the lowest court of all. Other types of court deal with a particular section of the law; the *Arbeitsgericht*, for example, hears disputes connected with employment and labour, the *Finanzgericht* with financial matters. Appeals against the decisions of these courts are heard in the first instance by the State courts such as the *Landesarbeitsgericht*; the supreme authority is the appropriate Federal High Court *(Oberes Bundesgericht)*.

In criminal cases the Public Prosecutor *(Staatsanwalt, Bundesanwalt)* institutes proceedings against the accused; in civil cases the plaintiff *(Kläger)* takes his grievance to court. Certain minor criminal offences are however outside the province of a Public Prosecutor; proceedings for slander, causing a disturbance and minor assault are brought by private individuals, who report the offender to the authorities. Minor road traffic offences are punished by on-the-spot fines, although in every instance the citizen has the right to insist on the judgement of a court. There is no capital punishment.

Laymen play a considerable role in the administration of justice, particularly in the lowest courts *(Landgericht, Amtsgericht)*, where they may act as assistants to the judges *(Schöffen)* or as jurors. Many minor disputes between individuals never reach a court. They are heard by a *Schiedsmann*, who is a respected citizen appointed to this honorary post to serve a certain area; his function is to persuade the parties to reach a reasonable settlement.

All citizens of the Federal Republic are equal before the law. It is the duty of those who enforce and administer the law to observe this fact and to grant a fair trial to anyone accused of a crime. Politics are permitted to play no role whatsoever in the administration of justice. The law is absolute and not open to drastic reinterpretation without new legislation from the *Bundestag*. However the law does not offer to the accused the same protection as does British law; there is no right of Habeas Corpus and the press is free to print what it pleases about him. A newspaper may for example report that 'the murderer' has been caught, and may publish details of the man's life and career which in Britain would have to be suppressed on the grounds that they could influence the outcome of the trial. People arrested on criminal charges are often kept in custody *(Untersuchungshaft)* for long periods before being brought to trial; investigations may take a year or longer.

The Law

German law is an attempt to regulate all aspects of society; it is codified and classified to include every possible crime or offence. Even minor infringements of traffic regulations are listed together with the appropriate fine; in Bavaria, for example, the list of 400 possible infringements is published as a paperback. The law is subdivided into civil and criminal law. The former is contained in the BGB *(Bürgerliches Gesetzbuch)*, the latter in the StGB *(Strafgesetzbuch)*.

On a personal level the law compels everyone to carry an identification card *(Personalausweis)* at all times; car drivers must also carry their driving licence and insurance certificate. All residents must register with the local police, who keep a record of all removals, lodgers and guests. Each family keeps a *Familienbuch*, in which entries are made officially by a registrar; besides births, marriages and deaths other important events such as christenings are recorded. Moves to make both sexes equal before the law now permit marriage at sixteen if one partner is at least eighteen. (Once girls could marry at sixteen, boys never before eighteen.)

Other laws impose upon the population an obligation to be quiet for an hour every afternoon and after 10 p.m., and to refrain at all times from causing even a mild nuisance, for example by shaking a duster from a window outside the prescribed hours or by playing a radio so loudly that it can be heard in the next room. In winter occupants of ground-floor dwellings must have the pavement clear of snow and sprinkled with salt or ashes by 8 a.m. In short, laws and regulations confront the citizen at every turn, leading him to believe that anything which is not expressly forbidden is actually permitted; it is thus necessary to state explicitly that parking on tramlines or in the centre lane of a three-lane road is forbidden.

The enforcement of these laws is, however, an entirely different matter. Minor transgressions such as the flouting of the quiet hour usually only come to light if someone reports the offence to the authorities, a procedure which is not uncommon. Most Germans delight in obeying the letter of the law and, apparently, in reporting those who do not. This explains the universal absence of laundry drying out of doors on a Sunday as well as the meticulous observance of no-smoking regulations. The offence of not possessing up-to-date identification papers, however, unless revealed by accident, frequently goes undetected, since it would need a large army of officials to keep abreast of the necessary paper work. It is rumoured that less than a quarter of the population of Hamburg is in possession of the correct papers.

The Police and Public Safety

The raising and organizing of a police force is the responsibility of each State. The duties of the force include traffic and crowd control, crime prevention and detection, the issue of identity cards and the recording of personal movements. The police can be investigated by the courts if they are accused of exceeding their constitutional role. In an emergency the central government can call directly on the services of the police; it is the duty of the States to have such a force to place at the government's disposal. This *Bereitschaftspolizei* is not a part of the normal police force.

The role of the *Bundesluftschutzverband* in time of war would be to warn of impending attack from the air; the *Technisches Hilfswerk* would bring relief to stricken areas.

In peacetime the former checks, for example, that building regulations have been observed (from 1968 all new houses must have an atomic shelter). The *Technisches Hilfswerk* is always ready to help after any natural catastrophe.

There are both full-time and voluntary fire services. It was once a matter of social prestige to belong to the voluntary fire service, but since it has become an ancillary branch of the professional service this is no longer the case. The State of Lower Saxony pioneered in Germany the formation of airborne fire-fighting teams, which now exist in several States. The fire service also provides ambulance facilities.

The Armed Forces

Between 1949 and 1954 the Federal Republic was not permitted to raise any armed forces. Gradually, however, the idea had been gaining ground that she should play some part in the defence of western Europe and in 1954 she became part of NATO (North Atlantic Treaty Organization). The constitution was altered to provide for the introduction of conscription, and in the following year the Federal Republic began to build up armed forces *(Bundeswehr)*. In 1956 an 18-month period of compulsory military service was introduced for all men reaching the age of twenty. In 1965 the age limit was reduced to eighteen to compensate for the shortage of manpower, due to the sharp drop in births at the end of the war. In 1972 military service was cut to 15 months.

The *Bundesgrenzschutz* is part of the army which concentrates particularly on securing the borders of the Federal Republic, normally patrolling a stretch of land 30 km. deep immediately behind the frontier. In time of peace its duties mainly consist in operating passport controls, but in an emergency the entire force could be mobilized and deployed throughout the country.

The *Wehrbeauftragter* is appointed by Parliament; he investigates the grievances of any member of the armed forces and keeps under observation the conduct of all aspects of military affairs.

No regulation concerning the armed forces is valid in West Berlin, since Berlin is still technically under Allied occupation. Residents of West Berlin are therefore automatically exempt from military service.

The Social Structure

When Berlin was still the hub of the Empire the upper classes enjoyed a brilliant social life, but Germany has like many other countries been affected by a social revolution which has altered the class structure. The leading role in the Federal Republic has been taken over by wealthy business-men and industrialists and society has lost much of its glitter. The old class system, which distinguished between the higher civil servants *(Beamte)*, white-collar workers *(Angestellte)* and manual workers *(Arbeiter)* has also virtually disappeared, although the position of *Beamte* still retains a degree of prestige. The gulf between the middle and lower classes has been much reduced by education and by the rise in wages, which has made the pay of manual workers completely comparable with that of white-collar workers and has all but abolished poverty. The working class now has a considerable share in the economic prosperity of the country and can afford to maintain a good standard of living; the West German manual worker is one of the most cultured in Europe.

Youth

There are many different youth organizations in the Federal Republic, some of which are allied to religious or political organizations, and all of which belong to the *Bundesjugendring* ('Federal Youth Union'). Great care was taken to prevent the formation of a nation-wide youth movement after the war, since it was felt that this could easily be taken over by unscrupulous elements and transformed into a political organization like the 'Hitler Youth'. There is no compulsion on any child to become a member of any group.

The government supports work amongst young people by subsidizing youth clubs; the States provide holiday homes in the country such as those regularly used by groups of schoolchildren as part of their education. There are also some 800 Youth Hostels in the Federal Republic. Some of the money for the facilities given to young people comes from the issue of special postage stamps which carry a small surcharge *(Jugendmarken)*.

Comprehensive legislation aims to protect young people from corruption and danger especially in public places; parents are expected to co-operate in the enforcement of such laws. Parents are frequently held to be responsible for the actions of their children; an accident caused by a child under school age crossing the road unaccompanied is said to have in fact been caused by the parents, since they should have been supervising the activities of the child.

The Organization of Labour

In the Weimar Republic trade unions had strong political or religious affiliations; the workers in any one industry might, for example, have the choice of joining a specifically Catholic, Protestant, Communist, nationalist, liberal or Socialist union. Hitler banned all these unions and replaced them by a single organization, the *Deutsche Arbeitsfront,* which claimed to represent both employers and employees. The Constitution of the Federal Republic granted to both employers and workers the right to band together to further their interests *(Koalitionsfreiheit)*. A new feature of the post-war trade union movement is the organization of all types of workers in any one industry into the same union *(Ein Betrieb, eine Gewerkschaft)*. A minority of workers belong to the trade union movement; the membership fee is one hour's pay per member per week. Sixteen unions, representing both manual and clerical workers, together form the Congress of German Trade Unions *(Deutscher Gewerkschaftsbund* or DGB*)* founded in 1949. Many office workers, however, prefer to join either the DAG *(Deutsche Angestelltengewerkschaft)* or the DBB *(Deutscher Beamtenbund),* both of which are outside the DGB. The Congress of German Trade Unions is completely independent of all governments, political parties, religions and employers. Besides seeking full employment, it strives to bring about an increase in the standard of living and a more just distribution of profits; it also aims to extend the right of workers to participate in management *(Mitbestimmungsrecht),* and it finances schools and educational and cultural enterprises. It sponsors the annual *Ruhrfestspiele* at Recklinghausen, owns a chain of shops and finances building projects, especially the erection of dwellings for the lower paid. It organizes celebrations marking the annual Labour Day (May 1st). The national congress is held every three years.

Participation of the workers in management is usually accomplished through the *Betriebsrat* or works committee, which by law must exist in all but the smallest firms to represent the interests of the workers to the management. Representatives of the workers must occupy half the seats on every supervisory board. Reports from the *Betriebsrat* and from the management are given to the regular meeting of all workers *(Betriebsversammlung)*; topics discussed include the economic situation of the firm, working conditions and social benefit schemes. Redundancy and unemployment have not been serious problems in the Federal Republic; there was for a time a shortage of labour despite the large numbers of foreign workers *(Gastarbeiter)* attracted by the relative affluence of German society. Since 1960 the unemployment figures have risen above 0·7% only occasionally; in 1967 they reached 2·1% and in 1975–6 they exceeded 5% for a time.

The main representative of employers and management is the *Bundesvereinigung der deutschen Arbeitgeberverbände*. One of its main functions is the training and re-training of workers; it also organizes research to ensure the further prosperity of industry.

The constitution of the Federal Republic does not expressly recognize the right of workers to strike, nor does it forbid a lock-out by the employers. However, strikes can only be called by a Union, not by a works committee or local group; unofficial strikes are illegal. The law safeguards the agreed working week and the right of workers to a minimum paid holiday, to safe working conditions, to adequate notice of dismissal or redundancy and to welfare facilities. It forbids the exertion of pressure on any person to take up a particular career, to undergo a course of training or to accept a position that he is offered. Agreements between employers and unions may be given the force of law.

Social Security

All working people in the lower income groups are compulsorily insured in the national scheme against sickness, accidents and unemployment; they are also required to contribute regularly to the pension fund. Extra private insurance against illness is however encouraged, since the State scheme pays only for necessities, such as third class hospitalization and basic preventive medicine. People not covered by insurance must pay for all medicines and medical services; if they are given a blood transfusion for instance, they pay for both the operation and the blood. A charge is also made for the use of the ambulance service.

The *Gesundheitsamt* ('Health Department') of each local council undertakes for example the screening of immigrants and also looks after hygiene standards in public places. Less than two-thirds of all hospitals are run by public authorities; churches and welfare organizations play an important role in all aspects of medical care.

Kindergeld (children's allowance) is paid to all families for each child; in 1975 a two-child family received DM120 a month. Cases of extreme need may claim *Sozialhilfe* (social aid). Various funds exist to help those who have suffered as a result of war, for example expatriates, former prisoners-of-war and those with physical disabilities. The most important fund is the *Lastenausgleich*, which makes available public money to those who lost property during the war, in particular to refugees.

One of the outstanding provisions of the welfare services is the scheme whereby old-age pensions are linked to one's former salary and the current cost of living, giving the aged a fairer share in national prosperity.

Taxation

Because West Germany is a federal state, the revenue from taxation has to be divided between the Federal and State governments. Before the First World War the income was divided equally between local authorities, States and central government, but this plan was clearly unsuited to the high expenditure at national level in the modern state. The Federal Government now receives the lion's share; its income derives from value added tax *(Mehrwertsteuer)*, duty on imports *(Zölle)* and purchase tax *(Verbrauchssteuer)*. It also receives a share of income tax *(Einkommensteuer)* and corporation tax *(Körperschaftsteuer)*. Value added tax was introduced by the Federal Republic in 1968 as part of the agreed policy of the Common Market; it displaced turnover tax *(Umsatzsteuer)*. The tax is calculated as a fixed percentage of the increased value of all goods at each stage in their manufacture.

The States are financed by a variety of taxes on income and property *(Besitzsteuer)*, on commercial transactions *(Verkehrsteuer)* and on such things as entertainments and motor vehicles. Local authorities receive the entire revenue from profit tax *(Gewerbesteuer)* and land tax *(Grundsteuer)* as well as the charges they levy for such services as garbage disposal, but since these sources only rarely provide enough money to cover expenditure, most authorities are heavily subsidized by their State.

This system does not apportion fairly between the States the revenue from taxation, since income depends upon population and not upon size; Schleswig-Holstein, for example, receives far less than North-Rhine Westphalia. It was therefore necessary to introduce a scheme which would achieve a more balanced distribution *(Ausgleich)*.

Tax evasion is practised to a considerable degree by large concerns, which are permitted to make expensive gifts and give lavish hospitality and set them off against tax, since these are considered legitimate elements in the conduct of big business.

Church tax *(Kirchensteuer)* is paid by over 90% of the working population, being deducted from salary at source. The revenue goes either to the Evangelical or Roman Catholic church, according to the faith of the taxpayer; members of other churches are not required to pay. The number of taxpayers does not reflect the size of the church-going population.

The Churches

Freedom of belief and of worship are guaranteed in Federal Germany; the government also undertakes to safeguard Sunday as a day of rest and to recognize certain ecclesiastical feasts. The Evangelical (*i.e.* Protestant) and Roman Catholic churches occupy special positions in West Germany, the relationship between them and the State being governed by laws and concordats; there has been no established church since 1918. Both churches receive grants from the States and central government as well as income from church tax. Ministers and priests are paid according to the salary scale applicable to civil servants *(Beamte)*. Over 90% of the population belongs to one or other of these churches; to opt out of Church membership it is necessary to appear before a judge *(Amtsrichter)*. For various reasons it is more convenient to remain in the Church even if this does mean that one is obliged to pay church tax, since to leave cuts one off from

Notices giving details of Protestant and Catholic church services are often to be seen as one enters a town or village

all the services and sacraments, including marriage and burial.

Once it was possible to identify exactly the religion of each area (see Peace of Augsburg 1555 and Treaty of Westphalia 1648), the people being compelled to adopt the religious beliefs of their ruler, but the geographical distribution is now by no means so clear as it was even before the Second World War, because the population has become much more mobile. Membership of the two main churches is about equal, the Evangelical Church having grown tremendously because of the influx of refugees from the former eastern provinces of the Reich. Roman Catholics, however, still predominate in the Rhineland and southern Germany, whereas Protestants are more numerous in the north.

Administratively the Protestant Church is divided into State Churches *(Landeskirchen)*, the States being those of the inter-war years, such as Hanover, Brunswick and Schaumburg-Lippe. The States have, however, no other function than to see that no law is broken. Since 1949 a convention *(Evangelischer Kirchentag)* has been held annually. Many of the Protestant churches of Germany are members of the *Evangelische Kirche in Deutschland*, which is a union of Lutheran, reformed and United churches headed by a Synod. Other unions of churches are the *Evangelisch-Lutherische Kirche Deutschlands* and the *Evangelische Kirche der Union*. Until 1961 the Protestant Church in the Federal Republic maintained strong links with churches in the Democratic Republic, but recently it has proved impossible because of restrictions imposed by the East German authorities to hold united meetings.

The Roman Catholic Church did not alter the boundaries of its bishoprics after the war and therefore includes territory outside the Federal Republic. The West German branch is centred upon the Conference of Bishops, which meets in Fulda and publishes the official attitude of the Roman Catholic Church on topics of current interest. The major meeting of German Catholics is the biennial *Katholikentag*, which was first held in 1848. All the major religious orders have houses in the Federal Republic and contribute to welfare and education services.

The Free Churches brought to Germany the concept of voluntary church membership, since at no time has anyone been compelled to belong to them. They have existed alongside the established church in some unusually tolerant areas since 1700, but their membership is still extremely small. They receive no financial support from public funds.

All the Christian Churches of the Federal Republic undertake social work amongst young people, the poor and in industry. They run libraries and book clubs, hoping to spread a love of good books; they offer criticism of films and books in the attempt to protect their members from corruption. Their evening courses supplement the public *Volkshochschulen*. Some of the Churches publish important newspapers, such as the Roman Catholic *Rheinischer Merkur*. In most States the Churches participate in the educational system; denominational schools are preferred for example in the Rhenish States.

The Jewish population of Germany now seems to have stabilized after the emigration and persecution between 1933 and 1945. Most large towns have a Jewish community; there are now approximately 30,000 Jews in West Germany.

Mass Media

In Germany there is no long tradition of free speech and of a free press. During this century there has been a twelve-year period of complete repression under Hitler which killed most of the newspapers and replaced them with organs for Party propaganda. The freedom of speech guaranteed by Article 5 of the Federal Constitution, and limited only by such considerations as the prevention of the corruption of young people, is therefore particularly precious. The government and people alike are so determined to maintain a free press that they will tolerate outrageous scandalmongering on the part of some unscrupulous editors.

The *Presse- und Informationsamt* of the government is not a political organization; it exists to publicize government activities, but it has no powers to compel anyone to print or broadcast its views. The *Deutscher Presserat* was set up voluntarily by publishers to protect the freedom of the press by condemning any misuse of this freedom; since its introduction in 1956 it has gained for itself a position of considerable influence.

There are many newspapers and periodicals in the Federal Republic, mostly run by private individuals; the largest and perhaps the most influential of all publishers at the moment is Axel Springer, whose organization publishes some 40% of all daily papers and the most important Sunday newspapers. Springer also publishes *Hör zu*, at $4\frac{1}{2}$ million copies Europe's largest selling magazine, which gives details of radio and television broadcasts together with serials and illustrated reports on topics of all kinds, and *Bild Zeitung*, a popular daily, which now sells $4\frac{3}{4}$ million copies. No serious paper achieves this size of circulation; the *Frankfurter Allgemeine*, a respected national daily, prints less than 300,000 copies. This is largely because many people prefer a local daily paper (there are about 400 of them) which, besides reporting local news, provides excellent world coverage. German dailies sell 19 million copies, the most on the Continent.

A selection of West German newspapers

In the *Deutsche Presseagentur* (dpa), founded in Hamburg in 1949, the Federal Republic possesses a news agency of international repute. The only widely read news magazine however is the frequently controversial *Der Spiegel*, whose penetrating reporting has often proved uncomfortable to the government.

Radio broadcasting is not controlled by either the State or Federal governments. The States organize their own regional broadcasting systems and appoint an independent administrator *(Intendant)*, who is advised by committees representing interested parties such as the unions, political organizations and the Churches. Exceptions are the stations *Deutsche Welle* and *Deutschlandfunk*, which are both run as national programmes broadcasting principally to an audience outside the Federal Republic. The broadcasting stations are guaranteed absolute freedom of news reporting.

There are at the moment three television channels, which form part of the Eurovision network. The 'First Programme' is put out by a consortium of all the existing State broadcasting stations transmitting as *Deutsches Fernsehen*. Any one evening's viewing will include programmes provided by different stations. The second channel puts out a single programme from Mainz. A third channel has been introduced on a limited scale, transmitting programmes of an educational or cultural nature. Commercial television is restricted to a short period of advertising on two channels in the early evening. Transmissions in colour began in 1967 using the PAL system.

Certain transmitters, such as Radio Free Europe and The Voice of America, and two in Berlin (RIAS—Radio in the American Sector and SFB—Free Berlin Transmitter) transmit programmes which aim to give citizens in the other part of Germany a glimpse of the western world. Two major radio stations, BFBS (British Forces Broadcasting Service) and AFN (American Forces Network) broadcast to NATO troops and their families stationed in West Germany. A feature of German radio are the 'service wavelengths' in each area, which carry for example road reports, SOS messages, weather forecasts for sportsmen, hints for tourists and news bulletins.

2. Berlin

Despite the sentimental attachment of many Germans to their pre-war capital, Berlin has no long history as the capital of Germany and emerged only comparatively recently as a great city and cultural centre. In the fifteenth century Berlin was the centre of the Province of Brandenburg-Prussia; between 1740 and 1786 Frederick the Great made Potsdam, just outside Berlin, the seat of his sparkling and highly cultured court. At this period a spate of building began to give Berlin the grandiose appearance it lost only in the bombing raids of the Second World War. Berlin's real rise came after 1871, when it was made capital of the Empire. After the abolition of the monarchy in 1918 Berlin became the artistic, industrial, scientific and transport centre of the Weimar Republic; in 1920 the city boundary was extended to form Groß-Berlin, and with four million inhabitants Berlin became the second largest city in Europe. The measures taken by the National Socialist government of the Third Reich to centralize administration focused more attention than ever on the city. It was this Berlin, embodying the national pride of the German people, which was bombed into submission and occupied by the advancing Russian troops in May 1945.

The London Protocol of 1944, agreed by the United States, Britain and Russia, proposed a special status for Berlin after the war. France gave her support to the proposal, which was eventually embodied in the Potsdam Agreement of August 1945. Berlin, an island some 160 km. inside the Soviet Zone, was consequently divided into four Sectors to be governed jointly by an Allied Control Council, helped at a later date by a German administration. Each of the Allies occupied one of the four Sectors, Russia being allocated the eastern Sector comprising eight of the twenty administrative districts of Groß-Berlin. Over a period of time, co-operation between the Soviet Union on the one hand and the United States, Britain and France on the other declined, and relations became extremely strained. The West German currency reform adopted in the Western Sectors of Berlin and the claim of the Soviet Commandant to control the whole city caused a worsening of the situation; the split was completed by the Soviet blockade by road and rail of Berlin, which lasted from June 1948 to May 1949.

Politically the two halves of the city were moving in different directions. By the end of 1948 the agitation of the Russian-backed Socialist Unity Party (*Sozialistische Einheitspartei Deutschlands* or SED) had become so strong in the Eastern Sector that the central administration of Greater Berlin

(Magistrat) felt unable to function properly in the City Hall in East Berlin and moved to Schöneberg Town Hall in the West. Although this freely elected *Magistrat* represented the whole of Berlin, the Russians then set up their own governing body for the Eastern Sector, its members drawn from the SED. In West Berlin, outside the Russian sphere of influence, the Socialist Unity Party failed to make any headway against the Social Democratic Party *(Sozialdemokratische Partei Deutschlands* or SPD*)*. Many citizens of the Soviet Sector resented the increasing political direction of their institutions and left to live in the West; in 1948, for example, many of the professors and students at the Humboldt University left East Berlin to found a new Free University with the aid of American finance in the West Berlin suburb of Dahlem.

The blockade of Berlin was in fact the culmination of various pressures applied by the Soviet authorities to the citizens of West Berlin in the hope of forcing them to consent to come under the control of Soviet and East German influence. The Western Allies, however, came to the rescue of the beleaguered city and for almost a year maintained an air lift *(Luftbrücke)* to keep life running with a semblance of normality. All three airports in the Western Sectors were in constant use; planes were landing every two or three minutes. Even when the blockade was lifted the city remained split; transport connections between East and West were cut except

The Kurfürstendamm is lined with shops, places of entertainment and cafes which spill out onto the pavement in good weather

for the underground *(U-Bahn)* and municipal railways *(S-Bahn)*. Gas, water and electricity supplies ceased to be available to West Berlin. The telephone lines were cut in 1952 and not restored until 1971.

When the Federal Republic was founded in 1949, West Berlin was included as a member state, although it could not, according to the four power agreements of 1945, be governed by the Federation. It sends observers to both the *Bundestag* and *Bundesrat* in Bonn, even though the laws passed there are not enforceable in Berlin unless they are passed by Berlin's own government, the House of Representatives *(Abgeordnetenhaus)*. Some laws, for example those introducing compulsory military service, are not under any circumstances enforceable in West Berlin. The citizens of West Berlin hold Federal Passports, although they are not allowed by the East German authorities to use them for transit across the Democratic Republic, which regards the passports as illegal documents and threatens to confiscate them. In 1957 Berlin was declared by the *Bundestag* to be the capital of the Federal Republic, although Bonn was to remain the seat of the Federal Government. From time to time official meetings, such as the election of the President, have been held

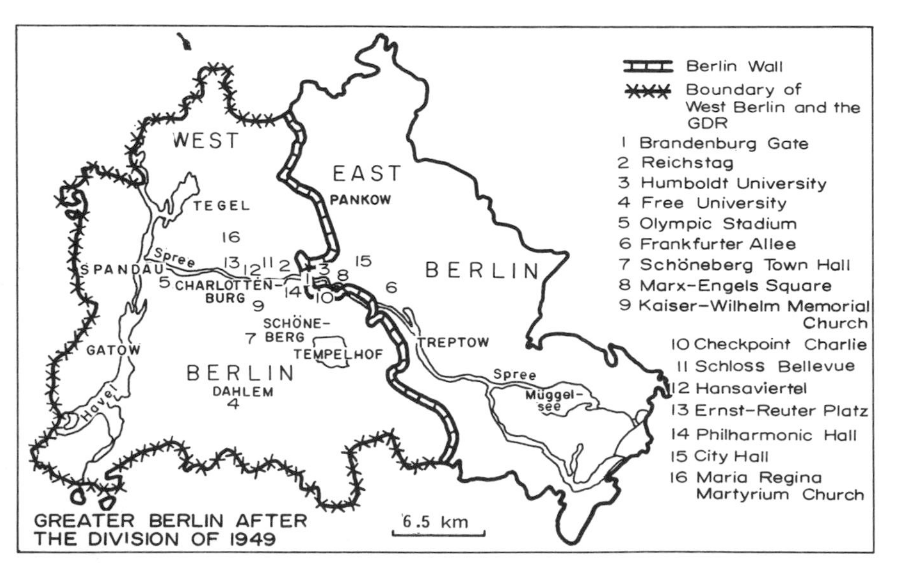

Fig 27

West Berlin: the Congress Hall (nicknamed 'the pregnant oyster' by irreverent Berliners)

in Berlin. The President has an official residence (Schloß Bellevue) in the city.

Because of her connections with the Federal Republic, West Berlin was able to benefit from the financial assistance given to Germany by the United States. The rebuilding of West Berlin was regarded as a matter of prestige; many famous architects contributed to making parts of the city into showplaces with the obvious intention of impressing the 'rival' authorities and of attracting tourists. West Berlin became noted for striking examples of modern architecture such as the Congress Hall and later the Philharmonic Hall.

East Berlin on the other hand was at first rebuilt in the stolid, unimpressive style we have come to expect from Eastern European countries; the then Stalinallee was officially described as 'the first Socialist thoroughfare'. Since about 1960, however, the standard has considerably improved and the newest architecture (Moscow Restaurant, Berolina Hotel, House of the Teachers) compares well with western building. The repair or reconstruction of the major buildings of historical or architectural importance was also slower in East Berlin, where the prevalent political ideology condemned them as symbols of the imperialist system. The greatest tragedy of all was the demolition of the Hohenzollern Palace and the Lustgarten to make way for a concrete wilderness where political assemblies could take place, known now as Marx-Engels Square.

Berlin has never long been out of the headlines; crisis after crisis has revolved round the 185 square miles of hotly-disputed territory. In June 1953 an undercurrent of discontent amongst East German workers led to the revolt on the 17th, when working people marched through the centre of Berlin bearing banners and slogans and demanding better working conditions and more food. The East Berlin authorities, being unable completely to rely on their own police force, called in Soviet tanks; the workers, armed only with sticks and stones, lost the unequal struggle.

For some years after this incident relations between the two halves of the city continued, even though they were extremely strained. It was still common for people to live in

East Berlin: new flats dominated by the Television Tower (which is over 330 metres high) and the Hotel Stadt Berlin

East Berlin, June 17th 1953: a crowd of demonstrators. (The banner reads: "We demand free elections")

one sector and work in the other; housewives crossed the boundary to shop, tourists to visit theatres and museums. This freedom did, however, lead to the defection of many East German citizens, almost three million in all, who found in Berlin a loophole in the otherwise closely guarded frontier. It was impossible to stop even the flow of news and money; the Democratic Republic claims variously that it lost between 30 million and 30,000 million Marks through this 'open frontier'. On August 13th, 1961 the border was suddenly and completely sealed; armies of workers were brought to the demarcation line to erect an ugly but effective wall of concrete blocks and barbed wire along its entire length of 45 km., leaving only a handful of carefully-controlled crossing points. For thirteen years citizens of West Berlin could no longer enter the Eastern Sector although exceptions were occasionally made by special agreements between the West Berlin Senate and the government of the Democratic Republic. The original hastily built wall has been reinforced and rebuilt after escape attempts and has been further secured by cleared, mined areas and a lighting system in stark contrast to the poor street lighting in all but the main thoroughfares. Undeniably the wall has done its job; the flow of refugees dried up immediately, the frontier was secured and the currency situation brought under strict control. Co-operation between the four Allies has virtually ceased, the sole remaining joint enterprise being the prison at Spandau, now housing only one inmate, the aging Rudolf Hess. Crises still arise from time to time, especially about the rights of access across the Democratic Republic to Berlin.

East Berlin has been incorporated into the Democratic Republic and has been described since 1949 as 'Berlin, capital of the German Democratic Republic', though this has long been resisted in Bonn. The constitution and laws of the Democratic Republic are valid within the city, which has become in everything but name the fifteenth District *(Bezirk)* of the GDR.

East Berlin has an international reputation as a cultural centre; the division of the city in 1945 gave to the East almost all the old theatres (Staatsoper, Komische Oper, Deutsches Theater, Theater am Schiffbauerdamm), the most famous museums and the old Humboldt University.

West Berlin has since 1950 been governed by a Senate *(Senat)* composed of eleven Senators and led by the 'Governing Mayor' *(Regierender Bürgermeister)*. There are 140 seats

East Berlin, November 1961 : Additional defences being erected behind the Wall

in the parliament *(Abgeordnetenhaus)*; extra seats are kept free for deputies from the other part of the city, should it ever be reunited. West Berlin shares the legal, financial and industrial systems of West Germany and most of its laws are derived from Federal legislation, although the occupying forces still retain important powers.

Large subsidies and tax concessions from the Federal Republic have transformed West Berlin into the largest West German industrial city despite the missing hinterland and the limited number of supply and delivery routes approved by the East German authorities. West Berlin has also achieved a considerable reputation for its intellectual and cultural life, although its theatre and opera do not stand out above the general high level of culture in the Federal Republic. It has however two great cultural assets: the magnificent art gallery of Berlin-Dahlem and the Berlin Philharmonic Orchestra, one of the finest in the world, both of which had to be rehoused after the war. There is also a new classical theatre (the Schillertheater) and a new opera house (the Städtische Oper, now renamed Deutsche Oper).

3. East Germany—the Democratic Republic

In the Zone of Germany occupied in 1945 by the Soviet Union the growth of Socialism and Communism was actively encouraged. In 1946 the Social Democratic Party (SPD) and the Communist Party (KPD) amalgamated under the title Socialist Unity Party (SED), led jointly by Wilhelm Pieck and Otto Grotewohl. The new party made plans to rebuild the whole of Germany, although their influence was at the time limited to the Soviet-occupied Zone. The Socialist Unity Party was ruthless in its purge of members of the National Socialist Party from high office and in the expropriation of war criminals. The land gained in the purge along with the expropriated estates of the great landowners was divided amongst peasants organized into co-operatives. Industry too was reorganized according to Socialist principles. The currency reform of 1948 introduced in West Germany was not accepted in the Soviet Zone, which immediately introduced its own reform. The foundation in 1949 of the Federal Republic was regarded by the East as a voluntary breakaway; it was answered a month later by the formation in the Soviet Occupation Zone of the German Democratic Republic *(Deutsche Demokratische Republik)*, described as sovereign, socialist and democratic and the 'first German Peace State'. Wilhelm Pieck became the first President; the national flag is black, red and gold with the State emblem in the centre field, a hammer and compasses surrounded by a wreath of grain around the lower part of which a black-red-gold band is wound. It is intended to signify the unity of action of all sections of the population.

Constitution

The original Constitution of the GDR was formulated by representatives of political parties and important organizations and was approved by the Third German People's Congress *(Volkskongress)*, a body elected on the single list system, in May 1949. Provisional organs of government were set up which adopted the Constitution as the basis of the newly founded Democratic Republic.

The wording of this constitution closely resembled that of the Weimar Constitution of the pre-Hitler era. Its meaning however differed considerably because of the re-definition of certain key words including 'democracy' and 'freedom'. According to Walter Ulbricht "the system of socialist democracy has the social function of forming the will of the whole society, in a form binding on everybody, in a uniform process with the creative co-operation of the citizens of the State, and to apply it in social practice." 'Freedom' as it is known in the West is condemned as impractical individualism; 'freedom' in Socialist terminology means "freedom in the interest of the people, the ability to participate fully in the building of Socialism, the need to put the common good before self-interest". In this light the freedom of the press, for example, guaranteed in the Constitution, is seen to be quite different from the freedom offered by the Constitution of the Federal Republic. In 1968 a new Constitution was adopted which, for example, further restricted the role of the Churches and abolished the right to strike. Amendments in 1974 altered the legal system and removed all mention of reunification as a constitutional objective.

The Government of the Democratic Republic is completely centralized. In order to accomplish the centralization, the

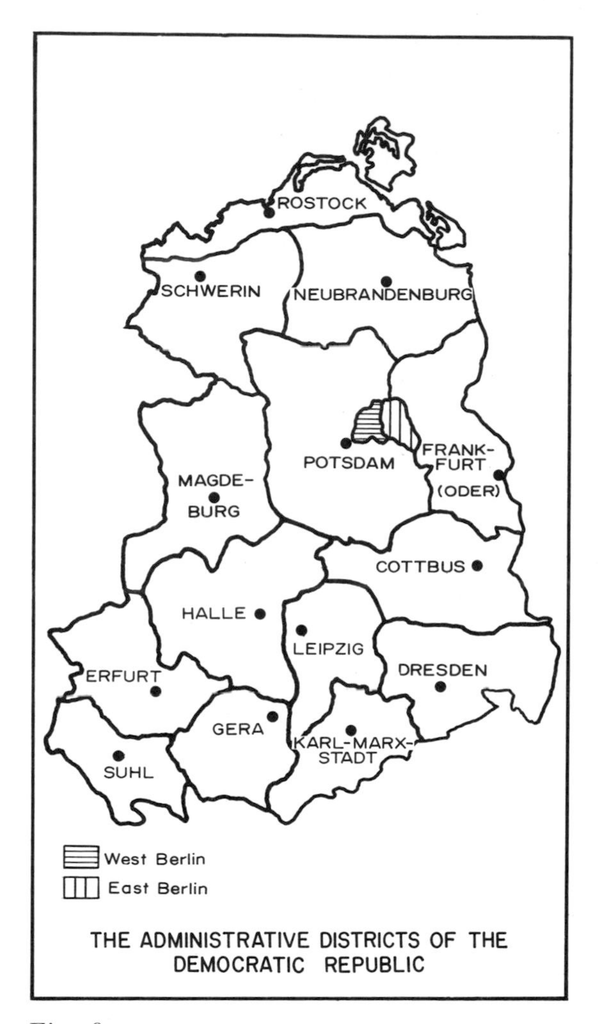

Fig 28

States which existed when the GDR was founded (Brandenburg, Mecklenburg, Saxony *(Sachsen)*, Thuringia *(Thüringen)*, and Saxon-Anhalt *(Sachsen-Anhalt)*) were abolished and their parliaments disbanded in 1952 when the country was divided into fourteen Districts *(Bezirke)*. The government thus also rid itself of the old second chamber *(Länderkammer)* which had similar powers to those of the *Bundesrat* in the Federal Republic. The District Assemblies *(Bezirkstage)* of the GDR are completely subordinate to the central government, whose plans and regulations they administer. The Districts are further subdivided into 217 urban and rural districts *(Kreise)*, each of which has its own local assembly *(Kreistag)*. All representative bodies are elected every four years in 'general, single-vote, secret and direct' elections from a single list of candidates.

From 1960 to 1973 Walter Ulbricht was the most powerful politician in the Democratic Republic. Before 1960 he had shared power with the President, Wilhelm Pieck, but when the latter died the opportunity was taken to alter the constitution. The post of President was abolished and his function replaced by a Council of State *(Staatsrat)*, composed of a Chairman, six Deputy Chairmen, sixteen members and a Secretary, all elected by the People's Chamber *(Volkskammer)* for a period of four years. Walter Ulbricht, First Secretary of the Socialist Unity Party, became Chairman of the Council of State. The Chairman and Secretary are the sole full-time members and so can steer the whole government machine. The Council exercises the usual functions of a Head of State and in addition issues directives to organs of local government and to the courts, interprets the Constitution and publishes laws. It also takes over the duties of the People's Chamber when this is not in session; resolutions of the Council of State have the force of law. In effect this body forms the actual government; it has reduced the powers of the Council of Ministers *(Ministerrat)*, which was given the responsibility of government by the original Constitution. In 1971 Erich Honecker became leader of the SED. When Ulbricht died in 1973 Willi Stoph became head of State. No one man any longer had absolute power.

The Council of Ministers has now become principally an executive organ responsible for carrying through decrees of the People's Chamber and the Council of State; its functions are usually carried out by a small committee of Ministers, the Presidium. It has several subordinate organizations, for example the State Planning Commission, the Agricultural Council of the GDR and the individual Ministries.

According to Article 50 of the Constitution the highest organ of power is the People's Chamber; it consists of 500 deputies as elected representatives of the people. There is a large proportion of women and young people. Most of the deputies belong to the Socialist Unity Party (SED), but other political, industrial and youth organizations are also represented. All the parties have identical policies and present a unified ('national') front; there is no official opposition.

The People's Chamber is not in permanent session, since the deputies each have a job of work outside politics. It has the power to pass laws, to see that they are carried out and to punish law-breakers; it exercises these functions by electing the members of the Council of State, endorsing the Council of Ministers and electing on the recommendation of the Council of State the Public Prosecutor, President, Vice-presidents and judges of the Supreme Court, all of whom are responsible to the People's Chamber. It also sets out directives for government policy, passes national economic plans and gives its approval to international treaties. Committees of experts advise the People's Chamber and prepare and draft all laws and decrees.

District and local assemblies take account of resolutions and directives issued by the central government and take the appropriate measure within their own sphere. Their decisions are binding on all the administrative bodies, organizations and citizens in the area.

The referendum is an important feature of political life in the Democratic Republic and has been used to make important alterations to the law. Resolutions put to the public are regularly approved by over 99% of the electorate.

Elections

Elections for all representative bodies are held every four years. Every citizen who has reached the age of eighteen may vote and may stand for election to local assemblies; at twenty-one he may be elected to the People's Chamber. Voting is compulsory. The Constitution states that every citizen has the right to vote and that this right to participate in decision-making is at the same time an obligation.

A single list of names is presented for the approval of the electorate, composed of candidates from the National Front and the Democratic Bloc and distributed amongst the parties according to a set pattern. Candidates may belong to a variety of parties, but as all the parties share a common policy there is no need for electioneering. It remains possible to indicate disapproval by spoiling one's voting paper or by voting against the official list, although there has recently been pressure to remove even this slight concession; the outcome of every election indicates that over 99% of votes cast support the official candidates. Elections are held in secret, but there is a growing movement amongst ardent supporters of the government to make them public.

Deputies elected to the People's Chamber continue their job of work; there are no professional politicians since they would have less contact with the working people.

Political Parties and other Organizations

A number of political parties exist in the GDR, united in effort under the leadership of the Socialist Unity Party (*Sozialistische Einheitspartei Deutschlands* or SED) in the Democratic Bloc. The permitted parties were founded in the years before the GDR came into existence; they are the DBD (*Demokratische Bauernpartei*—Democratic Peasants' Party), which mainly represents collective farmers, CDU (*Christlich-Demokratische Union*—Christian Democratic Union), representing Christians, LDPD (*Liberal-demokratische Partei*—Liberal Democratic Party), representing mainly craftsmen, small traders and members of the intelligentsia, and the NDPD (*Nationaldemokratische Partei*—National Democratic Party), which includes former supporters of the National Socialists amongst its members, and the above-mentioned SED, formed when the Social Democratic Party (SPD) and Communist Party (KPD) united. The DBD, CDU, LDPD and NDPD each hold 45 seats in the People's Chamber; the SED holds 111. The SED is described as the revolutionary fighting party of the working class, being founded on Leninist principles; it is led by the Central Committee (ZK), the nucleus of which is the *Politbüro*. The highest official organ is the Party Conference, which meets every four years. Also represented in local assemblies and the People's Chamber are the Confederation of Free German Trade Unions (FDGB), the Democratic Women's Federation of Germany (DFD), the Free German Youth (FDJ) and the German League of Culture (DKB). Other organizations with considerable political backing are the German-Soviet Friendship Society (DSF), the Society for Sport and Technology (GST), the Association of German Consumer Co-operatives, the Ernst Thälmann Pioneers and the artists', writers', journalists' and composers' unions.

The National Front unites all political parties and mass organizations in joint action for the development of a Communist society. The GDR described itself in 1957 as a People's Democracy, which was seen as a stage in the development towards a socialist and later Communist state. The GDR has been described since the new 1968 constitution as a German Socialist State; Communism remains a goal towards which all sections of the community are striving through the National Front. The political aims of the National Front are identical with those of the government.

Currency

Since 1968 the currency of the GDR has been the *Mark der Deutschen Demoktatischen Republik* (M, formerly MDN, *Mark der Deutschen Notenbank*). Officially it is exchanged for the West German mark (DM) at a parity of 1:1. Before tight currency controls were imposed the Black Market rate quoted 4 MDN to 1 DM; in this way the GDR lost vast sums of money, a loss which ceased in 1961 with the erection of the Berlin wall. The purchasing power of the East German mark compares unfavourably with that of the West German mark; the price of imported goods and luxuries (coffee, butter, chocolate, etc.) is high, whereas basic necessities (rye bread, sugar, milk, margarine) are relatively cheap.

The functions of the *Deutsche Notenbank* are to issue money, to give loans and credit to industry and to carry out all payments to and from foreign countries which derive from international trading. It acts as the State exchequer and is the only body in the GDR permitted to hold foreign currency and precious metals.

Policy

The leaders of the Democratic Republic have always insisted that there were two separate sovereign German States. They accordingly distinguish between German nationality *(Deutsche Staatsangehörigkeit)*, possessed by all citizens of both States, and citizenship of the GDR *(Staatsbürgerschaft der DDR)*. From the outset the GDR accepted the finality of the Potsdam Agreements and worked to persuade other countries to do the same. It was 1950 when she concluded a treaty with Poland in which the Oder-Neisse line was described as the permanent frontier between two friendly, peace-loving nations *(unantast-*

bare Friedens- und Freundschaftsgrenze).

At one time the GDR Government constantly abused the Federal leaders as 'militarists', 'fascists', 'capitalists', 'revanchists', 'imperialists' and 'neo-nazis'. Bonn's claim to represent the whole of Germany was taken to show her intention to invade the GDR and thus bring about nuclear war. The GDR accordingly fortified her frontier with West Germany. Even though relations between the two States are now more cordial, the defences remain unchanged. However, the GDR now allows more West Germans to cross this frontier in return for economic and trade concessions.

The Basic Treaty was a great landmark for the GDR because it gained her wide international recognition. Her industrial prowess increased her prestige still further. In these changed conditions the desire for reunification, once apparently so fervent, has faded. Reunification would only ever have been possible for the GDR under a uniform, and therefore Communist system. She could never have countenanced any form of federation. Reunification now seems to the GDR a supreme irrelevance; her future as an independent State is assured.

The government of the Democratic Republic insists that West Berlin shall remain quite separate from the Federal Republic, since it fears the use of West Berlin as a military bridgehead and a hotbed of espionage. It has suggested that West Berlin should become a Free City or that it should be incorporated into the Democratic Republic.

The Democratic Republic has received substantial financial aid from the Soviet Union; it is a member of the Council for Mutual Economic Assistance (Comecon) and of the Warsaw Pact, and pursues a policy of permanent friendship with the Soviet Union. It is now a member of the United Nations Organization.

The Legal System

The legal system is based on the political ideology of the government. The main criterion in the formulation and administration of the law is the amount of benefit to be derived by society from its provisions; the function of punishment is to reform the citizen so that he will be able to play a useful role in the socialist society. All punishments are recorded in the *Strafregister*; entries can however be erased after a period of satisfactory conduct. The death penalty is retained for serious crimes against the State, such as treason, which are tried with great publicity *(Schauprozesse)*. The interpretation of the Constitution and of other laws is therefore not fixed; it may be changed if it is considered that a change would benefit society. Political considerations are of extreme importance when the law is being interpreted; justice is said to be the will of the ruling class as enshrined in the law. A function of Trade Unions is to help shape the legal system.

A full-time judge presides over the courts aided by two lay judges appointed by District Assemblies to serve for four years. Only politically reliable citizens are appointed; they do not usually hold high legal qualifications although they may receive training after proving their worth in other professions. There are three types of court, and all judges serve in only one type. In passing sentence they follow the directives of the Supreme Court; where no precise directive exists, they are advised by inspectors from the Ministry of Justice. Anyone who feels that he has been unjustly treated by a judge may appeal to a committee of members of the same Assembly which appointed the judge.

Political and industrial offences are kept separate from each other and from other miscellaneous crimes. Minor offences may be dealt with by an 'arbitration commission' *(Schiedskommission)* meeting in a place of work or community centre in order to draw the attention of ordinary people to the law; irresponsible parents or the work-shy, for example, may be publicly rebuked and told to reform. Military courts have jurisdiction over the armed forces; they also try crimes such as espionage or sabotage alleged to have been committed against military personnel and installations. New criminal and civil codes introduced respectively in 1974 and 1976 were modelled on Soviet law.

The Law

It was the aim of the early governments of the GDR to create a Socialist society, and since the law was the main instrument at their disposal it could not be impartial. The detailed contents of the books of law are determined by the political objectives of the country's rulers; they contain elements such as the persecution of the remnants of the middle and upper classes ("Jedes Strafrecht hat Klassencharakter"). Acts liable to weaken the hold of Socialism on the population are described as 'crimes'. 'Incitement to boycott' includes taking Western newspapers into the GDR; 'sabotage' includes both the non-fulfilment of economic plans and the wilful damage or destruction of machinery. *'Republikflucht'* is the crime of leaving the GDR without permission, or aiding and abetting anyone to do so; this is punishable by up to three years' imprisonment, yet there were some two million offenders between 1952 and 1960. The Party (SED) also plays a considerable role in dealing with family troubles; official policy declares that it is pointless to attempt to perpetuate a family unit if it is no longer making a useful contribution to society. Divorces are granted on this principle, and neither partner is legally regarded as 'guilty'; a woman has no claim to be supported by her divorced husband.

All the citizens of the GDR are regarded as equal before the law. Women have been granted full equality of education and opportunity, and have largely been relieved of the burden of bringing up a family by the generous provision of day nurseries and play centres. They are expected to take an equal share of productive work and are widely employed in shipyards, mines, factories and on construction sites; they constitute 47% of the total work force. It has been made possible for a man to take a woman's surname when he marries her.

Everyone resident, even temporarily, in the GDR must at all times carry valid identity papers; this regulation is rigorously enforced. Close checks are kept on the movements of the population by the police; visits must be entered in a *Hausbuch*, kept in every block of flats by the warden *(Verwalter)*, and reported by him independently to the police.

The Armed Forces and the Police

When the Democratic Republic was founded, regulations were in force which prevented the country from raising an army, although there was no objection to the existence of a police force. The *Kasernierte Volkspolizei* was technically a company of police; it was, however, subject to military discipline and it was housed in barracks. In 1956 it was renamed 'People's Army' *(Nationale Volksarmee)*; a navy and an air force were created a little later. At first recruiting took place from the youth organization FDJ, whose members were persuaded that they had a moral obligation to serve their country. In 1962 an eighteen-month period of national service was formally introduced; conscientious objectors are given non-combatant duties. The defensive role of the armed forces is always stressed, especially in regard to the securing of national frontiers; the frontier guards *(Grenzpolizei)* are part of the army.

The police force is extensive and organized into several quite distinct branches. The *Volkspolizei* (People's Police) undertake the usual police duties; like the West German police they are armed. The Transport Police *(Transportpolizei)* supervise public transport and the travelling public. There is a large reserve force of police *(Bereitschaftspolizei)* composed of highly trained, politically trustworthy men kept in a state of constant readiness. Each factory has its own police force *(Betriebsschutz)* and emergency reserve *(Kampfgruppen)*; the latter carry out regular manoeuvres and can be armed in case of emergency such as social unrest. Their function is "to defend the achievements of the GDR". The political influence on police training cannot be over-emphasized; one of the functions of the force is to observe and report on unreliable elements within the population. In this they are helped by official 'auxiliaries' *(Volkspolizeihelfer)*, whose duties include checking identification papers and entries in the *Hausbuch* recording the names of visitors, and on attendance at political meetings. There exists also a secret police force *(Staatssicherheitsdienst)* of undisclosed strength.

The Social Structure

In the eastern part of Germany the class structure of society has been radically changed; whereas political power was formerly in the hands of the financially powerful, it is now wielded by an elite composed of ideologists and reliable Party workers. All the elements of the population are now drawn together by the slogan "Plan together, work together, govern together". The bourgeoisie has practically disappeared. *Beamte* were abolished in 1945 and renamed *Staatsfunktionäre*, losing with this change of name all the status and privileges to which *Beamte* had been entitled. The dominant class are the 'workers and peasants'; their children are chosen for higher education in preference to children of the middle classes and the intelligentsia.

Wages and salaries are linked to the productive value of

each job; most salaries are made up of basic pay, about 80% of the total, and bonuses for productivity. Salary levels are in general far below those in West Germany; the differential is greatest for white-collar workers, who earned in 1974 on average 820 M per month in the GDR and over 2400 DM in West Germany. For many years there was little competition to acquire consumer goods as status symbols since these were not easily available. As more were produced for the home market, ownership of cars and electrical goods increased dramatically, despite their relatively high price. Choice is still limited; there are no luxury homes or sleek cars available.

Youth

The GDR has invested vast sums of money in its youth, recognizing that young people are the citizens of tomorrow. They are given excellent opportunities and facilities to develop educationally, physically and politically. Their environment is closely controlled so as to avoid any exposure to 'undesirable' influences. Their parents, their school and the State (through the FDJ) co-operate to ensure that they behave responsibly and pass their time profitably.

The 'Free German Youth' *(Freie Deutsche Jugend,* FDJ) is the only permitted youth organization; children aged between 10 and 14 belong to its junior section, the 'Thälmann Pioneers'. The FDJ is represented in the government and has heavy political backing. Membership is expected of all young

East Berlin: Members of the FDJ at a demonstration in the Marx-Engels Platz

people between the ages of 14 and 25. One of its functions is to prepare its members for the *Jugendweihe* (see p. 202).

The organization of Labour

The right to work has been said by the leaders of the GDR to be the main basic right of every citizen, but the Constitution points out that everyone also has the duty to work. The workers have the right to participate in the planning, organization and management of industry; a constant flow of propaganda in the press and on radio encourages the workers to help increase productivity by any means compatible with official policy, since the country is heavily dependent on its industrial output. 'Norms' (standard working capacities) are set for each industry and each process; the norm is worked out as the mid-point between the output of an enthusiastic and of an average worker. An element of competition has had to be introduced to offer incentives and rewards to individuals and to groups who exceed their norm; an outstanding worker will receive the title 'Worker Hero' *(Held der Arbeit)*, together with a large sum of money.

"The free German trade unions, united in the Confederation of Free German Trade Unions *(Freier Deutscher Gewerkschaftsbund)* are the all-embracing class organization of workers, office employees and members of the socialist intelligentsia", according to Article 43 of the Constitution. The unions' role is to safeguard the personal, material and cultural interests of the workers; they enforce the 'Socialist Labour Code' and the workers' right of participation in industrial planning, they safeguard the principle of equal pay for equal work and the workers' right to leisure time and recreation. They also run the social insurance scheme (see below). The health service of the FDGB *(Gesundheitsdienst)* has the right to allocate all places at spas and seaside resorts. The unions play no part in negotiating salaries or conditions, which are regulated by law. They do, however, negotiate on the working and living conditions of the people. They have no right to call the workers out on strike; the revised Constitution of 1968 abolished strikes, declaring that since industry is owned by the people, they would in effect be striking against themselves. Trade union appointments must be approved by the leaders of the Socialist Unity Party; in this way close political control is maintained over the working force.

All the workers in any enterprise belong to the same union. Union congresses and meetings are frequently held; the Congress of the whole Confederation meets at least every four years. Membership of a trade union brings many benefits including travel concessions for the annual holiday; the unions run cruises, holiday homes and camping sites, 245 in all.

Finance

The government of the Democratic Republic does not publish detailed information about its finances, taxation system and economy. Statements made by former citizens point to the fact that taxation has been used as a political instrument to eliminate private enterprise by demanding the surrender of almost all the annual profit. Corresponding concessions are made to co-operatives and nationalized undertakings.

The Social Services

The trade union movement administers the social insurance scheme, which includes sickness, accident and old-age benefits. All production and office workers are compulsorily insured, paying 10% of their gross earnings up to a maximum of 60 Marks per month. Students are automatically insured free of charge.

There is a completely integrated health service with extensive facilities for preventive medicine. All treatment and medicines, even those available in sanatoria and spas, which have retained their popularity, are free of charge. The State makes efficient use of its medical personnel and facilities by running 'Polyclinics' *(Polikliniken)*, which give both initial consultations with a non-specialist doctor and specialized treatment to out-patients in every branch of medicine including dentistry. A dispensary is attached to each clinic. Whenever necessary, cases may be referred direct from the clinic to the local hospital of which the clinic is a branch.

The Churches

The revised 1968 Constitution requires the Churches to "arrange and carry on their affairs and their activities in conformity with the Constitution and the legal regulations of the GDR". State protection for the Church is abolished although freedom of conscience and religion for individual citizens is retained. Church activities are limited by the regulation requiring that permission for each service or other meeting must be obtained in advance.

Half the people belong to the Evangelical Church; 20 years ago membership was 80%. Once there were close links with the Protestant Churches of the Federal Republic. Now only the system of linking an individual church with one in the Federal Republic is allowed to continue.

The position of the Roman Catholic minority has been particularly difficult, since their dogmatic belief is completely irreconcilable with the politics of the GDR. Whilst religious houses and indeed the priesthood itself have not been abolished, it is virtually impossible for them to find new recruits.

Even the welfare role of the Churches has been restricted; to a great extent it was made superfluous by the extensive social services provided by the State, but the churches were willing to provide additional services of many kinds. Church activities have had to be curtailed because of the lack of money; once the State gave funds and subsidies to the churches, but these were discontinued and the churches' powers to collect money were limited.

Every opportunity is taken to persuade the population to abandon Christianity. Religious instruction has been removed from the school curriculum, Christian festivals are reviled and new rites substituted for the Christian sacraments of baptism, confirmation, marriage and burial. Baptism has become *Namensweihe*, or 'name-giving ceremony', at which the child is accepted into the Socialist society. Confirmation has been replaced by *Jugendweihe*, which takes place when the child leaves school and enters "active social life", usually at the age of fourteen. The child must swear "to work and fight for Socialism, to revere the revolutionary heritage of the nation, to co-operate at all times with one's comrades and always to combine personal happiness with the struggle for the happiness of the whole people". 'Socialist marriage' takes place after the ceremony held in the registry office, usually in the place of work of one of the partners, and includes a promise that the couple will work together to strengthen the Socialist worker-and-peasant State. Politics are even introduced in graveside speeches at a 'Socialist burial'.

Jugendweihe: Participants are congratulated after the ceremony by Young Pioneers

Participation in these ceremonies, especially *Jugendweihe*, has become expected of the people. A refusal can result in disadvantages, such as the non-fulfilment of the condition of political maturity required of all candidates for university education.

The Mass Media

The Constitution states that "Every citizen of the GDR has the right to express publicly and freely his opinion in accordance with the spirit and aims of this Constitution". This does not mean that there is freedom of speech as it is known in the Western World, since 'freedom' is a quite different concept in the Democratic Republic. Walter Ulbricht once said, "Freedom in the interest of the press is with us a freedom in the interest of the people and not a privilege for the arbitrariness of press trusts . . . against the people, against peace, against international understanding and humanism". 'In the interests of the people,' the SED tells editors which items to stress and which to play down. There is no formal censorship. Every opportunity is taken to attack capitalist press tycoons, especially the West German Axel Springer. There is no sensational popular press.

The press is controlled by the *Presseamt*, a department of the government which grants, generally to political parties and organizations, the licences to publish newspapers. The *Berliner Zeitung* and *Berliner Zeitung am Abend* are however published in East Berlin by publicly owned companies. Seven party newspapers are printed in East Berlin, including the SED's organ *Neues Deutschland*. There are altogether some 40 daily newspapers and almost 30 weeklies; there are many magazines of all types, some of which are of extremely high quality. Some eight million daily papers are sold.

Besides the state-controlled broadcasting network which covers the whole of the GDR, there are two stations transmitting programmes for listeners outside the country; they are *Radio Berlin International* and the *Deutschlandsender*. Since 1956 there has been a regular television service *Fernsehen der DDR*; there are two channels which transmit only partly in colour (Secam). The GDR belongs to the eastern European International Organization of Broadcasting Companies (OIRT) with whom it shares many programmes.

Extensive use is made of broadcasting facilities and newspapers to publicize the 'official' line on public affairs. The State exercises complete control over the editorial function of the press. The State-controlled news agency ADN *(Allgemeiner Deutscher Nachrichtendienst)* decides what news will be published and in what form. Only those items are published which "convince the reader of the rightness of the policies of the government". Besides long editorials, selected foreign news items, reports of industrial successes, transcripts of speeches, official notices and appeals, local news, cultural reports and readers' letters make up the content of all newspapers. Both the press and the radio are used to exhort the people to greater productivity and to arouse a feeling of national pride. A common feature of all reporting is the repetition of emotionally or politically charged phrases; common abusive terms for the Federal Government include 'militarists', 'capitalists', 'revanchists' and 'neo-nazis'.

In the towns of the GDR slogans ('Plan together, work together, govern together.' 'Onwards to the victory of Socialism!') are often posted in large letters in conspicuous places. They invariably hammer home some aspect of the government's ideology and political programme. Other types of poster which are highly critical of the West German government are also common.

4. The Iron Curtain

When Germany was originally divided amongst the Occupying Powers it was intended that the arrangement should be temporary. The demarcation lines between the British, French and American zones were abolished by 1953, but the 1,376 km. long western border of the Soviet zone has been transformed into the so-called Iron Curtain. It began to exist physically in 1946 when its route was marked by a barbed-wire fence, on the eastern side of which all the undergrowth was cleared. This fence was closely guarded at first by Russian army units and from 1948 by East German police. Gradually the structure was strengthened so that by 1952 the demarcation line had become virtually impenetrable. A 10-metre wide strip of land on the eastern side of the fence was kept freshly harrowed; all movement in the area within three-quarters of a mile from the border was forbidden during the hours of darkness and public meetings were banned. Most of the 32 railway lines and all the 31 main roads were cut, although three motorways remained open. In 1956 the line was first described as a 'national frontier' *(Staatsgrenze)* by the government of the Democratic Republic; the Federal Republic refused to accept this description, preferring the term 'zone border' *(Zonengrenze)*. Since 1961 the defences on the eastern side have been still further reinforced; buildings in which people might hide were demolished and observation was intensified. There are sophisticated devices such as tripwires combined with flares or teargas mines, electric fences and deep, concrete-lined ditches; the whole is guarded by patrols helped by dogs and, on isolated stretches, by helicopters. In an emergency, roads near the frontier can be blocked by carts laden with stones, held in readiness on specially prepared ramps by the roadside. Strict regulations on the movement of people are in force for some three miles behind the actual frontier; farmwork may only be undertaken during daylight hours and vehicular access is strictly limited. The special permits needed to enter the border area are only given to people who are not security risks. Despite all these precautions, attempts are still made to cross into West Germany; incredibly, some are successful. Meanwhile it is still possible from the western side to walk up to the original fence without being challenged by the West German border guards *(Bundesgrenzschutz)*, who unobtrusively patrol its whole length.

A much more concentrated type of defence was possible in Berlin, where the whole frontier has since 1961 been sealed by a closely guarded and fortified wall, consisting of concrete blocks over a yard thick in places. On the eastern side there is the usual cleared strip reinforced with mines, trip-wires, tank traps and barbed wire entanglements; there are guard dogs on long leads and batteries of searchlights. Additional precautions prevent escape over the rooftops and under water. Sentries are posted on both sides of the wall. They are armed and provided with powerful binoculars and two-way radio; they spend much of the time staring impassively at each other. The East German sentries are posted in pairs and are never allowed to remain together for more than one period of duty. The guards are most numerous at sensitive points such as the Brandenburg Gate and 'Checkpoint Charlie'. All the defences in Berlin are estimated by Western sources to have cost over 20 million DM.

Many visitors come to stare over the wall from platforms erected on the western side. Important official visitors to West Berlin are taken to the bullet-proof observation box near the Brandenburg Gate. Some of the platforms have been answered by baffles erected on the eastern side to prevent unwanted viewing. On both sides of the wall immense posters proclaim the policies of the respective governments; news headlines are flashed into East Berlin on banks of electric lights. At various points on the western side simple but poignant memorials mark the places where some of the people died who tried to cross the wall.

Together with the West Berliners, who may now visit the East, large numbers of other visitors go through the wall each year. 'Checkpoint Charlie' in the Friedrichstraße is the busiest crossing point. Vehicular traffic must pass through an extremely narrow gap in the wall and negotiate a series of obstacles erected to prevent cars accelerating past the guards. All vehicles are carefully checked on the eastern side to make sure they have no modifications which would enable them to secrete an illegal traveller. Rigorous checks of luggage and personal papers ensure that no forbidden objects or seditious literature enter or leave the East; all printed matter, however trivial, is liable to be confiscated when the temperature of the Cold War rises.

The Berlin wall is more than just a monstrosity; it has become symbolic of a divided Germany. The purpose it serves depends on the side from which it is viewed (see p. 209).

East Berlin: American jeeps passing through 'Checkpoint Charlie'

From the East it is seen as " . . . the anti-fascist protective wall along the GDR State Frontier with West Berlin." From the West it is seen as "a wall of shame, built by Ulbricht around his concentration camp."

5. The Situation Now

There are now two separate German States, and German territory is generally agreed to end at the Oder-Neisse line. The two German States are aligned with different power blocks, who themselves are at loggerheads; politically and socially, the two Germanies are totally incompatible. In West Germany there is an underlying sense of injustice at the division of Germany, especially at the restrictions on travel and communications with the East. Although there is some lip-service paid to the idea of reunification, it is doubtful if the majority of West Germans wish for a united Germany since it would reduce their standard of living and might even lead to a Communist State. Even some of the most ardent supporters of reunification—namely refugees from the eastern provinces—

privately express their unwillingness to leave the affluence of West Germany to endure the hardships of returning to recolonize the area.

Reunification is still part of the long-term policy of the Federal Government, though it is no longer the burning issue it was before about 1970. Even the CDU, once ardent advocates of reunification, are now prepared to consider alternatives in order not to jeopardize advantages gained by the SPD's *Ostpolitik*. In the GDR, however, reunification is no longer mentioned as a constitutional aim, and the Government would never allow the idea to become a rallying point for popular sentiment.

The extent of German territory has now been widely agreed internationally. The status of Berlin, in particular West Berlin, remains unsatisfactory, yet no plan for its future has so far proved acceptable to all the governments involved. It is in many ways a forgotten city, with an ageing population, its economy kept alive by huge West German subsidies. The Western Allies are still committed to defend its freedom.

Reunification looks at the moment a hopeless cause; it would only ever be accepted by either side on terms quite unacceptable to the other. Reporting in one part of Germany about current issues in the other is rarely objective and often amounts to sheer propaganda.

We in the West are apt to forget that there is another side to this problem, since we are as much caught in the western propaganda net as the citizens of eastern Europe are in a propaganda net of a different type. Let us therefore permit the respective governments to put their own point of view about two incidents, the workers' rising in East Berlin on June 17th, 1953 and the erection of the Berlin wall on August 13th, 1961.

June 17th, 1953

Reactionary elements start a fascist putsch attempt which had been prepared a long time in advance from West Germany and West Berlin to overthrow the workers' and farmers' power in the GDR . . . . The attempted riot collapses within a few hours because it was rejected by the great majority of the population. (From *GDR. A chronological table 1945–1965*, Verlag Zeit im Bild, Dresden).

After years of repression, exploitation and terror the working people rose up against their Soviet overlords and demanded the restoration of human rights . . . . The Soviet authorities, taken unawares by the uprising, succeeded in restoring the situation only with the use of extreme force. (Konrad Adenauer in a speech to the Bundestag on July 1st, 1953).

August 13th, 1961

In agreement with the Warsaw Treaty States a reliable guard and an effective control are established at the frontiers between the GDR and West Germany and the frontier with West Berlin such as are customary at the frontiers of all sovereign states. (From *GDR. A chronological table*).

The government of the Soviet Zone, controlled by the SED, erected the wall in order to impede personal, intellectual and factual contact between its vassals and the Western World. . . . Without any doubt the wall is a witness to the poverty of the Communist world. (*Berliner Begleiter*, Freideutscher Kreis, Berlin).

V Education in Germany

Between 1648 and 1933 education in Germany was the responsibility of each individual State. Even the foundation of the German Empire in 1871 did not bring a uniform education system; the standard of teaching varied, as did the curriculum and even the extent of compulsory schooling. 1933 brought a complete change; education came firmly under the control of a central government which used it as a means of spreading propaganda.

From mid-1945 education was organized by the Allies, first according to Zones of Occupation, then according to States or towns. The immediate aim was to 'de-nazify' the schools, and to do this much material from Russia, Britain and America was used. Reading matter was carefully selected and censored. There was a shortage of male teachers caused by the war and its after-effects, and schools had to function on a shift system because of the lack of suitable buildings. As time passed the education services of the Soviet Zone and of the Zones administered by the Western Allies developed along separate and quite distinct lines because of their differing aims and political beliefs.

Education in the Federal Republic

Decentralization of education was favoured after the experiences of 1933–45, since no one political party is likely to be able to exercise undue influence over the whole system. The Basic Law *(Grundgesetz)* of the Federal Republic states that each State *(Land)* is responsible for providing and administering its own education service. The one subject in which the States are obliged to provide instruction is religious education, although children are not obliged to attend these lessons if their parents prefer to withdraw them. Primary and secondary education services are free of charge, although most States do not provide books and materials. The right of all parents to choose the type of education that their children shall receive is also safeguarded, since provision is made in each State for the recognition of both private and denominational schools. However there are relatively few private schools, so that the choice between public and private education may in fact be unavailable in some areas without considerable difficulties for the parents.

Each State has a Ministry of Education *(Kultusministerium)* headed by the *Kultusminister*. The Standing Conference of Education Ministers *(Ständige Konferenz der Kultusminister der Länder)* in Bonn was until 1969 the only central organization. It tries to ensure a certain uniformity, but variations nevertheless occur; until 1966, for example, the States did not even share a common school year—some started in spring, some in the autumn. Even now teachers' salaries vary by as much as £10 per month, there are differing ages for transfer from primary to secondary education, differing syllabuses and differing regulations governing the training of teachers. This confusion creates enormous difficulties; children moving to another State are frequently at a disadvantage, and despite the shortage, many teachers find that their qualifications are unacceptable in another State. In an attempt to unify the education system, a Federal Ministry for Education and Science was created in 1969, but it can only make recommendations to the States.

Each State Ministry of Education determines all aspects of educational policy in the whole State and carries responsibility for the appointment and certification of teachers and for determining the standard of examinations. The State prescribes a standard syllabus for each subject together with a list of textbooks from which the teacher may make his selection, but examinations, the in-service training of teachers and the administration of junior schools are all controlled at local level. There are in Germany few kindergartens. Those that do exist are usually run privately and charge fees, although they are closely controlled by the State and may only employ fully qualified staff. As from 1971 however, a year of pre-school education has been compulsory in Schleswig-Holstein.

Primary Schools. Compulsory full-time education starts with the first new school year after a child reaches his sixth birthday; if a child is declared to be ready for school *(schulreif)* after being given a suitable test he may be admitted at the beginning of the year when his sixth birthday will fall. Very occasionally children are deferred until they are seven, in which case they may be placed in a *Schulkindergarten* to

Children at a primary school waiting to go back to their classrooms after the morning break

help them to adjust to the discipline of education. Formal education begins in the *Grundschule* or Primary School, which is the lower level of the *Volksschule*. Even the smallest children are given regular homework, which they do in the afternoons or evenings; normal school hours for all age groups extend from 8 a.m. (7 a.m. in some places during the summer months) to 1 p.m., including Saturdays. However the young children rarely have enough lessons to fill the whole of this period; in their first week they may have only an hour's school each day, and later they may begin as late as 10.00 or 11.00, or come home at 11.00 or 12.00 on several days. Saturday school rarely extends beyond noon.

Junior schooling lasts for four years except in West Berlin, Hamburg and Bremen, where it is six years; it is common to all children, and the schools are coeducational. The curriculum particularly emphasizes German and Mathematics, whereas little importance is attached to physical exercise and free expression. One of the most striking aspects of the first year syllabus is the teaching of longhand writing (instead of printing) and the use by even the youngest children of pen and ink.

From the outset great importance is attached to academic attainment; the system of marking is standard throughout the country and applies to all types of school. Marks range downwards from 1 to 6; 1 is very good *(sehr gut)*, 2 is good *(gut)*, 3 is satisfactory *(befriedigend)*, 4 is acceptable *(ausreichend)*, 5 is deficient *(mangelhaft)* and 6 is unsatisfactory *(ungenügend)*. Monthly tests are given in each subject, the results officially recorded and averaged at the end of term; the final term mark may however be slightly altered at the teacher's discretion. In order to qualify for promotion to a higher class at the end of the year, a pupil must achieve satisfactory marks. If during the year it seems likely that he will not do so, his parents will be warned by a 'blue letter' *(Blauer Brief)* that his transfer is endangered. Such a letter is dreaded by most parents, who regard it as a social stigma to be concealed if at all possible. Failures repeat the year in the same class; a pupil who fails for a second time is transferred to another school. A failure during the first four years of schooling automatically disqualifies a child from entry to a Grammar School *(Gymnasium)*.

Secondary Schools. Methods of transfer to a secondary school vary from State to State, but usually take into account the child's performance in school and the parents' wishes; many working class parents, for example, refuse to send their children to a *Gymnasium*. There is frequently a short trial period in a *Gymnasium* for borderline cases to allow the teachers to form an opinion of the child's potential.

Almost three quarters of all children transfer to the upper level of the *Volksschule*, or *Hauptschule*, where they stay for at least five years. The curriculum concentrates on providing a sound education in all the basic subjects and includes one foreign language, usually English. At the end of the course a leaving certificate *(Schulabgangszeugnis)* may be granted.

About a tenth of all pupils go to a *Mittelschule* or *Realschule* for a course lasting six years leading to a leaving certificate *(Mittlere Reife)* roughly equivalent to G.C.E. 'O' level, but in all the subjects in the curriculum, from German and Mathematics to Music and Sport. After leaving the *Mittelschule* most children enter business or industry; a few transfer to a type of *Gymnasium* known as the *Aufbauschule* or *Aufbaugymnasium*.

The *Gymnasium* is the most demanding type of secondary school. There are three distinct forms, agreed by the States: the *Altsprachliches Gymnasium* specializes in Latin and Greek, the *Neusprachliches Gymnasium* in modern languages and the *Mathematisch-Naturwissenschaftliches Gymnasium* in science

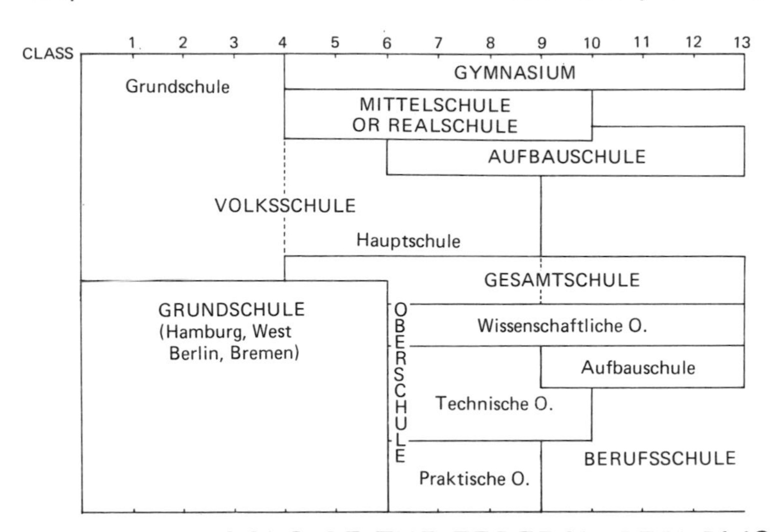

THE SCHOOLS OF THE FEDERAL REPUBLIC

Fig 29

and more practical subjects. It provides a nine-year course leading to the *Abitur,* the university entrance qualification and a pre-requisite for most professions, which is roughly equivalent to G.C.E. 'A' level. The provision of comprehensive education is not a basic political aim and progress towards it is slow, though Comprehensive schools *(Gesamtschulen)* now exist throughout Germany. Such schools are always carefully planned, purpose-built and generously equipped, yet ambitious parents are often reluctant to place their children there, in case the *Abitur* they get is later rated lower than the traditional *Gymnasium Abitur*.

Reform of the *Abitur* examination has begun; hitherto a candidate has had to perform adequately in subjects ranging from German and English, Science, Mathematics, History and Geography to Music, Art and Sport. He has also had to master Latin and Greek, or French, depending on the type of *Gymnasium* he has attended. This vast curriculum has been severely criticized because it leaves little time for independent thought; also many pupils need private coaching *(Nachhilfestunden)* in their weaker subjects to make sure of this vital qualification. As yet however there has been no agreement about which subjects to drop, although in some States the burden has been lightened to eight examination subjects, of which Social Science *(Gemeinschaftskunde)*, Sport and Music or Art are compulsory. The remaining subjects vary according to the type of school, German and Mathematics being common to all. The Federal Education Ministry has recommended reducing still further the number of subjects; it is hoped sometime to standardize the content of each course nationwide. A new examination, taken at 16, *Abitur I*, is in use in some States; for it all secondary pupils study a common syllabus and success in it qualifies them to study for *Abitur II* at 18 or 19.

The *Abitur* result is arrived at in three stages, in each of which a candidate must gain a third of the maximum possible marks. His basic subjects *(Grundkurse)* and examinations subjects *(Leistungskurse)* are tested at intervals throughout the year, and the marks averaged. Written examinations then follow, with a subsequent oral for candidates whose classwork and examination show an unexpected discrepancy. The written examinations are set by the *Oberschulrat*, who combines the functions of Director of Education, Chief Inspector and Chief Examiner, from questions submitted by the candidates' teachers. The examination is taken and marked in school and is then moderated by the *Oberschulrat*. The oral examination, conducted by the subject-teacher, can be rather daunting, as the whole staff and the *Oberschulrat* may be present. As the competition for university places increases, the importance of gaining high marks in the *Abitur* cannot be overemphasized. Students are constantly under considerable pressure both at home and at school, and some performances will undoubtedly suffer as a result.

The examination is usually followed by a Grand Ball *(Abiturientenball)*, attended by pupils, parents and staff. By far the majority (something like 80%) of these school leavers go on to some form of higher education.

Other types of secondary school cater for specialized interests or for pupils with special needs such as those with a physical or mental handicap *(Sonderschule* or *Hilfsschule)*.

1. The *Frauenoberschule* specializes in domestic subjects up to *Abitur* level; this qualifies girls to enter university to study a limited range of subjects.
2. The *Wirtschaftsoberschule* specializes in commercial subjects; the *Abitur* has again only limited recognition.
3. The *Einheitsschule* (multi-lateral school), also known as *Kombinatschule*, embraces all types of secondary education under one roof, usually in well defined streams, which

approximate to the *Gymnasium, Mittelschule* and *Volksschule* of other areas. Bremen and Hamburg have established many of these schools and isolated experiments are being conducted in other States.

4. *Bekenntnisschulen* or *Konfessionsschulen* (denominational schools) are preferred in districts where the majority of the population are devout members of the Roman Catholic Church, such as the Saar, North-Rhine Westphalia and Rhineland-Palatinate. Baden-Württemberg and Bavaria decided in 1967 and 1968 respectively to abolish their denominational schools and to provide non-denominational schools *(Gemeinschaftsschulen)* for all pupils.

5. Private boarding schools take more than a tenth of the pupils completing their primary education. Often these schools stress certain aspects of education such as the development of character; many follow the *Gymnasium* curriculum, often with small classes of children not accepted by a public *Gymnasium*.

In each case the syllabus and staff must be approved by the State's Ministry of Education.

All schools have certain things in common. The choice of clothes is left to the individual; no uniform is worn. School begins with registration in the first lesson; there is no assembly. There is a long mid-morning break when pupils eat sandwiches *(zweites Frühstück)*; no meals are provided in school since lessons always end by early afternoon. Every pupil is under pressure to do well; a complete record of his academic performance, his absences, misdeeds etc. is kept by the teacher, who is also his examiner. Nevertheless the atmosphere in the classroom is often happy and relaxed; no corporal punishment is allowed. The teacher is able to observe his charges both in and out of school, since a monthly outing and an annual long trip *(Klassenfahrt)* are usually compulsory. He will also accompany his class on any journey to the *Schullandheim*, a hostel where education in community living and outdoor activities are cultivated alongside book-learning. The classes in a German school have a great sense of unity. It is usual for a whole class (coeducational in most schools) to attend a ballroom dancing class; in later years class reunions play an unexpectedly large role in social life.

Any requests, or on occasion complaints, from a class are put to the teacher by an elected member of the class, the *Klassensprecher*. Little responsibility is given to pupils in the upper classes; prefects in the British sense are unknown. The idea of a School Council *(Schülermitverwaltung)* has been introduced in some schools, but since the scope of such a council is limited by the inflexible education system, the scheme has had little success. An important part of every school is the Parent-Teacher Association *(Elternbeirat)*, which has several functions. It aims to foster cooperation between parents and teachers and provides the parents with opportunities of discussing their child's progress. Teaching methods and aims are explained to the parents, who are allowed to make suggestions about certain aspects of school life. In addition to these regular meetings teachers have the right to summon parents to school as and when difficulties occur.

Regional variations on the outlined educational system are legion. Bremen, Hamburg and West Berlin provide a six-year basic education in the *Grundschule* to delay selection for secondary education, but this plan has not proved popular with parents since they feel that it does not suit gifted children. In Lower Saxony the first two years of secondary education are now seen as a trial period *(Orientierungsstufe)*. On the whole parents dislike the idea because of the constant testing, which never permits the children an 'off-day'. Some places have introduced wholeday school *(Ganztagsschule)*, in which afternoon classes during the week replace Saturday morning school. The *Aufbauschule* which caters for late developers who transfer at 13 plus and who wish to study for *Mittlere Reife* is common in the agricultural regions of southern Germany; those serving particularly scattered communities are boarding schools. In 1964 the *Hauptschule* was introduced to replace a number of small, inefficient village schools; instruction is given by specialist rather than class teachers. It is hoped that this type of school will increase the flow of candidates for *Abitur*, which in the rural areas of southern Germany was 30% below the national average.

In 1959 it was agreed in principle that all the State educational systems should conform to a basic plan *(Rahmenplan)*, which envisaged a four-year course in the *Grundschule* followed by a two-year period of orientation. Parallel types of school would then cater for all pupils up to the age of sixteen. Very little of this plan has in fact been implemented. In 1969 a Federal Education Ministry was established to try to alleviate the general "catastrophic state of education" *(Bildungsnotstand)*, but even its national plan is not being adopted with alacrity by all the States.

Vocational and Technical Training. Vocational training until the age of 18 has been compulsory for 50 years for all children not in full-time education. The schools which supply this training *(Berufsschulen)* give wide-ranging courses to groups of apprentices in allied trades; the aim is not only to impart specialized knowledge, but to continue a general education. One State gives as its aim "to educate students to be morally valuable members of society, filled with a love for their professional activities and conscious of their responsibilities as citizens of a democratic state". The courses at a *Berufsschule* are available to apprentices for six to twelve hours each week, so the major part of practical training is carried out by industry and commerce.

The standards of apprenticeship training are agreed nationally, and the courses are closely controlled. At the moment there are some 700 recognized branches of industry and commerce for which apprentices may train; recognition is agreed by industry and by the government. The premises and facilities of firms wishing to employ apprentices are inspected to see if they conform to national standards; only then will an apprenticeship be officially registered. Periodic checks are made to ensure that the apprentices are in fact being taught properly. The curriculum for each apprenticeship is required to be wide, so that later specialization or re-training is eased. Despite all the safeguards, however, industrial training has been found to be inefficient, and reform is thought to be essential.

Eighty-five per cent of all apprentices in the Federal Republic choose this form of training. For those who come from a *Volksschule* the apprenticeship lasts 3½ years; attendance at a *Mittelschule* or a *Berufsfachschule* may shorten this period. A *Berufsfachschule* provides full-time training in certain professions. There are three main types of course covering office and business studies, 'womens' subjects' and engineering. There are also specialist schools for music, acting, dancing, violin-making, etc.

Talented apprentices may transfer either during or after their apprenticeship to a *Berufsaufbauschule*. 3½ years' study enables a school leaver to reach the standard of entry to a *Fachschule, Wirtschaftsfachschule* or a Technical Institute. The *Fachschulen* of all kinds provide training, refresher courses and a general education for people with professional training and experience. From the *Fachschule* it is possible to proceed to a university; this is known as the 'second method of obtaining higher education' *(zweiter Bildungsweg)* and gives valuable opportunities to those who failed to gain entry to a *Gymnasium*. Pressure on university places has lately devalued this route to higher education.

University Education. The traditional pattern of German university education is based on the ideas of Wilhelm von Humboldt (1767–1835). He suggested four principles: the unity of all knowledge, the duty to educate rather than train, the unity of teaching and research and the necessity for academic freedom, meaning that professors should be free to teach whatever they liked and that students should be free to study whatever and however they chose. The older West German universities still pay lip service to these principles, which are however being eroded by changing circumstances. Knowledge has advanced so far that specialization is inevitable. The modern student is not usually concerned with education in the broad sense; he prefers to acquire such knowledge as will be useful to him in his future career. The pressure of numbers makes the students' participation in their professors' research quite out of the question; nowadays much research is in any case undertaken outside the university. Academic freedom has come to be regarded as a mixed blessing, for it has created many of the problems with which the German universities are now faced. The newer universities have departed from some of these traditions; some have even sacrificed the sacred cow of academic freedom in favour of planned courses.

There are (1976) 54 institutions with university status in the Federal Republic. These include Technical Universities *(Technische Hochschulen)* and Institutes of Higher Education now called *Gesamthochschulen*, as well as the traditional university *(Universität)*. There have been 13 new foundations since 1970. The largest university is Munich which has over 32,000 students. Universities are all self-governing, being administered by a Senate, but they remain under the supervision of the State Ministry of Education which finances them. In 1969 some State governments departed from the tradition of university independence by taking powers to compel universities to discipline unruly students. The State sets the qualifying examination for the professions *(Staatsexamen)*, which is, however, administered by the university. As from 1969 student representation on all university committees has been compulsory; on some appointment committees students occupy a third of the seats.

Until 1973 everyone holding an *Abitur* was allowed to attend a university; now students must apply for a university place via a clearing house *(Zentralstelle)* in Dortmund. Some courses, notably medicine, require very high marks, since laboratory space is limited; universities can turn students away if courses are full *(numerus clausus)*. Such is the demand for some subjects that even outstanding students with an average mark of 1·8 in *Abitur* are having all three permitted applications rejected. A student entering university will probably be bewildered by the complete freedom he enjoys, which is in stark contrast to the discipline of school. He is free to choose his own course and to decide how long he will study. The professors are equally free to teach what they please; they publish details of the lectures and seminars they intend to give, from which the student makes his selection. His choice is recorded in a *Studienbuch*, a document which later must be produced as proof of attendance at a minimum number of lectures and seminars. Theoretically the book should be signed at the end of each lecture, but because of the pressure of numbers they are usually signed by the lecturer once a term. All the lectures and seminars entered in the *Studienbuch* must be paid for; nevertheless there is a tendency amongst all new students to overload themselves with work, which only adds to the chronic overcrowding of lecture theatres. Lectures are the chief means of instruction; they are given by full-time members of the university staff and are in general interrupted only by applause, signified by banging on desks, or disapproval, shown by a scraping of feet on the floor. Seminars provide students with the opportunity of discussion with their teachers or of practising their newly acquired skills; although numbers are frequently restricted by admitting only the students who enrol early, seminars often prove so large that the majority of students cannot hope to attract the teacher's attention. In general there are no intermediate examinations, so students must present a minimum number of satisfactory pieces of work *(Seminararbeiten)* before being admitted to the final examination *(Staatsexamen)*. The Medical Faculties however have for many years had compulsory intermediate examinations *(Vorphysikum* and *Physikum)*, and many scientific faculties are now following suit. For most students the goal is the *Staatsexamen*, which is not an academic degree, but is sufficient to qualify the holder for entry into many professions, such as teaching. The only academic degrees are diplomas, M.A. *(Magister Artium)*, and the doctorate. Outstanding students study for a doctorate, which is still demanded by some professional bodies as a condition of entry; the examination therefore attracts a greater number of candidates than it does in Great Britain.

The university year is divided into two Semesters, November to February and May to July, and students may enrol in either Semester. The length of study is also reckoned in Semesters, not years; the minimum duration of each course is prescribed, but there is no limit to the number of years a student may spend preparing himself for his final examination. The average is now 6·6 years. Most universities are overcrowded. The increase in student numbers was planned and new universities were built, but existing places are not being vacated as quickly as was expected. There still remains a vast untapped reservoir of talent amongst young people however, since only 7% of students come from the working class (1976). Most students work to pay (at least in part) for their studies. The *Honnefer Modell* fund, founded by the Federal government in 1957, provides grants for about 15% of students, who are chosen by examination. Private or charitable sources help about 30% and some receive grants from the States. Some 60% of students are therefore supported by their parents and by what they themselves can earn both during the vacations and during term.

The freedom enjoyed by students has many drawbacks; much time is wasted by students who find difficulty in orientating themselves, and it is suspected that it is a contributory cause to the high failure-rate (40%). Counselling schemes for new students are now being tried. The practice of dividing one's studies between two or three universities, once encouraged to give a wider command of one's subject, has now died out. Among the most significant proposals for reform is a suggestion that there should be a two year planned course ending with an examination, followed by a period of free study for the successful candidates.

University Life. Lectures are held between 7 a.m. and 8 p.m. and are sometimes advertised to last two hours. However the letters "c.t." *(cum tempore)* after the title of the lecture indicate that it will begin 15 minutes after the advertised time; those described as "s.t." *(sine tempore)* begin on the hour. In the university library often only the most fundamental reference books are readily available; students have to find any other book in the index, order it and return on the following day to collect it.

A new student often finds difficulty in making social contacts, since the number of places where students meet is comparatively small; clubs and societies are relatively few in number. Cheap meals are provided in the university restaurant *(Mensa)*, but this is not usually a place for making contacts. Most universities have some hostel accommodation, but only for a small proportion of students; the modern universities such as Bochum, designed on a single campus, provide more halls of residence, but in general a student must still expect to lead a solitary existence in lodgings,

Munich: In a students' hostel

often situated at a considerable distance from the university buildings. *Verbindungen* however flourish, especially in small university towns; they are traditional student societies financed by 'old boys' and have private premises, which often include student accommodation. Under the National Socialists these clubs were banned on the grounds that they were privileged groups; indeed membership could, and still can, ensure entry to a profession. *Verbindungen* are common to all universities, so a member who moves to another university is sure to find immediate contact. They vary in nature and aim; some have a religious or political basis, others are reserved for the 'upper class', almost all are exclusively for men. A few still practise duelling *(Mensur)*, even though it is illegal. Most of them cultivate ritual beer-drinking.

The official student organization AStA *(Allgemeiner Studenten-Ausschuß)* looks after student interests in each university and sends representatives to the VDS *(Verband Deutscher Studentenschaften)*, which is the central organ of the student population. There are also two non-voting student representatives on the Senate, but legislation is in hand to give the students greater influence (see p. 220).

The late 1960s brought increasing student unrest in West Germany. Not only were the students dissatisfied with conditions in the overcrowded universities (in 1976 there were an estimated 850,000 students), they said their university studies were insufficiently job-orientated, and they sought a greater degree of responsibility for university organization.

The 'establishment' came in for severe criticism, for it was the political leaders who, it was claimed, bore the lion's share of the responsibility for the miserable state of affairs. The students also condemned the CDU for perpetuating an educational system which favoured children of the middle class and placed working class children at a complete disadvantage. Organized student protest (SDS and APO—see p. 162) was extremely left-wing, and it aroused the antagonism of the man in the street who feared a Communist take-over. In many cities protest marches and meetings turned into street fights, many of which were given considerable publicity because of alleged police brutality. Student protest in the mid-1970s has grown much less violent. Perhaps the greatest source of discontent is the shortage both of university places and of suitable employment for graduates, who are described as the '*akademisches Proletariat*' of West Germany.

Adult Education. Over 1,000 Evening Institutes *(Volkshochschulen)* cater for the education of adults in the Federal Republic. No entrance qualifications are required for any of the available courses, which range from the academic or semi-vocational, such as typing or languages, to political education, hobbies and pastimes. A much smaller number of residential institutes *(Heimvolkshochschulen)* provide more intensive courses for specific social groups. Both these institutes are financed from public money. There also exist similar facilities provided by religious organizations and the unions.

Mature students may study for the Abitur at evening classes *(Abendgymnasium)* as part of the *zweiter Bildungsweg* (see p. 219).

Teacher Training. People entering the teaching profession must decide at the outset in which type of school they wish to work, since the qualifications required of teachers differ; it is rarely possible to change to another type of school. In order to teach in a *Volksschule* a student must pass the *Abitur* and then spend two or three years at a College of Education *(Pädagogische Hochschule)*. There are some seventy of these Colleges in the Federal Republic, some of which already hold university status.

After completing the prescribed period of study the students begin a two-year trial period in school during which a much reduced timetable is taught to allow for further study. A new teacher can expect to receive help and guidance from the older staff; he must also write a thesis on some aspect of his profession. A final examination and a test of practical teaching complete the probationary period.

After several years' experience in a *Volksschule*, teachers in certain States can take a further examination and transfer to the *Mittelschule*. The remaining States require of this type of teacher a minimum of six Semesters' study at a university.

In order to teach in a *Gymnasium* a student will have to attend a university and complete the final examination *(Staatsexamen)*. It is possible in some universities to study education as part of the main course and to spend trial periods in schools. Two years' training is required after the *Staatsexamen*. During his probationary period the new teacher holds the status of *Referendar*; when he has completed his final examinations he becomes a *Studienassessor*.

Teachers employed in vocational training establishments

are required to hold differing qualifications according to the nature of their subject.

The German obsession with titles causes an intense awareness amongst children of the exact status of their teachers; the staff themselves perpetuate the hierarchy. Seniority is determined by length of service and there is nothing to be gained by moving from school to school, indeed only senior staff can at will—young teachers usually have to go where they are told.

The educational system in the Federal Republic is highly organized and wide-ranging; it produces specialists who have enjoyed a general education to a high level, but it favours children from middle and upper class backgrounds.

Educationalists are aware that there is much criticism of the existing system, but opportunities to experiment are limited by its very inflexibility. An unsolved problem is the position that political education should occupy within the curriculum. It is felt almost universally that some form of introduction to politics is desirable, but agreement on the form that this teaching should take has not yet been reached. It is in this respect that West German educationalists differ most widely from the unequivocating attitude of their East German brothers, who base their whole education system upon rigid political ideals.

Education in the Democratic Republic

At the beginning of September 1946 all levels of education in the Soviet Zone came under the direct control of the central government. The new educational system was modelled on that of the Soviet Union, being closely linked to the aims and needs of a Socialist society. In 1945 the Communist and Socialist parties had already called for a purge of the existing system and the introduction of a liberal, progressive and democratic education in which there would be equal opportunities for all; the children of farmers and factory workers were to be encouraged to make the best possible use of these opportunities. The new type of school created in 1946 *(Einheitsschule)* accepted all children of school age and retained them for their whole school career; it was utterly independent of any religious influence. Tuition and materials became completely free, and all schools were organized on the same lines, so that they could indeed offer equal facilities; small rural schools were closed (the last in 1956) and the children transferred to area schools, where the education they received was comparable to that in the towns. Certain subjects were made compulsory, including manual work and the study of Socialism; it was stated in 1949 that high political as well as professional qualifications would be required of all teachers. Political teaching is reinforced by the activities of the *Freie Deutsche Jugend* or FDJ (Free German Youth Movement), which co-operates closely with the schools.

In 1958 the principle of polytechnic education was introduced. The intention was to teach mathematics and science as applied to industry and to impart to the pupils a knowledge of the construction and function of important machinery and of basic industrial processes. The pupils were to be made familiar with tools, instruments and machines and were to be introduced to economics and the study of production methods. The very nature of this curriculum compelled the schools to forge and maintain close links with local industry. New schools were founded over the next six years as the plan was implemented and at the same time compulsory schooling was extended from eight to ten years. By 1965 a uniform system existed throughout the Democratic Republic; it was organized by the *Ministerium für Volksbildung* (Ministry of Education) and linked to the 5-year plan for the whole economy and to the nation's need for well-trained workers. The common curriculum *(Staatlicher Lehrplan)* unites all learning, general, vocational, moral and political, in the service of the community; each pupil is expected to aim at becoming a useful, model member of society. To remind older pupils that schools are a part of the working community, practical productive work is carried out, often under contract from a local industry; the senior classes spend one day each week working in a factory.

No social divisions are recognized by this education system; the children of manual and agricultural workers are however particularly encouraged, because the country needs to exploit every latent talent. There is ample opportunity for everyone to develop his particular ability to the utmost both during his school career and his working life; special facilities cater for anyone of outstanding promise. Responsibility is put squarely on the young to make the best possible use of every opportunity they are given.

As a place of education the family is of decreasing importance. Much of the responsibility for pre-school education and leisure time activity has been taken from it and given to schools and the FDJ; the family does however have a duty to support and reinforce the work done by schools and the youth movement.

Pre-school Education. In 1961 the government of the Democratic Republic decided to relieve women of their tasks as housewives and mothers in order to allow them to make a greater contribution to society; this was a necessary step in view of the labour shortage. Day nurseries *(Kinderkrippen)* were set up by factories and local authorities to look after the babies of working mothers returning to employment after 14 weeks' maternity leave. Some of the nurseries care for the children day and night; others exist only on a temporary basis, for example to release extra labour at harvest time. *Kinderkrippen* care for children up to the age of three; they form part of the national health service.

In these nurseries education begins on carefully defined lines. The aim is to develop the children's speech, their familiarity with the environment, their physical and mental faculties, their ability to mix with other children and their readiness to obey adults.

Children being looked after in the day nursery of a farm co-operative while their mothers work in the fields

From their third birthday the children may attend a kindergarten organized by the local authority or by places of employment. They receive here a type of education which will fit them to attend school when they are six; it is planned and controlled by the Ministry of Education. The children are encouraged to be attentive and to develop their imagination and memory. Daily games and exercise keep them physically fit, singing, music-making and poetry develop their linguistic ability; it is expected of the children that they show an eagerness to learn. Some aspects of character training are accorded special importance, namely ambition, self-discipline and respect for parents and working people. The children are encouraged to help each other and to carry out some of the daily tasks entailed in the running of the kindergarten.

Children who do not attend a kindergarten are encouraged to join a play group *(Spiel- und Lernnachmittag)* in the year before they begin full-time schooling.

Schools. Every child in the Democratic Republic begins his compulsory education at the age of six in a 'Ten-class Polytechnic High School' *(10-klassige allgemeinbildende polytechnische Oberschule)*; he receives a general education coupled with either a basic or complete vocational training and a thorough preparation for the world of work. One child in four can now expect to enter a college or university.

The first three classes (age 6, 7, 8) are grouped to form the Lower Level *(Unterstufe)*. The children are taught the basic subjects; they are required to think, to express themselves clearly, to love work, to exhibit patriotism and to prepare themselves to serve the community. High academic standards are expected; the method of marking tests resembles that used in the Federal Republic (see p. 213). The education given has the scientific, practical basis advocated by Marxist philosophy; from the beginning the ideological or political aspect of every subject is stressed.

The Intermediate Level *(Mittelstufe)* comprising Classes 4, 5 and 6 continues the type of education already established, although more emphasis is now placed on accurate factual knowledge. The first foreign language (Russian) is introduced in Class 5 and physics in Class 6; courses in these and other subjects are constructed with an eye to the needs of industry. Sport is also considered important, the emphasis being placed on competition and on improving personal techniques and performance. At this stage of their education the pupils are introduced to the various possible careers open to them; discussions involve both the pupils and their parents. Considerable effort is expended on attracting girls into technical and agricultural careers. The children are expected to engage in responsible cultural and political activities in their spare time through membership of the Pioneer movement *(Die jungen Pioniere)*, the junior branch of the FDJ. A Pioneer leader is always a permanent member of each school's staff.

Classes 7 to 10 form the Upper Level *(Oberstufe)*. The emphasis at this stage is on preparing pupils for their careers and on producing good citizens; education in citizenship *(Staatsbürgerkunde)* begins in Class 9. From the age of twelve each pupil learns technical drawing, chemistry and a second foreign language; increased emphasis is placed on mathematics and science, so that in Class 10 almost half the periods on the timetable are devoted to these subjects. Each pupil spends one day each week at work in industry or agriculture; the pupils are given experience of all types of industry and many of them are able to complete an apprenticeship by the time they leave school, whilst some others need only one year's further study to qualify. There exist also a number of 'extended' secondary schools *(erweiterte Oberstufe)*, where the pupils remain to complete twelve years' education leading to *Abitur*. In general they are organized along the same lines as other schools, but usually they specialize in a group of subjects such as mathematics and science, or very occasionally classical languages. Pupils can easily be channelled into careers where there is a shortage of manpower; care is taken to see that no vital branch of industry will be understaffed. Time is found for specialist training by allowing pupils to complete certain subjects before their final year. Sport is encouraged both in and out of school to maintain a good level of physical fitness amongst the population, but competition and high performance remain sport's main purposes. The *Sportabzeichen* (Sport Certificate) is intended to encourage the average performer to improve; outstanding performers train for the *Olympiaabzeichen*.

There is at present a movement to extend full-day schooling in order to help working mothers and to be able to provide additional leisure activities for the children. Centres already exist *(Horte)* to cater for some of these children by providing meals, facilities for homework and recreation.

Some special schools *(Spezialschulen)* have been founded

for children who are exceptionally gifted in a certain field such as mathematics, music, sport or ballet. The pupils take the normal *Abitur* examination and then a specialist examination one or two years later. Near Cottbus and Dresden there are several special schools for the Sorb minority group where instruction is given in their own language; in all other respects these schools conform to the normal pattern.

Handicapped children are educated where necessary in separate schools *(Sonderschulen)*; it is, however, the aim to integrate handicapped people into society wherever their disability permits, so these children are transferred to normal schools as soon as possible. It is intended that they should receive a vocational training commensurate with their disability so that they will eventually become self-supporting.

Orphans, or children from homes regarded by the State as unsuitable, are placed in special homes where they receive a full Socialist upbringing or re-education.

Every school in the Democratic Republic follows a common syllabus prescribed by the Ministry of Education. The Ministry also issues detailed instructions about the timing, nature and conduct of tests and prescribes the interpretations to be placed on, for example, literary or historical fact. The responsibility for ensuring that the syllabus is properly taught rests with the Headmaster and the local school adviser *(Kreisschulrat)*, who are directly responsible to the Minister. Each school must issue a plan of its year's work *(Jahresarbeitsplan)* and each class teacher must produce a similar plan for his class.

Every Headmaster has a panel of local factory managers, youth leaders and other important people to advise him. Each school has a Parent-Teacher Association *(Elternbeirat)* which meets about three times a year to discuss a previously prepared subject. Every month each teacher is available to meet parents; he may summon parents to consult him. It is one of the teacher's duties to get to know the parents of every child in his class and to secure their co-operation. Parents who do not co-operate are officially reminded of their duty to bring up their children in a responsible manner.

Social and political education is complemented by the FDJ and the 'Young Pioneers', with whom the schools have close links. They organize out-of-school activities which fill evenings, weekends and holidays, so that the children have ample opportunity for spending their spare time on approved pursuits. The children are prepared for *Jugendweihe* (the dedication of youth to the cause of Socialism—see also p. 202) both in school and in meetings of the FDJ. There is considerable pressure on children to take part, and most do, since to refuse would be to close the door to higher education and promotion. The ceremony itself takes place at about the time of leaving school and entering employment.

Vocational Training. Everyone in the Democratic Republic must receive some form of education until he reaches the age of 18. Those who leave school at 16 must attend a *Berufsschule* on two days each week to continue their general education and to receive tuition in their chosen career. Basic vocational training begins in the ninth and tenth school Classes; since 1964 it has been possible to complete an apprenticeship during the last three years at an 'extended' school. Entry to every career is controlled by a law which requires the registration of apprenticeships. This is a safeguard against overstaffing in any one sector, since permission to enter into an apprenticeship contract may be refused. Apprenticeships in the private sector are only permitted when those in the public sector are adequately filled.

Because it depends heavily on the productivity of its workers, the Government insists that all of them shall be fully qualified, in whatever field they are employed. Retraining schemes which anticipate redundancies caused by improved production techniques are given official backing. Each factory and village has its own educational establishment *(Betriebsakademie, Technische Betriebsschule, Dorfakademie)*, which exists primarily to offer the workers the opportunity of gaining higher qualifications. Village academies also cater for the social and cultural needs of a rural population.

Over 200 specialist schools *(Fachschulen)* exist, which give further training to outstanding workers who already hold the minimum qualifications. Many kinds of course are provided; study may be full-time, part-time or by correspondence. Students can, if they wish, go on to study their special subject in a shortened course at university, but most students return from the *Fachschule* to fill key positions in industry.

Universities. The requisite qualification for entry to a university may be obtained in several ways by people of all ages (see Fig. 30). Social maturity is considered when the

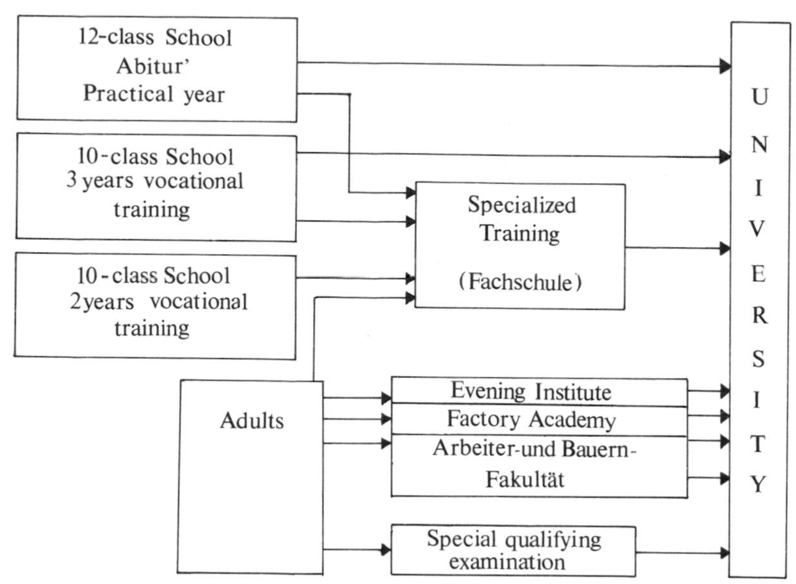

The Educational System of the Democratic Republic

Fig 30

award of the *Abitur* is discussed and politically immature students are not allowed to qualify. Holders of the university entrance qualification must apply for a place at a university; the selection process enables the authorities to ensure that the required balance is kept between faculties and to exclude students with unorthodox political ideas. 85% of students come from the working class. Before beginning his course every student must spend at least one year working in industry. This practical year is often supervised by the university and it may count towards fulfilling course regulations. Military service obligations must also be met.

Several types of institution hold university status; besides the traditional universities there are scientific and technical universities *(Wissenschaftliche Hochschulen)* and specialist academies *(Fachhochschulen)*, each for a particular subject, such as medicine, agriculture or politics. The Ministry of Education controls them and specifies both the subject matter to be taught and the nature of the research to be carried out by each faculty or institute; university research is in general linked to the needs of local industry. The University of Halle-Wittenberg for example concentrates on applied chemistry to help the Leuna Works. From 1968 the universities have received additional finance from industrial enterprises to help research and to pay for the training which many of their staff receive.

The aim of university education is to produce highly qualified specialists able to use their knowledge to improve the country's economy; the 1968 reforms aim to integrate completely science and productivity, university and industry. The practical part of a course is therefore regarded as specially important; the students are expected at every stage to prove their ability to apply their knowledge. In technical faculties, first year students spend alternate weeks studying and working *(Praktikantenzeit)*, for which they are paid a token wage. All students must take annual examinations which determine whether or not they will be allowed to continue; grants towards living expenses are withdrawn from students who fail. At least one year before the end of his course a student will be channelled into a suitable position where he may use his knowledge to the best advantage.

In addition to his special subject, every student must complete a basic course *(Grundstudium)* in Marxist-Leninist thought; he must also take part in sport and cultivate a working knowledge of Russian to enable him to read technical texts within his own field of specialization. In general, university studies are shorter than in the Federal Republic, lasting between four and six years; each academic year lasts ten months. Tuition is quite free of charge. Courses usually lead to the final examination *(Staatsexamen)*, occasionally to a doctorate.

The 1968 plan for university reform, made to forestall student unrest, foresaw future academic courses divided into four phases: basic, subject, special and research. Stages one and two together last four years and they give all students a broad education which will fit them to change careers should it ever become necessary. The third stage will lead to an academic qualification (Diploma), and it is regarded as a period of selection for the few who proceed to take a doctorate. The reforms also abolish Faculties and Institutes, establishing Departments in their place; Senates are replaced by councils, which are advised by the Heads of Departments, Professors, students, and representatives from industry, the State and political organizations.

Students are closely controlled, being divided into groups of between twenty and thirty, with their work under constant supervision. Talented students are in this way revealed and given special opportunities; leisure time activities can also be observed.

Student representation and activities are organized by the FDJ, which, along with the Trade Unions, has seats on the administrative board of every university.

Adult Education. The education of adults is closely linked to vocational training, since every worker is expected and encouraged to improve his qualifications. Evening Institutes *(Volkshochschulen)* run courses leading to the same level as 10 or 12 class schools. Specialist courses are run by a *Fachschule*. Factory and village academies cater for vocational and cultural activities. An integral part of every course is a general education, including a study of politics and Socialism.

The newly created 'Worker and Peasant Faculty' *(Arbeiter- und Bauern-Fakultät)* gives to good workers the chance to gain their *Abitur* in one to three years. Often the workers are sponsored by their factory; political reliability is essential. Once qualified, these workers may transfer to a university to study their special subject.

Teacher Training. Teacher training in the Democratic Republic is rigidly controlled, yet the system is flexible enough to give the most suitable training to every type of teacher. The *Pädagogische Schule für Kindergärtnerinnen* runs courses for kindergarten teachers. Three years at an *Institut für Lehrerbildung* will qualify a student to teach Classes 1 to 4; the same Institute also runs courses for 'Pioneer' leaders. In order to teach Classes 5 to 10 a student must attend a *Pädagogisches Institut*. Other teachers are trained at either a technical or traditional university according to their special subject. Outstanding workers are encouraged to become teachers in both ordinary and vocational schools, since their experience is invaluable; they first receive a short course in education.

An integral part of every teacher training course is Marxist-Leninist thought. Students also continue to receive a general education and they are given a thorough grounding in the psychological, methodological and practical aspects of their chosen profession. High academic standards are demanded. Most teachers must complete a two-year probationary period; only occasionally is it reduced to twelve months. Practical teaching is inspected and controlled by the State Planning

Commission *(Staatliche Plankommission)*. The law states that teachers are expected to be conscientious and to keep abreast of the latest developments in their special subject.

Headmasters and organizers must qualify for their promotion by further study of all aspects of teaching and of scientific organization and leadership. There is constant encouragement to all teachers to extend their knowledge and improve their work. Innovators *(Pädagogische Neuerer)* are particularly welcome and are granted special facilities for study. Senior positions *(Oberlehrer, Studienrat, Oberstudienrat, Professor)* carrying an increased salary are available for the most successful teachers, the success of teaching being measured by the later performance of their pupils in adult life.

If education is defined as the introduction of the young into an existing society, then the monolithic education system of the Democratic Republic is completely successful. It is constructed and controlled so that it will produce a steady flow of good and highly qualified workers and gives genuine opportunities for everyone to develop to the full any talents they possess. The basis and aim is unequivocally political, since it is intended to strengthen the establishment of a Socialist society.

VI Meet the Germans

1. The German Character

*What are the Germans like? What, if anything, is typically German? What impressions might a visitor take home with him?**

First impressions

The visitor can hardly fail to be impressed by the Germans' efficiency; wherever he goes he will find prosperous cities, clean, smoothly run hotels and restaurants, punctual public transport, knowledgeable and helpful shop assistants, punctilious policemen and a profusion of instructions and prohibitions. He will experience the legendary German love of bureaucracy. He will be flattered by the polite attentions he receives, amused by the constant handshaking and he will admire the slight, rather stiff ritualistic bow with which man greets woman. He is certain to note that this extreme formality and perfect courtesy contrast strangely with the undignified scramble which is the German version of a queue. He will observe the Germans' pride in their personal appearance and in their tastefully furnished homes, and will find ample evidence of the impressively high standard and wide appeal of cultural activities. He will applaud performances of traditional songs and dances, attend folk-festivals and photograph fetching girls going about their daily business in local costume, wondering that such things have persisted so far into the twentieth century. He will marvel at the quality and quantity of food that the Germans eat, envy the apparent affluence of the people and attribute their prosperity to their legendary capacity for hard work.

Second thoughts

On closer acquaintance the visitor will discover that the apparent efficiency of the Germans sometimes conceals a morass of administrative muddle. The issue of identification

---

*The remarks in this chapter refer in the main to the Federal Republic.

papers to the whole population, the registration of personal movements with the police, the issue of new number plates when a motor vehicle changes hands or when the owner moves to a different area, all serve a purpose, but they produce such mountains of paper-work that they have become unenforceable by the available manpower. It has already been decided to abandon the registration of overnight guests, for example, which was purported to help apprehend criminals, for by the time the wads of forms had been checked on the following morning, the bird had usually flown. Public offices, too, are overwhelmed by the products of their own red tape and are relentlessly grinding to a halt; the taxation department is almost two years behind in some of its routine business. Motorists in particular are confronted with a multiplicity of regulations covering every conceivable situation which they must learn in order to pass the driving test (would *you* know what lights to use if at night you saw a ship approaching alongside the road?), yet many accidents are attributed to people's obstinately observing these regulations instead of tempering them with common sense. The police pounce remorselessly on all offenders, collecting fines on the spot according to a fixed scale of charges *(Bußgeldkatalog)* for minor infringements. This ruthless efficiency earns the respect, but not the friendship, of the public despite the slogan which sought to portray the police as 'friends and helpers' *(Die Polizei, dein Freund und Helfer)*.

Even quite ordinary activities are restricted; it is an offence to disturb the daily 'quiet hour', to hang out washing on a Sunday, to shake a duster or beat a carpet except in the early morning, to play a radio loudly, to make a noise after 10 p.m.—except on one night each year when the tenant of a flat has the right to make as much noise as he likes, provided that he informs his neighbours beforehand. The enthusiasm with which such laws are invoked leaves the impression that they are totally necessary and that without them the whole population might revert to savagery, shaking their dusters at each other at noon and encouraging the children to play rowdy games at midnight.

The conspicuously correct behaviour of the Germans derives from an obsession with the niceties of etiquette, which is most pronounced in, although by no means confined to the older generation. People like to use whatever titles they have earned, they insist on '*Sie*', the formal style of address, they dress tastefully, not flamboyantly, and they expect children to conform to the standards of adult behaviour. They observe the most intricate procedure when effecting introductions, and ask the escort's permission before inviting a woman to dance. It is extremely easy for a stranger to give offence through ignorance of the appropriate behaviour.

One cannot but admire this high standard of social intercourse, but odd incidents give one the uncomfortable feeling that with too many people good manners are only a veneer; the inability to queue sensibly has already been mentioned, and the fact that a number of seats on public transport are reserved for certified cripples and invalids does rather suggest that they would otherwise have to stand.

A longer stay in Germany confirms the first impression that the average level of culture is remarkably high. There is an amazing number of major theatres (about 200) including many in towns apparently too small to support them; the fact that 100 theatres were built in 10 post-war years gives some indication of the popularity of the medium. The existence of 60 operatic ensembles in Germany shows that opera, too, has a wide appeal. Interest in the arts amongst the general public is fostered by subscription schemes offering reduced terms for season tickets *(Volksbühne)*. Even though performances are well attended, 80% of all seats being taken on average every evening, considerable subsidies are needed; grants

The new theatre at Stuttgart forms part of a complex which includes the old opera house and government buildings for the state of Baden-Württemberg

for the arts rank high on the list of priorities in both municipal and State administrations.

Concerts are also popular. There are about 90 permanent orchestras in the Federal Republic, and many towns have their own choir; some of these have become internationally known. Even more impressive however to the English observer is the amount of amateur music-making for pleasure.

The general quality of television programmes is admirable; a comparatively small proportion of time is allotted to pure entertainment (despite the country-wide popularity of *The Avengers, Maigret* and Francis Durbridge serials), and a great deal to important artistic performances, to informative programmes and to political discussion. The medium has been developed primarily as a vehicle for culture and information, and as such it is extremely successful.

There is ample evidence in Germany of a widespread sense of form and design, which compares favourably with the general standard of taste in Britain. Homes are frequently more tastefully furnished and are rarely cluttered with cheap ornaments. The average woman dresses fashionably in well-cut clothes, avoiding garish colours and cheap prints, though jeans and shirts are of course popular with the young. The general design of goods on sale is incomparably higher than in Britain, and they are usually better displayed. Of course plenty of trash is sold, notably in popular holiday areas, and there are still countless devotees of dangling ornaments in car windscreens and dozens of dwarfs in suburban gardens, but the overall impression is that good taste prevails.

Why is the cultural level so high? Perhaps it is because German children receive a wide education during the whole of their schooling, and are introduced to all branches of the arts. The interest in music and the theatre awakened at this impressionable age is carried on into adult life and is reflected not only in the good attendance at plays and concerts but also in the popularity of evening classes. Amongst the general public culture is regarded as a status symbol; it is the key to a better way of life.

The German likes to preserve his past, or the past as he imagines it, because beneath his efficient, formal, precise exterior he is an incurable Romantic. Hitler was able to take advantage of this trait to develop a tremendous feeling of nationalism to serve his sinister purpose. Since 1945 the idea of preserving traditions has had a new significance;

many Germans had to leave their homes in eastern Europe and they wanted to retain their culture and sense of community for the day when they would return. At first the Allies fought the move to found clubs of exiles, fearing that this would lead to a rebirth of nationalism, but the *Landsmannschaften* were founded and have so far not proved dangerous. Refugees do, however, form a large and potentially influential pressure-group.

Most traditions are much less inflammatory; many have become commercialized and have lost their original character as, for example, the pre-Lent Carnival *(Fasching)* in the great cities and the Passion Play at Oberammergau. Genuine traditions do, however retain a firm footing in the villages, where superstition and legends are very much alive. The folk dance and folksong are actively cultivated; each region has its own evocative, nostalgic verses which arouse in local people a sentimental yearning *(Heimweh)* for their homeland *(Heimat)*. Almost without exception the Germans retain a special affection for the place where they were born, especially if they can no longer live there. Germany without the cult of *Heimat* is unthinkable.

The Germans do indeed consume immense quantities of food of excellent quality. The choice of dishes in cafés and restaurants puts English catering to shame. The skill of confectioners and pastrycooks is almost unbelievable; enormous quantities of fresh cream go into their elaborate creations, but even so it is not uncommon to see an extra

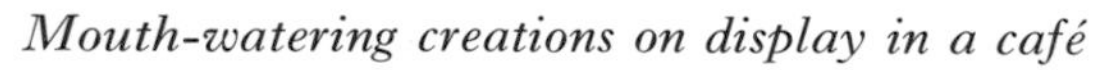

Mouth-watering creations on display in a café

portion of cream served with a slice of cream cake. At home the Germans eat less extravagantly but no less heartily; potatoes, noodles or bread form the basis of virtually every meal. The German housewife is proud of her cooking and can produce tempting meals from quite ordinary ingredients; vegetables for example are made appetizing by being served with a wide variety of sauces.

The present vogue for eating sumptuously, facetiously described as the *Edelfreßwelle,* befits a country with such a high standard of living, but its roots go back to the days of famine during and after the war when the only foods were turnips, potatoes and offal. When the days of plenty returned, people were determined to make up for this deprivation.

Maybe it is because so many people tend to overeat (and suffer from the effects of overwork) that the Germans are obsessed with their health; the most overworked adjective on food advertisements is *gesund* ('healthy'). Great faith is placed in health foods, herbal remedies and spas, which claim to cure everything from the effects of overeating to chronic rheumatism. Spas flourish in enormous numbers, patronized by all sections of the population; they form a considerable part of all health services. Undoubtedly many people benefit from their stay in a spa, but it seems likely that they would derive equal benefit from any restful, open air holiday away from the frantic pace of daily life without taking part in the ritual cleansing.

By international standards Germany is a rich land, but then so is Britain. What is it about Germany that gives the impression that the Germans are so much more prosperous?

Their towns are clean and smart, the shops are well stocked with luxury goods beautifully displayed, people appear to have plenty of money. Incomes are just as high as one might expect in view of the high standard of living; status symbols are everywhere. Among the less well-off it is however a matter of pride to conceal poverty by being clean, caring for one's clothes and presenting a neat appearance. For this the efficient German *Hausfrau* must take the credit; she has learned, sometimes through personal experience of slumps and shortages, how to budget sensibly and to save regularly. A national survey revealed that 60% of German men considered thrift to be the most important quality in a wife. The 'Bingo' craze and the hire purchase mania have not smitten German society; despite the existence of a national lottery, gambling comes very low on the list of priorities. In short, it is a common sense attitude to money, plus the national policy of encouraging regular, long term saving, which accounts for the high standard of living.

2. Everyday Life

The working day

The working day begins early for children and adults alike; the Germans have a saying that one must have earned one's salary by 11 a.m. Schools, shops and offices open at 8 a.m., earlier in summer in some parts of the country. The Germans eat a light breakfast of fresh rolls (bakeries open at 7 a.m.), butter, jam and coffee, and take with them a 'second breakfast' usually of substantial sandwiches to eat in the morning break. Many workers commute for considerable distances; they are pleased to put up with the inconvenience to enjoy the peace of the suburbs in their free time. Children only attend school when they have lessons, and since the younger ones at least have a number of free periods, they are to be seen going to and fro throughout the morning. Busy roads are sometimes patrolled by specially trained pupils (*Schülerlotsen*), who hold up traffic to let their friends cross in safety.

Lunch is often eaten late, occasionally even after 2 p.m., to coincide with the end of school, and is generally still the most substantial meal of the day, consisting usually of two courses. During the afternoon children are occupied with homework, which is given to all, even the beginners; most children can expect considerable help from their parents. What few extra-curricular activities there are, including sport, also take place in the afternoon.

The working day ends for most people at 5 p.m., and the evening meal is taken about 7 p.m. In the southern part of Germany this is generally a cooked meal, but in the north, as its name *Abendbrot* suggests, it often consists mainly of bread with a variety of cooked meats, cheeses or 'salads' eaten as open sandwiches with a knife and fork. Sometimes it may be supplemented with fried potatoes or other left-overs from midday. Weak tea without milk is the usual adult alternative to beer, the national drink, which is produced in vast quantities by over 2,000 major breweries.

The evening is regarded by the German as a time to relax; he calls it *Feierabend*, evoking with this word his own parti-

A road sign warning motorists that schoolchildren may be controlling pedestrian crossings in the area

cular idea of comfort and pleasure, and a feeling of satisfaction at having done a good day's work. He may spend it in the family circle, perhaps reading the newspaper or watching television, but almost certainly drinking a glass of beer, or wine if it is a special occasion. He may, however, prefer to go to a nearby pub *(Wirtshaus)* for his beer, his newspaper, his television and a game of cards; if he is a regular customer a table *(Stammtisch)* will be reserved for him and his friends. There are plenty of opportunities for the increasing number of people, especially those in sedentary occupations, who wish to take a little healthy exercise. Some are satisfied with a leisurely game of skittles, whereas others aim at the standards set for the various grades of Sport Certificate *(Sportabzeichen)* which have been awarded since 1952 in order to encourage ordinary people to improve their personal performance. Football is the most popular sport of all, but facilities exist for almost all other sports (except cricket, of course!). Bedtime for many is early, about 10 or 10.30 during the week; this is reflected in the early close-down of television, although radio broadcasting often continues into the early hours.

The weekend

For the children the weekend begins with Saturday morning school, which lasts until about midday; for the housewife it begins with shopping, as shops and stores close at 2 p.m. except on the first Saturday in the month. Saturday afternoon is spent pottering around the house or garden; it is the time when preparations are made for Sunday. In the Elbe Marsh-

The terrace of a café at a popular beauty spot

lands near Hamburg for example, the people carefully rake patterns in the sandy paths in their gardens, which they sit and admire in the evening and on the following day. Some families make a regular Saturday pilgrimage to the churchyard to tend the family grave. Many people take the opportunity of having an afternoon nap at the weekend before enjoying a pleasant stroll (or car ride) to a local beauty spot, although the main purpose often seems to be to sample the catering (especially the cream cakes) at a nearby café or restaurant. The list of Saturday evening activities is almost endless; this is the time when the Germans enjoy themselves. Many people like to visit their friends; the theatre and cinema are popular, as are certain pubs. Dancing is a favourite choice in both town and country.

Sunday is still a day of rest and by no means quite what the Englishman envisages when he thinks of a 'Continental Sunday'; the laws preserve peace and quiet in residential areas but permit professional sport in the afternoon. For many people car-worship has replaced the Sunday church service, but the washing, polishing and vacuuming is over by noon. In some areas it is not permissible to hang out washing or do any work out of doors on a Sunday; whilst these bye-laws are not always rigidly observed, there remains the possibility that they can be enforced. When so many activities are restricted, it seems strange that shops selling cakes and flowers should be allowed to open for several hours, but both commodities are regarded as essentials!

The most popular time for visiting is Sunday afternoon. No visitor ever comes empty-handed; one is expected to produce a bunch of flowers, conforming, needless to say, to certain conventions. There must be an odd number of blooms, usually 5 or 7, they must not be red roses unless the donor wishes to express an unusually deep affection for his hostess and at the same time to offend her husband, and the wrapping paper must be dexterously removed and concealed in the split second before they are presented. Once this ceremony is over and a few polite remarks have been exchanged, the guest will be regaled with strong coffee and incredible quantities of cake. An evening visit proceeds along the same lines, but the refreshments are completely different; beer, wine or liqueur will be served, with dainty biscuits, both sweet and savoury, or open sandwiches, or nuts. It is important to know that an empty glass will always be filled, but a half-empty one will not be topped up, so anyone preferring to go home sober must take care to leave a small amount in the glass until the end of the evening.

It is the custom in Germany to wish each other a 'nice Sunday'; this dates back to the days before most people could enjoy a full weekend's leisure and the expression has now come to include Saturday. A public holiday is also sometimes described as a 'Sunday', indicating that shops will close and that public transport will operate reduced services; it is puzzling at first to hear in the middle of a week that 'tomorrow is Sunday'!

The family

In rural Germany the word 'family' still describes the large unit to which three or more generations belong. Many of these families still reside under one roof, working together on the land and raising new generations to take over the farm in turn. The urban family has become a smaller unit; sons no longer follow the same careers as their fathers and frequently move away from home to get work, founding a family unit of their own.

German families are in the main patriarchal. Father likes to feel that he is master in his home and undisputed head of the family—he secretly thinks of himself as the founder of a dynasty, wishing for nothing more than the birth of a son and heir *(Stammhalter)*. He demands respect from his wife and children. Of recent years he has however been prepared to leave more and more of the upbringing of his children to his wife, as the increasingly exhausting pace of business life takes a greater toll of his energy and temper. A German wife is expected to be an efficient housekeeper and a conscientious mother, but very much the junior partner in marriage. The skill of many a woman lies, however, in making all the decisions, whilst at the same time persuading her husband that the ideas were entirely his own.

The attitude of parents and other adults towards children is extraordinarily ambivalent. Children are treated as miniature adults and are expected to conform more exactly than adults themselves to adult standards of behaviour. They are often repressed at home, partly because of cramped living conditions in flats, which cause neighbours to complain whenever children reveal their natural exuberance, and partly because the law holds parents responsible for the actions of their offspring. In well over three quarters of all families, corporal punishment is used as the chief means of disciplining children. School offers little release, for it is an inflexible environment with the serious purpose of training the mind; little time remains for the children to pursue personal interests or work off excess energy. Even on holiday children are unwelcome guests in too many hotels; the situation has become so acute that the Federal Government has begun to build a series of family holiday homes. The Federal Republic has earned for itself amongst German parents the reputation of being an uncongenial country for children.

At times when children are not expected to behave like miniature adults, they are being discouraged—in the preschool period at least—from growing up before their time; they are given six full years of freedom before they start school, and so at seven they are less sophisticated than their Anglo-Saxon contemporaries, having enjoyed childish pastimes for a longer period. At certain seasons of the year family celebrations centre around children; during Advent, for example, most children spend a great deal of time with their mother making small Christmas presents or decorations, talking and singing all the while about the coming festive season.

The German family is a closely knit community in which the young learn to respect their elders and in which everyone can feel secure.

Family celebrations

Important events in the lives of members of the family are celebrated by family reunions. The first milestone is the christening of the newest arrival, to which are invited close relations and the baby's godparents, one of whom must be a member of the Church into which the baby will be received; only members of a Christian Church may act as godparents. From the child's point of view the function of godparents would seem to be the provision of special presents for Christmas and birthdays, although officially the godparents share the parents' responsibility for the Christian education of the child.

The first day at school, said to be the beginning of the serious business of living *(der Ernst des Lebens)*, is made into a memorable occasion. The new pupil proudly carries to school an enormous cone filled with sweets *(Schultüte)* given by his family to divert his attention from the onset of his 9 or 10-year sentence to hard labour. It marks the child's first step towards maturity.

The godparents play an important part in the renewal of baptismal vows and the admission of the child to the Church. In the Roman Catholic Church this ceremony takes place on the first Sunday after Easter *(Quasimodogeniti*

The first day at school

The first communion

or *Weißer Sonntag)* when the child is about seven years old. Little girls are dressed in white and wear garlands in their hair, boys dress sometimes in black, sometimes in white; all carry tall white candles. In the Protestant Church confirmation takes place later in life, usually at about 13 or 14 years of age, after a two-year period of preparation; the ceremony takes place shortly after Easter. In contrast to the almost bridal appearance of the Catholics, the Protestant confirmands make a very sombre show with their dark colours, occasionally relieved by garlands or posies where local custom permits.

Engagements and weddings are also occasions for family reunions, the latter for a celebration lasting many hours. An engagement is not merely a convenient arrangement, it is an official bond between two people indicating their declared intention to marry. During the period of the engagement the couple wear a simple gold ring on the fourth finger of their left hands, usually with some legend engraved on the inside; especially in South Germany, they are still referred to as *Braut* and *Bräutigam* ('bride' and 'groom').

The wedding itself usually consists of two separate ceremonies. The couple must first be married by the registrar at his office *(Standesamt)*; then, if they wish, they can be married in church. The civil ceremony is often held on the day before the church wedding and may be followed by the *Polterabend*, if this has not already taken place. This strange custom is founded on the superstition that the shattering of pottery and glassware brings good fortune by frightening away the devil. Neighbours, friends and relations come to take part in the commotion and they are invited to enjoy the often lengthy celebrations.

For the religious wedding the bride and groom enter the church together preceded by two or three small children scattering flowers; the bride is usually dressed in white with a veil and bouquet and the groom wears a black suit, white shirt and silver tie, or sometimes even a dinner jacket. During the ceremony the plain gold rings hitherto worn on the left hand are placed on the couple's right hands; both of these rings will be worn by whichever of the partners outlives the other. As they leave the church their way may be barred by a rope held by local children, who drop it only when the bride and groom distribute coins or sweets. The wedding reception is a festive occasion, with speeches and light-hearted jibes at the bridal pair and their families.

The merrymaking continues until the early hours, but generally the bride and groom manage to slip away before the end. There exist many strange and picturesque traditions in the country, where weddings are particularly gay and colourful. The beautiful and elaborate costumes peculiar to the occasion are now rarely seen, but weddings remain vast affairs to which over 200 guests may be invited and which are celebrated over at least two days.

Wedding anniversaries, in particular the 25th, the 50th and 60th, are also family occasions. Birthdays too are celebrated, and not only for children; the 60th, 70th, 80th and 90th birthdays merit special festivities because old people are proud of their age and families are proud of their oldest members. Civic dignitaries bring birthday greetings to those who reach an extremely advanced age; the mayor himself visits centenarians. It is usual for children to receive presents from their family and friends, and a garland bearing a candle for each year of their life; they are sometimes excused homework so that they can enjoy their party. Older people also receive presents; sometimes a short entertainment is given in their honour by the children, consisting of short recitations or musical items and doggerel verses composed at home. Devout Roman Catholics prefer to celebrate on the day sacred to the Saint whose name they bear *(Namenstag)*.

Funerals are the occasions for solemn and respectful family reunions. Friends are notified of a death by large announcements placed in the local newspaper by the family and colleagues of the deceased, containing a brief eulogy and details of the funeral arrangements; close friends receive intimations on black-edged notepaper. In the country, news of a death is taken round the village by a neighbour, who invites everyone to attend the burial; those who receive the intimation are expected to send a wreath or other floral tribute unless expressly asked to contribute to some charity. It is usual for close relatives to wear full mourning for at least six months, up to two years in country districts; widows often wear mourning for the rest of their lives. It is customary for the family to tend the grave regularly as a sign that the memory of the departed is still honoured.

The urban scene

A stranger alighting at the main line railway station of a large German town will be impressed by the multiplicity of

A chimney sweep complete with a (rather battered) top-hat and briefcase

facilities provided on the station for the travelling public. There are shops selling all manner of commodities from flowers to works of literature, there are banks and buffets, baths and bars, an office where one can book accommodation, and at least one excellent restaurant, run on behalf of the *Bundesbahn* by a concessionaire and open most of the night, if not all night. On emerging from the station into a busy street the stranger may take a moment to stand and stare. He will see that pedestrians keep to the right hand side of the pavement and that men walk on the left of women; hardly anyone will be smoking. Certain aspects of dress may strike him; many men carry a briefcase (sometimes concealing sandwiches), some women, especially in South Germany, wear a traditional dress-and-apron *(Dirndlkleid)*, and the police carry firearms. Some professions wear distinctive clothing; many a chimney sweep has a top hat, and sometimes a journeyman joiner still wears a large black hat and velvet trousers with wide bottoms.

The interior of an articulated bus

The traffic too has a quite distinctive appearance; in almost every town buses have only one deck, but, like the trams, some tow an extra passenger unit. The newest buses and trams are articulated, the two parts being joined by a short flexible corridor *(Gelenkautobus)*. Most operate on the pay-as-you-enter principle, but where there is a conductor he usually sits at a desk next to the entrance (generally at the rear of the vehicle) to collect fares. The majority of passengers stand. Public transport is only considered full when no one else can be squeezed in, so it is fortunate that smoking is forbidden. All vehicles owned by the Post Office are painted in the characteristic yellow and have the registration letters 'BP' *(Bundespost)*. Police cars, fire engines and ambulances flash a blue light and sound a two-tone siren *(Martinshorn)*. Cyclists often use cycle tracks alongside the pavement and it therefore pays to walk warily. On the pavement there may be telephone kiosks, booths selling hot sausages and kebabs *(Schaschlik)*, or flowers and lottery tickets; it is likely that the main square will contain an ornamental fountain *(Brunnen)*. Hoardings covered with large posters are rare; instead there are at the edge of the pavement sturdy pillars about 9 feet high *(Litfaßsäulen)*, plastered from

Lottery tickets being sold in aid of the German Lifeboat Rescue Service

A street corner with a tram stop, street sign and Litfaßsäule

top to bottom with placards and advertisements. The plaque bearing the name of the street often includes brief details of the person, place or event from which the street takes its name. The bustling crowds are extremely well disciplined. Road crossings are controlled by pedestrian lights and the pedestrians dutifully line up on the pavement awaiting the 'green man'; to cross when the pedestrian lights are red is to invite an on-the-spot fine.

It is rewarding to examine the shops in a German town, particularly the smaller ones, since department stores do not vary significantly from country to country. Window dressing is generally excellent, whatever the type of shop. A bakery displays an amazing variety of bread from fresh white rolls to black pumpernickel; the confectioner's window is filled with a mouth-watering display of plaster-of-Paris cakes—the genuine article is carefully refrigerated inside the shop. Fish shops are fascinating; plaice flap around on the slab and freshwater fish such as trout and carp are kept alive in huge tanks awaiting a blow on the head which barely stuns them before their guts are ripped out. A box of wriggling, writhing eels completes the display. Butchers still make their own sausage in dozens of varieties; it is often wiser for the squeamish not to enquire too closely into the ingredients, although one may be sure that they are officially approved and pure, *and* perfectly fresh!

Where the climate permits, pavement cafés and beer-gardens flourish. Respectable public houses-cum-restaurants

The pedestrians, having dutifully awaited the 'green man' signal to cross, charge at each other like opposing armies in battle

A fishmonger offering live eels, carp and trout

A variety of sausage types in a butcher's window

(Wirtshäuser, Gasthäuser) abound in every town. They serve snacks and alcoholic drinks at any time and hot meals at midday and in the evening; many *Wirtshäuser* and most *Gasthäuser* also provide bed-and-breakfast accommodation. It is quite usual for women to frequent such places, but they would not normally go to a *Schenke,* which more nearly approximates to the English public house. Inns are easily recognized especially in old towns by their often elaborate signs. The most common names (such as Star, Lamb, Lion, Eagle, Ox) have a religious significance, reminding us that many were in medieval times monastic hostelries; the *zur Post* sign indicates that the inn was once a stage for the post-coach. In old towns many of the shops have fine wrought iron signs; a key indicates a locksmith, a pestle and mortar

A locksmith's sign in Celle

a chemist, a pretzel (a crisp, knot-shaped biscuit, flavoured with salt) a bakery and a boot is the mark of a shoemaker. Barbers' shops display a small silver dish, once used in blood-letting.

Homes

Since the war the cost of owning a home has risen so much that most people are unable to buy either a house or a flat until comparatively late in life, so most German families must live in rented accommodation. Rents, especially in the big cities, are not low and in addition tenants may have to pay a substantial deposit *(Baukostenzuschuß)* which entitles them to a slight reduction in rent and helps the landlord to recover quickly some of his expenses so that he can build yet more accommodation. Large-scale housing projects, usually consisting of tall blocks of flats, are financed by trade unions as well as private individuals, industry and local authorities. Even now the housing problem is still acute in some areas; publicly financed flats *(Sozialwohnungen)* are allocated to those in greatest need according to a points system. Most flats are astonishingly small, but the Germans have become accustomed to living in a confined space and make themselves extremely comfortable by using devices such as folding beds and dual purpose furniture.

Because of the nature of their accommodation, flat-dwellers are organized into a unified community. Communal facilities such as washing and drying rooms are allocated on a rota system, and all tenants must contribute towards services such as heating, lighting in the staircase, and the fees of a resident caretaker if one is employed. Where there is no caretaker each flat takes it in turn to clean the stairs; it is a matter of pride to keep them spotless, since those responsible are identified by the sign *Kehrwoche* hung alongside their door. Flat-dwellers must also comply with additional regulations imposed by the landlord or developer which prohibit, for example, the hanging of washing on balconies and can compel the redecoration of the interior every two years. Owner-occupiers in flats form a special committee *(Hausgemeinschaft)* to make such regulations as they find necessary.

A visitor to a block of flats in Germany will notice first of all a battery of letter boxes and name plates each with its own bell beside the front door. Having rung the bell he will be asked his business by a voice from the house telephone, an installation which saves people the journey to the ground floor to answer the bell. If he is to be admitted, a strange buzzing sound indicates that the front door is being operated by remote control and will open if he gives a slight push. Should it be dark inside he will easily find the luminous light switch; the lights will be switched off automatically after a suitable interval. The sign *frisch gebohnert,* which often hangs in stairways and public places, warns him to beware of newly polished floors; this absolves the owner from responsibility in case of accident. Once the visitor has reached his hosts's flat, he may be subjected to further scrutiny through a glass peep-hole in the door. If the Englishman's home is his castle, the German's flat is an impregnable fortress.

Until recent years there were few housing estates in Germany, but large developers are now building attractively designed estates on which detached houses and bungalows are mingled with terraced houses and blocks of flats; terraces are a post-war innovation in Germany. Much attention is paid to landscaping these estates and to the provision of shops, schools, churches and other facilities so that they form pleasant, self-contained residential units. Communal television aerials are a valuable innovation, preventing the otherwise inevitable clutter of private aerials. There is considerable interest in preserving mature trees, especially

A detached house on a modern housing estate (with terraced housing behind)

where new housing development is taking place, so one rarely sees a concrete jungle; it seems that the German cannot be happy unless his surroundings are aesthetically pleasing.

Detached houses are usually individually designed and built to the specifications of the first owner, although prefabricated building systems are gradually bringing about a greater degree of uniformity. Private development is most often seen in the suburbs, where land is not quite so expensive. It is not uncommon to see standing amongst elegant bungalows a shack housing a family which is saving hard to build a fine house on the same plot. Intending house-builders and buyers must often raise two or three mortgages and a considerable deposit. Refugees may turn to sources such as the *Lastenausgleich* fund ('Equalization of burdens'); the government subsidises people who undertake to keep the house in the family for long periods. It is therefore a moment to be remembered when one's own house is nearing completion; the erection of the roof timbers is a significant point, marked by the topping out ceremony *(Richtfest)*—the hoisting of a decorated wreath or small tree above the building and the provision by the owner of a large quantity of beer for the building workers.

The interior of a German home contains many interesting features. Central heating is almost universal. In a modern building it may be run on oil, gas or electricity, or it may even be supplied by a central unit heating hundreds of houses and flats; in older buildings it is run from a rather hideous solid fuel stove. Open fires are a luxury which can be afforded by few, but a strange regulation states that all dwellings must have a chimney in case one is ever needed, and chimney sweeps are municipal employees. Floors are almost always concrete, on which may be laid rubber, stone, or wooden tiles; fitted carpets are not very common.

Most buildings have a cellar, which is not a dark, dank dungeon but a space well used to store food, in particular winter supplies of potatoes and preserves, to do laundry and to house the heating boiler. In blocks of flats cellar space is also used for garages, and for gas, electricity and water meters, the rest being divided amongst the tenants to use as they please. After the war attics were pressed into service to provide additional living quarters; roof space is still never wasted in Germany.

The living room will generally be tastefully furnished. The furniture may be heavy and dark *(Stilmöbel)* or modern

A typical middle-class living room furnished in contemporary style

and light, both extremes being popular. It will probably be arranged around a low table since there is no fireplace to provide a focal point. Windows are large, curtained with elegant drapes and nets which filter the sunlight; in most buildings they will be double-glazed to keep cold and noise at bay. The windows open inwards to facilitate cleaning; professional window cleaners are virtually non-existent. A large window, with a wide sill and a sunny aspect may be used as a miniature conservatory, crowded with plants which flourish in the warmth and light. The decor of the room will be reserved, and there is not likely to be a clutter of ornaments; a pot plant or two or an elegant candle are favourite choices. Lighting will be soft and muted; wall lights and standard lamps are both popular. It is still the custom in many households to keep the living room permanently in a state of readiness to receive visitors.

The typical German bedroom causes consternation to British visitors. The most striking feature is the enormous double bed, which on close examination proves to be two single beds fastened together. On top of the bed is a mountainous bag of feathers *(Federbett)* under which one is expected to sleep. The stranger complains of cold feet for a few nights, since this voluminous eiderdown does not tuck into the bed, but with a little practice it becomes a snug and adaptable covering, cool in summer and warm in winter.

Very few families are lucky enough to have a garden,

THE NORTH GERMAN HOUSE

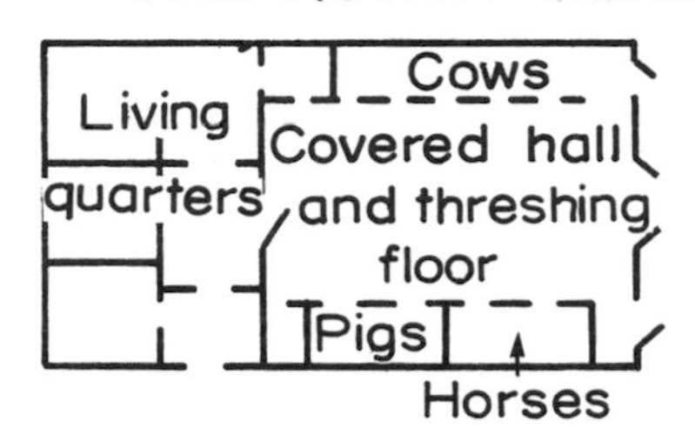

2. Ground plan

THE BLACK FOREST HOUSE

2. Section

Fig 31

CENTRAL GERMAN FARMHOUSE

1. Exterior

BAVARIAN HOUSE

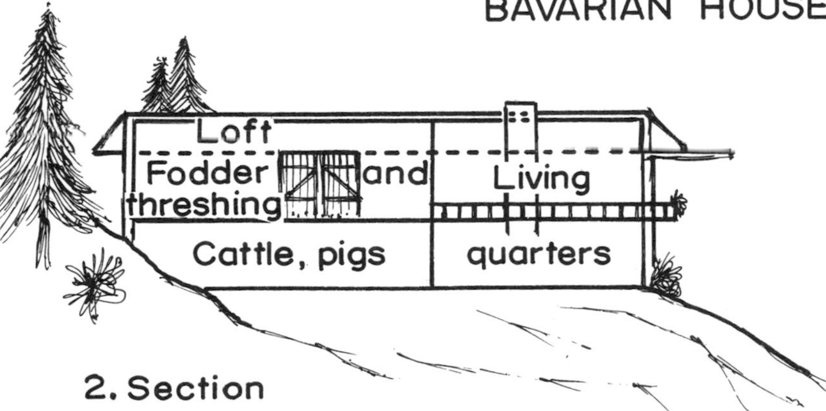

2. Section
from lower down the mountain

Fig 32

although many are able to grow a few flowers in window boxes or on a balcony. Gardens are highly prized and consequently well kept. Some families who live in a flat in town cultivate a patch of garden *(Schrebergarten)* in the suburbs to provide themselves with relaxation, flowers and a few fresh vegetables. These allotments are not eyesores, but pleasant and secluded gardens with smart summerhouses standing amongst mature trees.

In rural areas houses vary from region to region. Farmhouses in particular have evolved to suit each area; many of them are vast buildings, housing the family, the animals and the fodder under a single roof so that the animals can easily be cared for in the worst weather. In North Germany the farms are only one storey high; the living quarters occupy one third of the building whilst the remainder is given up to stalls and an enormous covered hall. Hay is stored under the thatched roof, which is surmounted on the outside by a pair of carved wooden horses' heads, formerly charms against ill fortune. In the mountains of Bavaria, farmhouses are usually two storeys high; they are now constructed of stone, which is whitewashed and decorated with designs and pictures. The roof is tiled, but older houses had roofs of wooden shingles weighted down with small boulders. The living quarters are again at one end, but on two storeys. The animals occupy the ground floor at the other end and the upper storey is a fodder store and threshing floor with direct access from outside up a ramp. The most picturesque of all farmhouses is the Black Forest house, adapted to its almost inevitable situation on a sloping hillside. Under the large thatched or shingled roof is the store of fodder, reached directly from the hillside at the rear of the house. Some of the animals are kept on the floor below, where the living accommodation is also situated, but mostly they are kept on the ground floor beneath the living quarters. The central German farm has proved to be the most practical of all and it is still being widely built. Here farmhouse and buildings are grouped around a square courtyard which has direct access to the road. The traditional buildings are half-timbered, but new ones are being built of modern materials.

Village types, too, differ from region to region according to the geographical situation and to the kind of farming suited to the area. In the eastern parts of Germany settlements were usually planned, often with an eye to defence; the *Rundling* for example was a circular village with only one

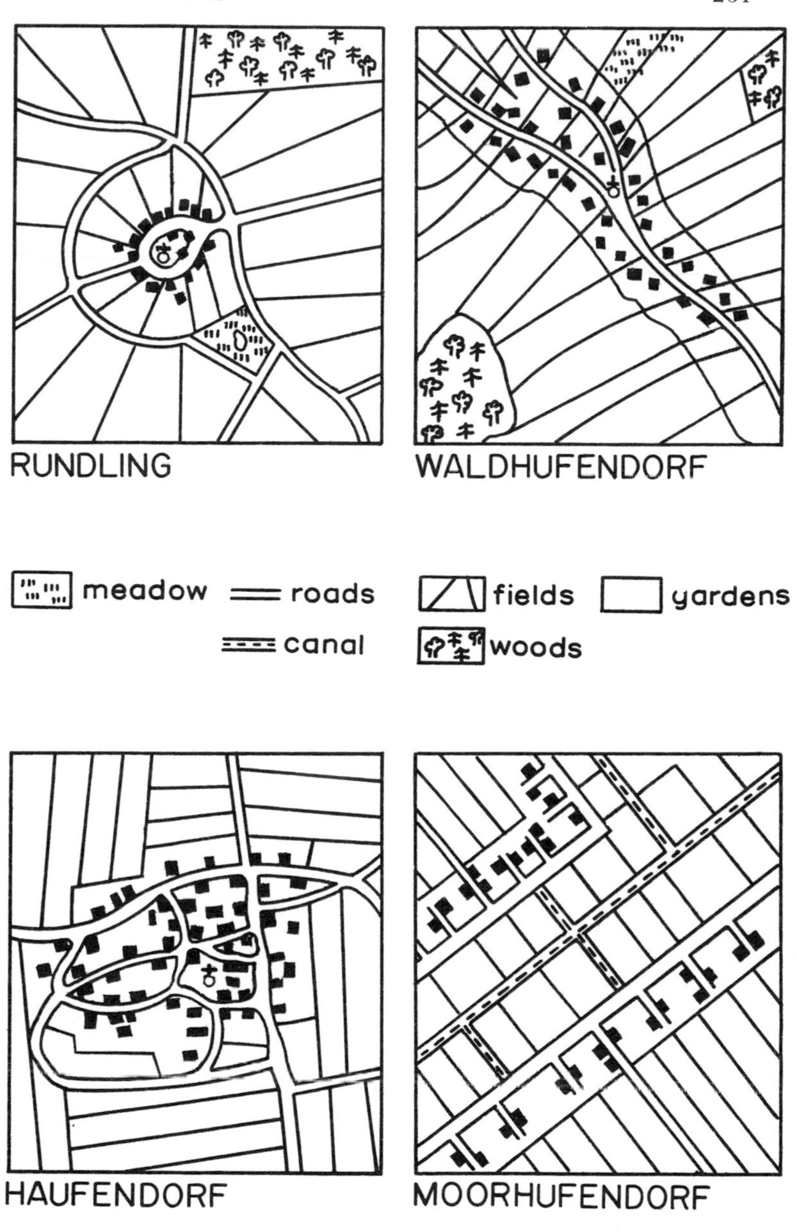

VILLAGE TYPES

Fig 33

entrance. West of the Elbe, however, communities grew organically; the *Haufendorf*, a cluster of farmsteads, is a common type on fertile, relatively flat land. The *Hufendorf* grew wherever land had to be cleared or reclaimed; it is an elongated community whose land stretches away from the main road in narrow strips. The *Waldhufendorf* is common in the central uplands and forested areas, the *Marschhufendorf* along the North Sea coast and estuaries, and the *Moorhufendorf* on the peaty moorland of northern Germany. Villages are rare in mountainous areas, which can only support isolated farms.

3. Living Customs

The rural regions of Germany are rich in folklore and traditions, which are for the most part kept very much alive. The heavily decorated costumes which were once the everyday dress have now become treasured heirlooms, worn only on special occasions, for no one now has the time to embroider the elaborate bodices and blouses or to make the

Varieties of German dress (left : traditional costume from the Bückeburg area ; centre : the ubiquitous leather shorts ; right : a dirndl dress)

dainty laces, but some forms of regional costume, such as the dirndl dress, are still widely worn for work, most especially in Bavaria. The variety of costume goes back to the days when the subjects of each Prince had to dress alike, but even within one area there is a considerable difference between the beautiful clothes reserved for special occasions and the plainer more serviceable version worn for work. There are still some differences in dress in different parts of Germany. A Bavarian man, for example, might wear grey and green leather trousers, a waterproof woollen jacket and a green felt hat with a plume of chamois bristles; a North German on the other hand prefers a dark blue jacket and trousers and a peaked cap. Most people, however, prefer to dress in the ubiquitous western European style although leather shorts and the dirndl dress, both of which are adapted from southern German costumes, remain peculiar to German-speaking lands.

Germany's rich heritage of folklore has preserved for us many interesting customs, sometimes derived from heathen times or superstitions, sometimes commemorating real or legendary events or advertising local attractions or products. Harvest festivities, the celebration of the summer solstice (now called *Johannisfeuer* and linked to the Feast of John the Baptist) and certain of the traditional games played on New Year's Eve all have their origins in pre-Christian practices. Commemorative traditions include the various Passion Plays, and the re-enactment of the legend of the Pied Piper of Hamelin. The heather festival at Schneverdingen on the Lüneburg Heath and the various wine festivals in and around the Rhineland are examples of festivals advertising local attractions. Most of these festivals are by their very nature limited to a small area, but others, especially those connected with the Christian calendar, are common to the whole country, although they are by no means always celebrated in the same way. The more important of these festivals have been declared public holidays throughout the whole of the Federal Republic, whereas others such as the Feast of the Epiphany and the Day of Prayer and Repentance (*Buß- und Bettag*) are holidays only in some States according to whether Catholics or Protestants predominate. To these religious holidays have been added others with purely political origins, such as Labour Day on May 1st.

New Year's Day is a public holiday throughout Germany, but January 6th, the Feast of the Epiphany, is a holiday only in the predominantly Roman Catholic south. In memory

JAN

of the Three Kings Caspar, Melchior and Balthasar the letters C M B are chalked on the front door; in country areas the children dress up as the Three Kings and, carrying a star, go from house to house singing carols and hymns.

FEB

Although it is celebrated all over Germany, *Karneval* or *Fasching* is particularly typical of the Catholic Rhineland and southern States. Proceedings begin officially in November, but gain momentum only when the Christmas festivities are over, reaching a climax in the week before Lent begins. During the 'drei tolle Tage' or last four *(sic)* days, the merry-making never ends. There are fancy dress balls, attended by the Prince and his (often male) Princess and their fools; there are banquets followed by a succession of outrageous and amusing speeches. On the final 'mad' Monday *(Rosenmontag)* there are the processions, extravagant, spectacular and great fun for both participants and spectators. Carnival as celebrated in the big centres of Mainz, Munich and Cologne has become commercialized and has lost much of its original flavour; the old customs are better preserved in smaller places such as Rottweil on the Neckar.

APRIL

By Ash Wednesday the Carnival is over and there follows a period of calm. Towards the end of Lent Palm Sunday is marked in some Roman Catholic areas by a procession and by the blessing during Mass of sprigs of leaves which are later placed in houses and stalls to protect their occupants. In parts of the Black Forest poles decorated with garlands and ribbons or trees with only their top branches remaining are blessed in church and then erected outside each home.

Good Friday *(Karfreitag)* is a public holiday and the most important feast in the Protestant church; it is observed by many as a fast, or meatless day. Easter Sunday, the most important feast in the Roman Catholic year, is in contrast a day of happiness, especially for children, who love to search house and garden for the Easter eggs brought in the night by the *Osterhase* ('Easter hare'). It is still the custom to decorate hard-boiled eggs for Easter, although the intricate traditional patterns have given way to bright, simple colours applied by the children themselves. In many places customs are still observed which originated in heathen celebrations for the arrival of spring; examples are the bonfires lit in parts of Hamburg and the flaming wheels rolled down the hillside in some villages in Westphalia. Easter Monday is also a public holiday and is the occasion for egg-rolling competitions. The Sunday after Easter *(Weißer Sonntag)* is for many Catholic children the day of their first communion, which is marked by celebrations both in church and in the family circle.

The night of April 30th is Walpurgis Night, when witches and the devil are said to congregate in the Harz mountains to celebrate heathen rites on the Brocken. The following day, May 1st, is Labour Day, a public holiday throughout continental Europe; the morning is devoted to parades and speeches and the afternoon to diversions sometimes specially arranged by the trade union movement. In country areas May Day is still celebrated as the occasion of the arrival of spring. Ascension Day is a public holiday; in addition to its religious significance it has in recent years come to be observed as Fathers' Day. At about this date Catholic villages stage processions of supplication for divine blessing on the crops. At Whitsuntide houses and churches are decorated with young trees, usually birches, in full leaf; Whit Monday is a public holiday.

MAY

Trees are again used as decorations on the Feast of Corpus Christi, celebrated only in Catholic areas; it is a public holiday in southern Germany, the Saar and the Rhenish States. Near Speyer, for example, elaborate altars and pictures made from flowers are set up along the roads; elsewhere statues and sacred relics are carried in procession to bless the land and the people. June 17th was until 1968 a public holiday marking the Berlin uprising of 1953 and called the Day of German Unity. When it was realized that people were using the occasion for merrymaking instead of for solemn remembrance, the holiday was abolished. June 24th is both Midsummer Day and the Feast of John the Baptist; most of the customs connected with the Feast are heathen in origin, notably the bonfires and balls of fire rolled down the hillsides during the preceding night in parts of southern Germany.

JUNE

Throughout the summer and early autumn clubs and societies hold their annual festivities. Shooting clubs, for example, which exist principally in northern Germany,

A 'Schützenkönig' wearing his symbols of office, which he retains for a year

elect a Queen to preside over the week's activities. Competitions are held to find the champion marksmen in various categories, and the overall champion or King *(Schützenkönig)*. The week ends with a great procession through the town to a large marquee where dancing and drinking continue until well into the night. Summer is the most popular time for the annual excursion which every employer must arrange for his employees; it is sometimes an educational tour, sometimes a joy-ride, always a merry occasion. Such is the proliferation of celebrations that many large inns, often situated in some beauty spot at a convenient distance from the town, cater specially for them.

Wine festivals *(Winzerfeste)* are a feature of the late summer and autumn in grape-growing regions; they fulfil several functions, the most important one being to publicise the most recent vintage of the local wines. Often a Queen is

SEPT

chosen to lead the festivities and to help advertise the wine during the following year. Enormous quantities of wine are consumed, partly by professional tasters, but mostly by the local people and tourists who can buy cheaply the *Heurige* (new, immature wine) and inferior or mixed wines contributed by the growers to help finance the festival.

As autumn approaches, festivals of light get under way, reminding us that pre-Christian man sought through them to lighten the darkening days. These festivals vary greatly in character from spectacular events as held along the Rhine ('The Rhine in Flames') involving major firework displays, to simple parades of children carrying candle-lit paper lanterns in the dusk. The sole public holiday in August, observed only in Bavaria and the Saar, is the Feast of the Bodily Assumption of the Virgin Mary *(Mariä Himmelfahrt)*.

In southern Germany preparations for winter begin in September. The cattle are brought down from the mountain pastures where they have spent the summer months; they are garlanded with flowers and greeted with general rejoicing in the village.

In late September or early October the nation-wide harvest thanksgiving is held; in the country the two-day celebrations begin with a procession of decorated carts

OCT

through the village, followed by dancing and drinking until the early hours. Harvest festivals are held in church on the next day. October is also the month of the *Oktoberfest,* the world-famous beer-drinking orgy in Munich. The last day of October is kept by Protestants as Reformation Day, commemorating the events of 1517 when Luther nailed his theses to the door of the church in Wittenberg. Schools in Protestant areas remain closed and the children attend church.

November 1st is the Roman Catholic Feast of All Saints, observed as a holiday in the Saar, the Rhenish States and Bavaria; it is followed on November 2nd by the Feast of All Souls. In preparation for these Feasts the churchyards are tidied and the graves decorated with wreaths and candles which burn for two days in memory of the departed souls. The Feast of St. Martin on November 10th is observed by Catholics and Protestants alike, although the latter are at the same time remembering another Martin, Martin Luther. The children go from house to house singing and collecting sweets and fruit, then at dusk 'St. Martin' rides through the streets followed by the children, each carrying a lantern.

NOV

At exactly 11.11 a.m. on the 11th of November, the eleventh month, Carnival traditionally begins, but apart from the ceremonial opening there is little evidence of it until after Christmas. The end of November is in fact a very solemn time, coinciding as it does with the end of the Church Year. The penultimate Sunday is *Volkstrauertag,* a day of remembrance for the victims of war; three days later comes *Buß- und Bettag,* a Protestant day of prayer and repentance, and a public holiday everywhere except Bavaria. The last Sunday before Advent is *Totensonntag,* when the dead are honoured and the graveyards tidied up for the winter.

At the beginning of Advent all thought of sadness is forgotten, for this is a time of preparation for the great festival of Christmas. The Germans have preserved much of the traditional spirit of Christmas, which has elsewhere been lost as the Feast has been increasingly commercialized. During Advent spirits rise as the preparations gain momentum. At the beginning of December the children receive an Advent calendar, on which they can open a series of windows, one for each day until Christmas, and on the first Sunday in Advent most families make an Advent wreath from fir branches and four candles, one of which is lit at dusk to the accompaniment of carols. December 6th is the Feast of St. Nicholas, and on the previous evening the children put out their shoes or socks in the hope that they will be filled with apples, nuts and sweets. St. Nicholas (or Santa Claus as we call him), who traditionally brings these gifts, is, according to legend, accompanied by his servant Ruprecht. The latter carries a cane with which he threatens to punish the children who do not promise to be good.

DEC

Preparations for Christmas meanwhile continue; families sit around making presents and decorations for the tree, the children learn poems and carols, the house is filled with the aroma of baking. Each Sunday one more candle on the Advent wreath is lit until by the last Sunday all four are burning. During Advent Christmas bazaars are held, the most famous being the Christkindlesmarkt in Nuremberg, which begins on December 4th. In many theatres the matinee performances are devoted to special Christmas plays for children. To finance the merrymaking, most workers can look forward to a Christmas bonus *(Weihnachtsgratifikation)* as part of their negotiated salary; it is often equivalent to a month's pay.

Christmas proper begins on December 24th. During the afternoon the children are excluded from the living room whilst the Christmas tree is decorated. The type of decoration, home made in most instances, varies from region to region and family to family; some people prefer to use only one colour or restrict themselves to stars made of straw, but where there are children the decorations are usually gay and include shiny red apples, gilded nuts and chocolate figures. Beneath the tree there is often a crib. At dusk the candles on the tree, still generally preferred to electric lights, are lit and the children are allowed into the room to sing carols before the whole family goes to church. By this time all the shops and places of entertainment have closed and most public transport has stopped. The churches are filled to overflowing; they, too, are decorated with a crib and Christmas trees.

After the service the family returns home to unwrap the presents mysteriously left in the living room by the *Weihnachtsmann* (Father Christmas) or *Christkind* (Christ child), depending on whether one is in north or south Germany. In addition to his presents everyone receives a dish of sweets, spicy biscuits and marzipan from which he can nibble at will during the whole of Christmas. The day often ends with a second visit to church for the midnight service. Many interesting customs are observed in country districts; in the south for example some families lay a place at table on Christmas Eve for the Virgin Mary.

Most people spend Christmas Day at home, but children are often taken to see their grandparents to receive their presents. There is no one national Christmas dish, although goose and carp are popular; each region has, however, twelve traditional dishes, one for each of the twelve days of

Christmas. December 25th and 26th are both public holidays.

New Year's Eve, the Feast of St. Sylvester, is usually celebrated with close friends at home, although New Year's Eve balls are growing in popularity. It is the custom at this time to take a light-hearted look into the future with games such as *Bleigießen*, when hot lead is poured into cold water in the hope that it will form a picture of the future. At midnight bells ring out and the New Year is greeted with fireworks and cannon fire; shortly before midnight people climb on to chairs so that they can leap into the New Year. Even young children are roused so that they can enjoy the fun—and a sip of champagne.

It is obvious that the Germans love to celebrate and that many celebrate extremely frequently. This is doubtless an antidote to and a necessary release from their often staid and exacting working lives; their motto seems to be work hard and play hard.

4. Language

In the early eighteenth century German was thought by many members of the aristocracy to be fit only for the lower classes; French was the chosen language in court circles. However the great achievements of later eighteenth century writers such as Goethe proved once and for all that the language was capable of expressing philosophical ideas, poetic sentiments and scientific discoveries. In the late nineteenth century a standard written German had evolved and this became an important factor in helping to unify the German Empire, founded in 1871. This language *(Hochdeutsch)* contained many regional variations of spelling and pronunciation, neither of which was fixed until the turn of the century, although the basic grammar had been unaltered since about 1750; its advantage lay in the fact that it could be understood by most Germans, whether they came from Saxony, Bavaria, the Rhineland or the coastal regions. *Hochdeutsch* however remains primarily a written language, despite the fact that for some 70 years it has been taught in its present form in schools throughout the country. Dialect is still the usual means of communication between local people in many areas, who use *Hochdeutsch* as a second language; elsewhere *Hochdeutsch* has been modified and enriched in colloquial speech by the addition of dialect or slang words and expressions, and it is frequently spoken with a strong local accent.

Before the Second World War German was spoken not only in the German Empire and in Austria, but also in parts of France, Belgium, Switzerland, Czechoslovakia, Rumania and Poland. The shift of population after the war caused the virtual extinction of *Hochdeutsch* and German dialects in the former German-speaking areas of Eastern Europe, so that the political boundary with Poland and Czechoslovakia has now become a linguistic boundary. Outside Germany itself variations from *Hochdeutsch* are legion, especially in vocabulary; Swiss and Austrian German, for example, contains many French words. Even within present day Germany, the linguistic unity, so recently attained, is threatened by the political division, which is exposing the language to two totally different influences. The language of the GDR is subject to periodic modifications *(Sprachregelungen)* carried out by a government department. New words are introduced and old ones redefined along Party lines. 'Freedom' is defined as 'the appreciation of necessity' ("die Einsicht in die Notwendigkeit"—Friedrich Engels (1820–95)); 'peace' as a 'state existing between two countries which can be achieved and maintained only by political battles or the use of force'. New words have come from Russia; others have fallen into disuse. Russian sentence constructions are becoming more common and many typically Russian turns of phrase are being literally translated. A Party jargon formed mainly from abbreviations, *e.g.* FDJ *(Freie Deutsche Jugend)*, and from new words, *e.g. Ultras, Zeitnormative, kulturelle Massenarbeit,* has appeared which is incomprehensible to the outsider. A pejorative noun or adjective is formed by prefixing *un-* or *nicht-* to a word; thus an *Unzeitschrift* is a periodical disapproved of by the Party. Certain adjectival expressions have become clichés peculiar to East Germany, *e.g. ruhmreiches Sowjetvolk, sozialistische Hilfe.* Also typical is the tendency to repeat the genitive where a West German would make use of the alternative *von* plus the dative, *e.g.* "der Stellvertreter **des** Vorsitzenden **des** Staatsrats **der** DDR . . .".

The main influence on West Germany comes from Britain and America; it has grown ever stronger as the youth of Western Europe fell increasingly under the spell of 'pop' culture. The largest group of foreign words concerns pastimes popular among young people, *e.g. die Party, der Jazz, baby-sitten.* Science took over many words, *e.g. Laser,* and translated many others, *e.g. Raumschiff*. Tourism too has played its part; Germans can eat *Donats* and *Toast,* they can say that things are *O.K.* and *smart.* Teenage culture has brought a new phenomenon, a 'literature' written in teenage slang which prides itself on being *up to date.* Whilst the adoption of many of these words is quite justified, the present vogue for using English words at every opportunity sometimes produces a debased language almost unrecognizable as German.

The diverging trends in the German language are recognized by scholars and politicians and the whole problem is being analysed, but it is doubtful whether their efforts can overcome the rift between the two states. Since the frontier became effectively sealed, all contact between ordinary people has ceased, creating ideal conditions for the separate development of the language.

The influence of German on the English Language

Philosophy and science have benefited most from German words; the former has *Weltanschauung* and *Leitmotif,* the latter has mostly words derived from the names of inventors, *e.g.* Diesel, Bunsen and Wankel. Tourism too has played its part: English restaurants serve schnitzel and torte and offer kirsch or schnaps to drink. There are numerous German words in specialized fields such as geography ('hinterland'), skiing ('sitzmark'), mountaineering ('abseilen') and walking ('rucksack'). We take our children to the kindergarten, speak of having the wanderlust, wear dirndl skirts, laugh at the antics of poltergeists and eat frankfurters bought at a delicatessen. Certain German words which were in current use during the war (1939–45) are now less familiar; people talked of U-boats, the blitz and the Luftwaffe. They took refuge in bunkers from V-bombs, and called the Germans 'Kraut'.

American English has been affected to a greater extent because of the numbers of Germans who have at various times found a new home in the United States.

Characteristics of the German Language

1. German is an inflected language having 4 cases and 3 genders. Each gender declines differently, and there is a

separate form for the plural; there are seven different renderings of English 'the'. In short, modern German is not so highly developed as are other Germanic languages which have discarded inflection.

2. Genders frequently take no account of the nature of the object, *e.g. das Kind.* A fondness for diminutives produces a neuter word to describe a person, *e.g. das Mütterchen.* Lifeless things are not always neuter, *e.g. der Tisch.*

3. Typically German are compound nouns built up from smaller elements, *e.g. Fernsprecher,* literally 'distant speaker', *i.e.* 'telephone'. These words indicate the intended meaning instead of veiling it beneath Greek and Latin roots. Compound nouns occasionally get out of hand, *e.g. Bundesstraßennummernschild, Wiedergutmachungsgespräche, Spezialempfängeranschlußschnur, Schützengrabenvernichtungspanzerkraftwagen.* Some of these lengthy words have been virtually replaced by abbreviations; *PKW* and *LKW* are so much easier to say than *Personenkraftwagen* and *Lastkraftwagen.* Some of the abbreviations have themselves been used to form new words; *die Flak* derives from a shortened form of **Fl***ieger*-**a***bwehr***k***anone.*

4. Compound adjectives are built in a similar way, giving extremely picturesque and poetic descriptions: *funkelnagelneu, kohlpechrabenschwarz, mucksmäuschenstill.*

5. Onomatopoeic words abound: *summen, zwitschern, quietschen.*

6. Particles, a peculiarity of the German language, are widely used: "Das hätte man *denn doch wohl auch* sagen können".

7. A German will often use an almost tautologous pair of words to add emphasis to what he is saying, *e.g. Haus und Hof, Sang und Klang, null und nichtig.* Rhyming pairs which are opposite or complementary are also popular, *e.g. Sein und Schein, Rat und Tat.*

8. German is generally spoken energetically; most Germans articulate precisely. Vowels are pure; consonants are pronounced more emphatically than in English. The glottal stop is used, preventing *ein Apfel* from becoming *ei napfel.* Thus one does not hear nearly so much slovenly speech as in Britain.

9. The multiplicity of inflexions and the unnatural word order of German are pedantic. In the hands of a clumsy writer the compound nouns (see 3 above) and highly favoured participial phrases (*e.g.* "der aus den Alpen in die Nordsee fließende und wegen seiner Schönheit besungene Rhein")

can easily give an air of pomposity, which is unfortunately typical of much German officialese, business letters and public speaking, but it has become much less common in literature and colloquial speech. Officialese also uses seven words where one is adequate: "Diese Frage ist mit ‚ja' zu beantworten" ('yes').

10. In dependent clauses the verb comes at the end. This construction can at times be confusing, but it can be used to effect by orators who gather the verbs and then hammer them home one after the other. There is however a movement to simplify German; in the spoken language one often hears the verb in a more natural position instead of in its grammatical place at the end of a sentence: "Das Stück wurde gespielt vom Kölner Rundfunk-Symphonieorchester". Such changes as one may hear today in Germany are by no means to be regarded as correct at this stage. They may never become acceptable even though remaining in current use.

Dialects

Dialects are still very much a feature of modern Germany, being spoken by a considerable percentage of the population. Dialects preserve much older forms of German than the modern written language; some German dialect forms have existed since early medieval times. Even until the inter-war years there were clear-cut distinctions between the languages spoken in different parts of the country, but because of the influx of refugees and the migration to industrial areas, some of the distinctions have become blurred.

The classification of the dialects of German into High and Low German is based on a change in consonant sounds known as the High German Sound Shift, which occurred between the fifth and eighth centuries. From the dialects which underwent the shift (though they were not equally affected by all the changes) has developed modern (or New High) German. The dialects of Northern Germany were not affected by the sound shift; they are known as Low German. The consonant shift altered chiefly the sounds *p, t* and *k,* which became *f/pf, ss/z* and *ch* respectively. Low German therefore retains words such as *slapen, Appel, Water, Tid* and *maken;* in High German these same words became *schlafen, Apfel, Wasser, Zeit* and *machen.* The boundary between Low and High German runs approximately from

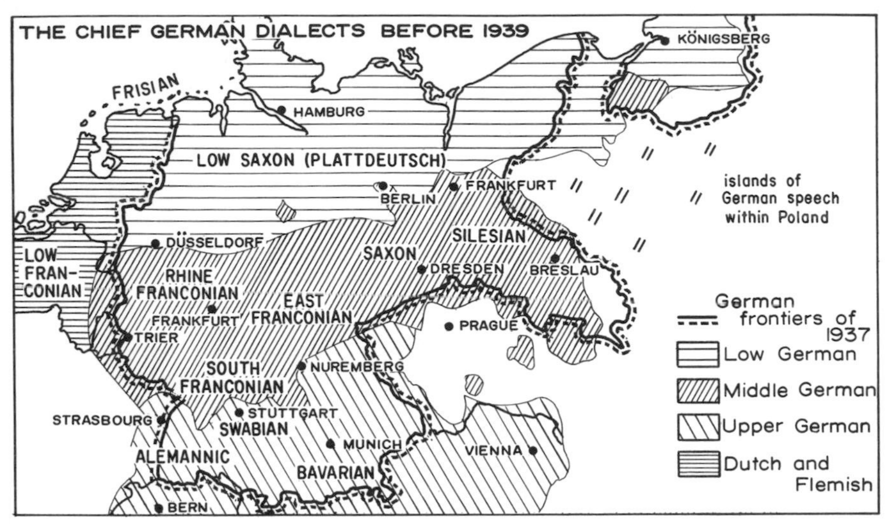

Fig 34

Aachen to Frankfurt-on-Oder; its course is somewhat arbitrarily fixed, since some unshifted words are in common use in central Germany.

The chief group of Low German dialects is *Plattdeutsch,* spoken throughout the North German Plain except in certain coastal areas, where Frisian has survived. *Plattdeutsch* has become modified, for example in Hamburg, into a language more easily comprehensible in the rest of the country and known as *Missingsch.* High German dialects are subdivided into two main groups, *Mitteldeutsch* (including the dialects of the Moselle and Rhine valleys, Thuringia and Saxony), and *Oberdeutsch* (including the dialects of Alsace, Switzerland, Swabia, Bavaria and Austria).

There is in general little social stigma attached to either dialect speech or regional accent, although some, for example Saxon and Bavarian, tend to arouse a jocular animosity in citizens of other regions. People do not try to conceal their accent; Konrad Adenauer was easily identified as a Rhinelander by his speech. Dialects are in fact regarded as a valuable part of Germany's heritage. In the Nazi era they were encouraged, since they bred national pride, and since the war they have been preserved by refugees coming from territories once part of the German Empire as nostalgic souvenirs of the lands they were forced to leave, where, incidentally, the dialects have died out. Dialect articles still appear in major newspapers *(e.g. Hamburger Abendblatt)* and in some places, notably in the Frisian islands, children are being given lessons in dialect so that it may be kept alive. Each region has its own tradition of popular literature and its own particular brand of humour or humorous characters; 'Klein Erna' for example belongs to Hamburg and 'Tünnes' to the Rhineland. There are six major dialect theatres in the Federal Republic and countless amateur dialect authors. It is therefore unlikely that dialects will be allowed to die out in the near future.

Bibliography

BITHELL, JETHRO: *Germany. A Companion to German Studies* (Methuen)
KOHN, HANS: *The Mind of Germany* (Macmillan)
ELKINS, T. H.: *Germany* (Chatto and Windus)
R. B. TILFORD AND R. J. G. PREECE: *Federal Germany: Political and Social Order* (Wolff)
D. CHILDS: *East Germany* (Benn)
HORNSBY, LEX (ed.): *Profile of East Germany* (Harrap)
WALTON, HENRY: *Germany* (Thames and Hudson)
SINNHUBER, K. A.: *Germany—Its Geography and Growth* (Murray)
POUNDS, N. J. G.: *The Economic Pattern of Modern Germany* (Murray)
CARR, W.: *A History of Germany 1815–1945* (Arnold)
PASSANT, E. J.: *A Short History of Germany 1815–1945* (Cambridge University Press)
ROBERTSON, J. G.: *A History of German Literature* (Blackwood)
COLLINSON, W. E.: *The German Language Today* (Hutchinson)
PILKINGTON, ROGER:
Small Boat through Germany
Small Boat to Bavaria
Small Boat to Northern Germany
Small Boat on the Moselle (Macmillan)

GOVERNMENT PUBLICATIONS

1. West Germany
Germany Reports
Facts about Germany
(Federal Press and Information Office, Bonn)
In the heart of Germany in the Twentieth Century—the Zonal Border (Federal Ministry for German Internal Relations, Bonn and Berlin)
Meet Germany
These Strange German Ways
(Atlantik-Brücke, Hamburg)
2. East Germany
Meet the GDR
The Constitution of the Socialist State of the German Nation
Berlin. Capital of the GDR
GDR Review (monthly)
(Verlag Zeit im Bild, Dresden)

Abbreviations

ADN	Allgemeiner Deutscher Nachrichtendienst
APO	Außerpolitische Opposition
AStA	Allgemeiner Studentenausschuß
BGB	Bürgerliches Gesetzbuch
BRD	Bundesrepublik Deutschland
CDU	Christlich-Demokratische Union
COMECON	Council for Mutual Economic Assistance
CSU	Christlich-Soziale Union
ct	cum tempore
DAG	Deutsche Angestelltengewerkschaft
DBB	Deutscher Beamtenbund
DBP	Demokratische Bauernpartei
DDR	Deutsche Demokratische Republik
DFD	Demokratischer Frauenbund Deutschlands
DGB	Deutscher Gewerkschaftsbund
DK	Deutscher Kulturbund
DKP	Deutsche Kommunistische Partei
DM	Deutsche Mark
dpa	Deutsche Presseagentur
DSF	(Gesellschaft für) Deutsch-sowjetische Freundschaft
FDGB	Freier Deutscher Gewerkschaftsbund
FDJ	Freie Deutsche Jugend
FDP	Freie Demokratische Partei
GDR	German Democratic Republic
GCE	General Certificate of Education
GST	Gesellschaft für Sport und Technik
HO	Handelsorganisation
KPD	Kommunistische Partei Deutschlands
LDP	Liberaldemokratische Partei
LPG	Landwirtschaftliche Produktionsgenossenschaften
MDN	Mark der Deutschen Notenbank
NATO	North Atlantic Treaty Organization
NDP	Nationaldemokratische Partei
NPD	Nationaldemokratische Partei Deutschlands
NSDAP	Nationalsozialistische Deutsche Arbeiterpartei
OIRT	International Organization of Broadcasting Companies
RIAS	Radio im Amerikanischen Sektor
SA	Sturmabteilung
S-Bahn	Stadtbahn
SBZ	Sowjetische Besatzungszone
SDS	Sozialistischer Deutscher Studentenbund
SED	Sozialistische Einheitspartei Deutschlands

SFB	Sender Freies Berlin
SPD	Sozialdemokratische Partei Deutschlands
SS	Schutzstaffel
st	sine tempore
StGB	Strafgesetzbuch
U-Bahn	Untergrundbahn
VDS	Verband Deutscher Studentenschaften
VEB	Volkseigener Betrieb
VVB	Vereinigungen Volkseigener Betriebe
ZK	Zentralkomitee

Index